D0026595

The Judicial System

Books in the **Contemporary World Issues** series address vital issues in today's society such as genetic engineering, pollution, and biodiversity. Written by professional writers, scholars, and nonacademic experts, these books are authoritative, clearly written, up-to-date, and objective. They provide a good starting point for research by high school and college students, scholars, and general readers as well as by legislators, businesspeople, activists, and others.

Each book, carefully organized and easy to use, contains an overview of the subject, a detailed chronology, biographical sketches, facts and data and/or documents and other primary source material, a forum of authoritative perspective essays, annotated lists of print and nonprint resources, and an index.

Readers of books in the Contemporary World Issues series will find the information they need in order to have a better understanding of the social, political, environmental, and economic issues facing the world today.

The Judicial System

A REFERENCE HANDBOOK

Michael C. LeMay

ABC-CLIO®

An Imprint of ABC-CLIO, LLC

Santa Barbara, California • Denver, Colorado

Copyright © 2022 by ABC-CLIO, LLC

All rights reserved. No part of this publication may be reproduced, stored in a retrieval system, or transmitted, in any form or by any means, electronic, mechanical, photocopying, recording, or otherwise, except for the inclusion of brief quotations in a review, without prior permission in writing from the publisher.

Library of Congress Cataloging-in-Publication Data

Names: LeMay, Michael C., 1941– author.
Title: The judicial system : a reference handbook /
  Michael C. LeMay.
Description: 1st Edition. | Santa Barbara, California : ABC-CLIO,
  LLC, 2022. | Series: Contemporary world issues | Includes
  bibliographical references and index.
Identifiers: LCCN 2021043844 (print) | ISBN 9781440874574
  (print) | ISBN 9781440874581 (ebook)
Subjects: LCSH: Justice, Administration of—United States—
History. | Courts—United States—History.
Classification: LCC KF8700 .L46 2022 (print) | LCC KF8700
  (ebook) | DDC 347.73—dc23/eng/20211004
LC record available at https://lccn.loc.gov/2021043844
LC ebook record available at https://lccn.loc.gov/2021043845

ISBN: 978-1-4408-7457-4 (print)
       978-1-4408-7458-1 (ebook)

26 25 24 23 22   1 2 3 4 5

This book is also available as an eBook.

ABC-CLIO
An Imprint of ABC-CLIO, LLC

ABC-CLIO, LLC
147 Castilian Drive
Santa Barbara, California 93117
www.abc-clio.com

This book is printed on acid-free paper ∞

Manufactured in the United States of America

Contents

Preface

By intentional design, the United States has a very complex system of government. Given their experience with an oppressive English government and the king's appointed colonial governors, the Founding Fathers feared the potential for a national government to become too powerful and oppressive. To limit the power of government, they designed the federal system with a checks and balances system. It divided power into three levels of government: local, state, and national (federal). It further divided government into three coequal branches of government: legislative, executive, and judicial.

Because each state establishes its own judicial system as to courts, judges, methods of selecting judges, other officers of the court, and the jurisdiction of the courts at the various levels, the U.S. judicial system can be bewildering and confusing to navigate. Since each state designs its judicial system, they use different terms or names for their courts, and the terminology varies from state to state so that different states use the same name or designation for different courts, and in other cases, different names for the same level or type of court. There is extensive variation in the jurisdiction of the various levels of courts and what sorts of fines, penalties, or terms of imprisonment are associated with what types of criminal behavior. And as is true for virtually all matters of law, the judicial system uses specialized terminology or "jargon" that can be confusing or even impenetrable to someone not trained in the law.

The Judicial System: A Reference Handbook is designed to help the reader cope with that complexity. In the United States, law is influenced by English common law, and so it reflects "judge-made" law. The use of precedent and of the judicial principal of "stare decisis" mean that judges and courts follow the decisions of preceding rulings of that court and comply with the decisions handed down by higher-level courts. *The Judicial System* also uses institutional analysis to clarify the elaborate systems used to structure judicial power by the national and state governments. The various courts in the judicial system all play a role in the checks and balances system intended by the founders to limit the power of government.

As this volume hopefully makes clear to the reader, the basic constitutional documents of America's federal and state governments intentionally allowed for the evolution of the nation's judicial system. As the United States expanded its frontiers, as its population became ever more demographically diverse, and as its economy became more complex, the judicial system evolved as well.

Like all volumes in the Contemporary World Issues (CWI) series, *The Judicial System* follows a set format for the structure and content of each chapter.

Chapter 1 discusses the history and background of the U.S. judicial system and the political factors that have shaped its character over the decades. It spans the colonial period and the pre-constitutional period (Articles of Confederation), through the establishment and amending of the federal judiciary to modern times. It also provides details on state and local court systems in each of the fifty states.

Chapter 2 discusses significant problems facing the judicial system as well as proposed reforms and solutions. Chapter 3 is comprised of nine original essays that provide perspectives on a wide range of issues confronting national and/or state judicial systems.

Chapter 4 presents brief profiles of key organizations and actors who are stakeholders in judicial politics. Some are advocacy organizations participating in judicial electoral politics or lobbying legislatures to amend laws; others represent the "think-tank" approach offering scholarly analysis of controversial issues facing the judicial system. The chapter also profiles individuals who have had a significant impact on the judiciary, including chief justices and associate justices of the U.S. Supreme Court, the two most recent presidents, members of the influential Senate Judiciary Committee, and one individual plaintiff in a federal case (*Gideon v. Wainwright*) that proved enormously influential in shaping criminal law and how state governments and state courts handled criminal case procedure. Arguably, the entire public defender system now so commonly used emerged because of the *Gideon v. Wainwright* decision.

Chapter 5 presents data and documents, including five graphs, tables, and ten primary sources, that span the history of the American judicial system from 1789 to the present.

Chapter 6 provides annotated bibliographic citations for a wide assortment of books and scholarly journals that exemplify the scholarly literature on the judicial system. It lists thirty useful websites that the reader is encouraged to visit for further study, as well as two documentary films that give "life" to the print sources.

Chapter 7 is a handy chronology of key events shaping the American judicial system at all levels of government from 1641 to 2020.

The book concludes with an extensive but accessible glossary of key terms used throughout the book and a detailed subject index.

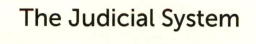

The Judicial System

GEORGE SHIRAS, JR.

HORACE GRAY.

STEPHEN J. FIELD.

RUFUS W. PECKHAM.

DAVID J. BREWER.

CHIEF JUSTICE FULLER.

EDWARD D. WHITE.

HENRY B. BROWN.

JOHN M. HARLAN.

JUSTICES OF THE
United States Supreme Court.

x

Introduction: An Overview of the Judicial System

An essential part of a federal form of government, the judicial system in the United States is enormously complex. Tracing its origins to the traditions of the judicial system of England, the U.S. judicial system evolved over time and across the nation with a strong emphasis on precedent and on "judge-made" law (Bach 2010; Barton 2010; Mays and Fidelie 2016; Scheb and Scheb 2015). Moreover, some states of the South reflect their French and Spanish colonial histories in their judicial systems. Louisiana, for example, calls their local courts parishes. Another important aspect of the judicial system is that it is one of three coequal branches of the federal government—executive, legislative, and judicial. These branches were designed by America's Founding Fathers to limit the power of government by establishing checks and balances among the three branches. The judicial system is also based on an adversary system of justice, where opposing lawyers compete to argue their side of a case (Kubicek 2006).

The judiciary features many important positions that add to the complexity of judicial system politics and play significant roles in the wider world of American politics (Buenger and De Muniz 2015; Corley, Ward, and Martinek 2015; Neubauer and Meinhold 2009). Federal judges are lifetime

---

In 1896 there were nine justices on the Supreme Court. Chief Justice Fuller and eight associate justices. The Court's size over the years ranged between 5 and 10. (Library of Congress)

political appointees, whereas most judicial positions at the state and local levels are popularly elected positions. Elected judges reflect the values and biases of the population that elects them; as a result, they can reflect the racial, ethnic, and cultural biases prevalent in their electorate (Van Cleve 2016). These aspects of courts at the differing levels of government impact judicial independence in significant ways; for example, by displaying racial bias in the rates of conviction and the length of sentences imposed (Shugerman 2012).

State courts were established in the original thirteen states even before the U.S. Constitution came into being. These state-level courts hear the most litigation in the United States, estimated at more than 95 percent of cases. State courts have various names and structures. For example, states maintain courts of special jurisdiction to hear a variety of misdemeanor matters, such as traffic citations and small-claims civil disputes. They also have courts of general jurisdiction that hear cases for more serious disputes involving both civil and criminal law. State courts are the courts of original jurisdiction in all but a few matters specified in the Constitution to be heard at the U.S. Supreme Court level. They operate under the dictates of state constitutions and laws.

All the courts within the American judicial system are closely linked and are hierarchical in structure. State (and territorial) courts established after the Constitution was adopted in 1789 are governed and determined by state constitutions. Those constitutions have been modeled on the U.S. Constitution. In U.S. law, when statutes refer to the courts of the United States, those laws are referring only to federal government courts.

Federalism divides power and governmental sovereignty between the national-level government and those of states and territories. As a result, state courts are free to operate in ways different than those of the federal government. In practice, however, most states have adopted judicial systems that divide courts into three levels that resemble the U.S. constitutional distinctions for federal courts. State courts have trial courts that first hear cases. Those cases may then be reviewed by "appellate courts," which are the next highest level. Finally, states have state supreme courts or courts of final appeal, also known as courts of last resort. Several states operate under two supreme courts—one for civil matters and the other for criminal case review. Federal courts hear cases on appeal involving litigants from two or more states. They also consider alleged violations of U.S. federal laws, cases involving challenges based on the U.S. Constitution and its constitutional protections, cases involving the admiralty (maritime law), and bankruptcy cases. Approximately 80 percent of cases before federal courts are for civil matters and 20 percent are for criminal matters. Federal civil cases typically involve civil rights matters, patents, and issues concerning Social Security. Criminal cases at the federal level typically involve tax fraud issues, robbery of federally insured banks, counterfeiting, and federal drug cases.

The trial courts of the federal system are called U.S. district courts, and as of 2021 the U.S. federal court system is divided into ninety-four district courts (see Figure 5.1). If judgments handed down at this level are challenged on legal grounds—a step known as an "appeal"—the case is considered again by an appellate court. The nation's ninety-four district courts are arranged into twelve circuits, each of which has an appellate court. Only a tiny fraction of cases heard at the appellate level are appealed to the U.S. Supreme Court, which is the highest and most powerful court in the land. In a few very rare matters of law, however, the U.S. Supreme Court has original jurisdiction, meaning such cases go directly to it.

To better understand the judicial system of the United States as it currently exists, it is useful to review the historical background of the structures, procedures, and practices of the judicial system, and their establishment as states were added to the union. It is also helpful to examine the evolution of U.S. jurisprudence over time. Finally, because of the important impact of federalism on America's court system, the interrelationships between and among local, state, and federal judicial systems warrant discussion.

Pre-Constitution Judicial System

Colonial Era: 1600 to Late 1700s

The thirteen colonies had their own judicial organizations, but the British government claimed the sole power to establish courts, and until the mid-1700s, they were created by colonial governors' action. But the British crown paid little attention to colonial courts after their initial establishment, and by the seventeenth century, problems arose concerning jurisdiction of various courts. In England, probate matters (legal issues concerning wills) fell within the jurisdiction of ecclesiastical courts (held before clergy such as a local bishop, rather than in a civil court of law). In the colonies, they were handled by the governor. The colonial governments had no separation of powers between branches, though, and officials could and did operate in several positions simultaneously.

By the mid-1700s, courts were formalized by legislative action and jury trials become more common (Surrency 1956). Judges of this period were seldom trained in the law and were often religious or political officials. The use of juries and lawyers was somewhat rare. Juries typically only served when the death penalty was involved. For minor (petty) crimes, a local magistrate heard the case and decided a verdict.

Magistrates firmly believed their role was to enforce God's plan, and they sought to convince the accused to confess and repent their sins. The goal in these early courts was less about punishment than about bringing order back to the colony. Often the defendants spurned jury trials. They often relied, instead, on the mercy of judges who often handed down more lenient sentences to people who emphasized their willingness to obey his authority. By the early 1700s, as the colonies grew in population, courts became more similar to those operating in England. Juries became more common, and defendants were allowed to have defense lawyers. Following English common law tradition, law was often "judge-made," that is, where the precedent set by one judge determines subsequent decisions.

The Articles of Confederation Period

To better pursue the War of Independence from the British crown, the thirteen states adopted the Articles of Confederation late in 1777 and ratified them in 1781. Under the Articles of Confederation, the national government was centered in the "Congress of the Confederation," where each state had one vote. It provided for the annual appointment of delegates to the Congress but had no permanent national judiciary. However, the Congress of the Confederation was authorized under the articles to create courts to adjudicate cases concerning the capture of enemy commercial vessels on the high seas, called "prize" cases. The confederation had no chief executive or president, but the Congress did annually elect an individual to serve as the president of the Congress. The position, however, had no broad executive powers, unlike those found in the modern presidency.

The Congress had the authority to declare war in case of invasion, and the national government could conduct foreign affairs. But the states also retained authority to send and receive ambassadors and other diplomats with the approval of the Congress and could regulate interstate movement of the mails. It did not have the power to raise taxes directly. It could and did settle disputes over the division of the western lands surrendered by Great Britain after independence. This transfer of land was stipulated in the 1783 Treaty of Paris. This treaty, negotiated on the American side by Benjamin Franklin, John Adams, and John Jay, brought the Revolutionary War to a close.

Four years after the Treaty of Paris, Congress passed the Northwest Ordinance, which established provisions for the disposition of public lands in the west and set parameters for the organization of territorial governments, including their courts. The ordinance also established the federal court of appeals to settle prize cases (disputes over captured ships), providing the precedent for the later establishment of the federal court system under the U.S. Constitution, as well as the precedent for the idea that the union formed by the states was "perpetual." The Articles of Confederation had no Bill of Rights, however, and its many other limitations—including its silence on many areas of potential conflict, both among states and between states and the federal government—led the Founding Fathers to push for the creation of a new U.S. Constitution and Bill of Rights.

The Federal Court System Established by the U.S. Constitution

Article III of the U.S. Constitution has three sections that provide the constitutional authority for the federal court system (see Document 5.1). It specifies the establishment of a supreme court and authorizes the Congress to ordain and establish lower federal courts. It details the types of cases over which the federal judiciary has jurisdiction. Federal courts established under Section 2 were empowered to hear cases involving ambassadors and other public ministers (i.e., what became known in today's parlance as the cabinet secretaries), cases of admiralty and maritime jurisdiction (since the high seas was not considered to be the purview of any one state, but of the nation as a whole), and disagreements between two or more state governments and between citizens of different states. Section 3 specifies that the U.S. Supreme Court has original jurisdiction to try the crime of treason, and it defines that crime.

The trial courts of the federal court system are U.S. district courts, followed by the several U.S. courts of appeal, and then the Supreme Court of the United States. Appellate courts and the Supreme Court review the work of the lower courts (Carp, Manning, and Stidham 2016; Corley, Ward, and Martinek 2015; Mays and Fidelie 2016; Posner 2017).

The number of justices comprising the U.S. Supreme Court is not fixed at nine. Indeed, the size of the court has been changed a number of times, ranging from the original six to a low of five and a high of ten justices, the latter occurring briefly during the Civil War. The Judiciary Act of 1789 (Act of September 24, 1789, 1 Stat. 73) set the number at six justices. Twelve years later, the Federalists, to limit the appointments of incoming president Thomas Jefferson (leader of the chief opposition party at that time, the Democratic-Republican Party), passed the Judiciary Act of 1801 (2 Stat. 89), also known as the Midnight Judges Act. This legislation set the number of Supreme Court Justices at five and created sixteen new judgeships in six new circuit courts. In 1802, the Congress, then controlled by the Democratic-Republicans, put the number back to six by the Judiciary Act of 1802 (2 Stat. 158). In 1807, the Democratic-Republican-controlled Congress added a seventh Supreme Court Justice and a seventh federal court circuit. In 1837, with Congress under the control of the Jacksonian Democrats, two more justices were added, bringing the total to nine (Judiciary Act of 1837, 5 Stat. 176). The size of the court was driven by political party considerations.

During the Civil War, Congress added a Tenth Circuit district and added a tenth justice to the Supreme Court (Judiciary Act of 1863, 14 Stat. 209). In 1866, Congress passed the Judicial Circuits Act (Act of July 23, 14 Stat. 209), which gradually reduced the number of circuit courts and Supreme Court seats. The Act of July 27, 1866 (14 Stat. 306) removed certain cases from state courts, transferring jurisdiction to the federal courts. One year later, Congress enacted the Judiciary Act of 1867 (14 Stat. 385), also known as the Habeas Corpus Act. The act concerned Supreme Court review of state court rulings. The 1869 Judiciary Act (15 Stat. 44) set the number of justices on the Supreme Court back to nine. In the Judiciary Act of 1891 (26 Stat. 826), Congress amended the circuit courts of appeals. This legislation is also known as the Evarts Act after its primary sponsor, Senator William M. Evarts (R-NY). The Judiciary Act of 1925 (43 Stat. 936) made further changes to the jurisdiction and processes of federal courts. The 1925 Act is also known as the Certiorari Act or the Judges' Bill Act. These post-Civil War changes reflected changing workloads of the federal courts.

Since 1869, the number of seats on the U.S. Supreme Court has remained at nine. That does not mean, though, that there have been no bids to change the high court's structure. In 1937, for example, President Franklin D. Roosevelt became so frustrated with the conservative-leaning court's rulings against his New Deal policies to combat the Great Depression that he sought to add six more justices, to "pack the court" with judges friendlier to his New Deal programs and expand the size of the court from nine justices to fifteen. The plan was opposed by Chief Justice Charles Evans Hughes (appointed to the court by Republican president Herbert Hoover) and Justice Louis Brandeis (appointed to the court by Democratic president Woodrow Wilson) and failed to gain traction in Congress.

Despite his failure to get his court-packing plan through Congress, President Roosevelt saw the Supreme Court change dramatically during his terms as president. Court historians believe that the threat itself may have made the court more reluctant to strike down his administration's New Deal initiatives. In addition, numerous vacancies on the court enabled President Roosevelt to nominate and appoint a record nine justices to the court between 1937 and 1943, thereby replacing the conservative justices who had been opposing his New Deal law proposals. This made the demise of his court-packing plan a moot issue. Although Roosevelt lost the battle, he won the war, so to speak (National Constitutional Center 2019: 2; see also Crowe 2012; Landis and Frankfurter 2017; Ragsdale 2013; Rosen 2007; Surrency 2002; Wheeler and Harrison 2006).

The constitutional basis for the U.S. Supreme Court that determines its structure and jurisdiction has evolved since America's earliest days. The institution has been significantly impacted, for example, by the leadership of several of the chief justices of the Supreme Court. Since its inception in 1789, seventeen jurists have served as chief justice of the court (see

Table 5.5). Of those seventeen, a half-dozen (profiled in Chapter 4) were particularly influential: John Marshall (who served as chief justice from 1801 to 1835), Roger Taney (1836–1864), William H. Taft (1921–1930), Charles E. Hughes (1930–1941), Earl Warren (1953–1969), William Rehnquist (1986–2005), and John Roberts (2005–). The impact on the court of these chief justices stems from several factors, including their length of service, landmark decisions handed down by the court under their stewardship, and the impact of their ideological or judicial philosophy on the court's deliberations.

In addition to the amending judiciary acts that have impacted the Supreme Court over the decades, Congress was empowered by Article III of the Constitution to create several "inferior" courts: thirteen courts of appeal (also known as circuit courts of appeal), established between 1789 and 1911. Congress also created the U.S. Court of Customs and Patent Appeals in 1909 and the commerce courts in 1910. Over time, as the nation expanded across the continent, Congress has also created ninety-four district courts, as the federal courts of first jurisdiction or general trial courts.

Congress from time to time also created specialized appellate courts, panels, or boards. These include the Bankruptcy Appellate Panel (created in 1978), the U.S. Court of Appeals for Veterans Claims (1988), and in 1951, the U.S. Court of Appeals for the Armed Forces (which includes one for each branch, the U.S. Army, the Navy–Marine Corps, the Air Force, and the Coast Guard Court). Congress also established the United States Tax Courts (1924), the U.S. Court of International Trade (1980), the U.S. Court of Federal Claims, an Article I tribunal (1855), the U.S. Foreign Intelligence Surveillance Court (1978), the Trademark Trial and Appeal Board (1999), the U.S. Merit System Protection Board (1979), and the U.S. Alien Terrorist Removal Court (1996).

Over the years, as the United States acquired more territories by treaty acquisition or war, U.S. territorial courts were added. Currently, the Courts of the Territories of the United States include American Samoa, Guam, Northern Mariana Islands, Panama Canal Zone, Puerto Rico, and the United States Virgin Islands. Specialty courts of limited jurisdiction or duration that no longer exist today included the U.S. Court of Private Land Claims (1891–1904), the U.S. Court for China (1906–1943), the U.S. Court for Berlin (1955–1990), and the U.S. District Court for the Canal Zone (1982). Other specialty federal-level courts include the U.S. Court of Military Commission Review, the Civilian Board of Contract Appeals, the Armed Services Board of Contract Appeals, the Office of Dispute Resolution for Acquisition, the Board of Immigration Appeals, and the Board of Veterans Appeals (U.S. Courts.gov 2020a; see also Corley, Ward, and Martinek 2015; Koelling 2016; Mays and Fidelie 2016; Neubauer and Meinhold 2009; Posner 2017).

Over the years, Congress established the U.S. Circuit Courts of Appeals (see Figure 5.1). The first nine of the U.S. Circuit Court of Appeals were created by the Judiciary Act of 1891 (the Evarts Act or the Circuit Court of Appeals Act, 26 Stat. 826). Each circuit court has appellate jurisdiction over a certain number of states (except the thirteenth, which has a nationwide jurisdiction over specialized subject matters). The First Circuit covers Maine, Massachusetts, New Hampshire, Rhode Island, and Puerto Rico. U.S. Court of Appeals for the Second Circuit covers Connecticut, New York, and Vermont. The Third Circuit includes Delaware, New Jersey, Pennsylvania, and the Virgin Islands. The U.S. Court of Appeals for the Fourth Circuit covers Maryland, North Carolina, South Carolina, Virginia, and West Virginia. The Fifth Circuit hears appeals from Louisiana, Mississippi, and Texas. The U.S. Court of Appeals for the Sixth Circuit covers Kentucky, Michigan, Ohio, and Tennessee. The Seventh Circuit hears appeals from Illinois, Indiana, and Wisconsin. The Eighth Circuit Court of Appeals covers Arkansas, Iowa, Minnesota, Nebraska, North Dakota, and South Dakota. The Ninth Circuit hears appeals from Alaska, Arizona, California, Hawaii, Idaho, Montana, Oregon, and Washington. The U.S. Court of Appeals for the Tenth Circuit was established in 1929, and covers Colorado, Kansas, New Mexico, Oklahoma, Utah, and Wyoming. The U.S. Court of Appeals for the Eleventh Circuit was created in 1981 by subdividing the Fifth; it includes Alabama, Florida, and Georgia. The U.S. Court of Appeals for the District of Columbia was established in 1893. The Federal Circuit, the thirteenth, was established in 1982 by the merger of the U.S. Court of Customs and Patent Appeals and the U.S. Court of Claims. As of 2021, there are 179 judgeships authorized by Congress in the circuit court system. Each circuit includes a court of appeals consisting of judges in regular active service.

District Courts

The workhorses of the federal judicial system are its general trial courts, the U.S. district courts. They hear both civil and criminal cases, and are courts of law, equity, and admiralty, meaning they are responsible for adjudicating cases arising on the high seas, outside the territorial jurisdiction of any one state. Each state has at least one district court (and federal district courthouse), and there is one in the District of Columbia, and one for the territories. The territorial courts (of Guam, the Northern Mariana Islands, and the Virgin Islands) are called district courts and have the same jurisdiction as the other district courts, but their judges serve ten-year terms instead of lifetime appointments. American Samoa does not have a territorial court, so federal cases arising there are heard in the District of Columbia or Hawaii. There are eighty-nine district courts distributed among the fifty states. They are also referred to as statutory courts since they are based on acts of Congress rather than directly by the U.S. Constitution.

The first Congress created the district court system by the Judiciary Act of 1789. Congress first established thirteen districts among the first eleven states that had ratified the Constitution, and then added two more when North Carolina and Rhode Island ratified the Constitution. Federal district court judges are Article III judges who serve until death or retirement, providing they meet terms of "good behavior." They are appointed by the president with the advice and consent of the Senate. They may retire at age sixty-five or can go on senior status and keep working. They may be removed involuntarily only by impeachment in the U.S. House of Representatives followed by conviction in the U.S. Senate. To date, twelve federal district judges have been impeached, and seven have been convicted in U.S. history. Senators representing the state from which a nominee is selected have, by a tradition known as senatorial courtesy, wielded unofficial veto power over nominees they find unacceptable (U.S. Courts.gov 2020e).

District judges manage their court, supervise trials, write opinions, and at their discretion may assign routine tasks to magistrate judges. Magistrate judges are appointed for an eight-year term; they may be reappointed for an additional term, but they can also be removed at any time for incompetency, misconduct, neglect of duty, or physical or mental disability. As of 2021, there are 677 authorized district court judgeships across the United States.

Each district court has an appointed clerk who oversees legal filings; maintains the court's records; processes fees, fines, and restitutions; and manages nonjudicial work of the court such as information technology (IT), budget and procurement, human resources, and related financial matters for the court. The district court may appoint deputies and other clerical assistants, and by authority of the Judiciary Act of 1789, they may serve as clerk of the corresponding circuit court. The clerk issues writs summoning juries for jury trials. Clerks are appointed by and may be removed by order of the entire court (sitting as a panel of judges), and they serve the entire court. Each judge has a law clerk to assist in conducting research and preparing drafts of opinions.

The jurisdiction of federal district courts is limited to subjects explicitly assigned by the Congress. The courts conduct trials in cases dealing with the following matters: civil actions arising under the Constitution, laws, and treaties;

civil actions between citizens of different states or citizens of a state and a foreign country; civil actions under admiralty or maritime jurisdiction of the United States; criminal prosecutions brought by the United States; civil actions to which the United States is a party; and assorted other types of cases and controversies that from time to time the Congress has assigned to district courts. They also have appellate jurisdiction over a limited class of judgments, orders, and decrees.

Appeals from district court rulings in civil or criminal cases may be appealed to the court of appeals in the federal judicial circuit in which the district court is located, except for certain specialized matters that must be appealed to the U.S. Court of Appeals for the Federal Circuit (located in Washington, D.C.). On rare occasions, the appeal may be taken directly to the U.S. Supreme Court.

The Central District of California is the largest federal district based on population. New York City and its surrounding area are divided between the Southern District of New York (SDNY) and the Eastern District of New York (except New York suburbs located in Connecticut and New Jersey that are covered by the district courts in those states respectively). California and the SDNY have the largest number of judges—at twenty-eight each. Several district courts in the District of New Mexico, the Western District of Texas, the Southern District of Texas, and the District of Arizona have, since 2007, become the busiest for criminal felony cases, with heavier caseloads related to prosecutions of illegal immigration (Howard 2014; Koelling 2016).

Special Courts

There are several special courts with special jurisdictional responsibility in the federal judicial system, each of which is briefly discussed here.

The U.S. Tax Court is a federal trial court that specializes in adjudicating cases in which taxpayers contest Internal Revenue Service (IRS) interpretations of their tax obligations. These suits are generally heard by the court before the taxpayer prepays any portion of the disputed taxes. It was established by the Revenue Act of 1924 (26 U.S. C. 7441), also known as the Mellon Tax Act. Currently, it is comprised of nineteen judges who serve for a term of fifteen years. The U.S. Tax Court is housed in a building in Washington, D.C., but its judges also travel to hear cases in other federal district court buildings. Appeals of tax court judgments go to the U.S. Court of Appeals. The responsibilities and operations of the tax court were amended in 1942 and 1969.

The Patent Trial and Appeal Board (PTAB) is located within the U.S. Patent and Trademark Office (USPTO). The PTAB decides appeals of patent application rejections from the USPTO and determines the patentability of issued patents by third parties in post-grant proceedings. It has existed in some form or other since the 1800s, and its operations were most recently revised in September 2012 as part of the America Invents Act. It is comprised of statutory members and administrative patent judges appointed by the secretary of commerce. All judges on the board must have technical expertise as well as a law degree. The PTAB decides about 12,000 appeals and 1,500 trial proceedings annually (USPTO 2020a).

The International Trade Commission (USITC) is an independent, nonpartisan, quasi-judicial federal agency. It investigates and makes determinations in proceedings involving imports claimed to injure a domestic industry or that violate U.S. intellectual property rights. USITC provides adjudication, research, and analysis, and maintains the Harmonized Tariff Schedule (a tariff schedule or list that sets up a hierarchical structure for describing all imported goods). It is headed by six commissioners appointed by the president and confirmed by the Senate. USITC was first established in September 1916, but has been amended by subsequent legislation in 1930, 1933, 1962, 1974, 1979, 1984, 1988, and 1994. ITC commissioners serve nine-year terms that are staggered so that terms overlap and provide ITC continuity from year to year (USITC 2020).

The United States Court of International Trade (USCIT) was established under Article III of the U.S. Constitution. It has nationwide jurisdiction over civil actions that arise from customs and international trade laws. CIT traces its history back to 1890 and was expanded on by Congress in 1926. It was reorganized in 1956 as an Article III court, and most recently in 1980 when the CIT was amended as part of the Customs Court Act. It is comprised of nine judges who have lifetime appointments. They are appointed to the court by the president with the advice and consent of the Senate. The chief judge of the CIT is a statutory member of the Judicial Conference of the United States, the principal policymaking body concerned with the administration of U.S. courts. CIT is located in New York City (U.S. Courts.gov 2020c).

The U.S. Court of Federal Claims, known as "the People's Court," hears monetary claims against the U.S. government. It is the direct successor to the U.S. Court of Claims established in 1855 (28 U.S.C. 1491). It was amended in 1866 when President Abraham Lincoln insisted that Congress give it the power to render final judgments. In 1953, the number of jurists on this court was expanded to fifteen, and in 1977 to sixteen. The court's judges serve for fifteen-year terms and are appointed by the president with the advice and consent of the Senate. Judges can retire at age sixty-five or continue to serve as "senior judges." The court has concurrent jurisdiction with the U.S. district courts and has nationwide jurisdiction to hear cases on a wide variety of monetary claims against the federal government. For example, in the past the court has heard monetary claims against the U.S. government by Japanese Americans interned during World War II, as well as suits against the federal government arising out of the National Childhood Vaccine Injury Act of 1986 (U.S. Courts.gov 2020h). The 1986 law was passed to protect vaccine manufacturers from lawsuits that might otherwise keep them from vaccine research and production.

The U.S. Foreign Intelligence Surveillance Court was established in 1978 (50 U.S.C. 1801–1885). The court considers applications made by the U.S. federal government for approval of electronic surveillance, physical search, and other similar investigative actions for foreign intelligence purposes. The court is comprised of eleven federal district court judges designated by the chief justice of the Supreme Court. They serve for seven years on staggered terms and must be drawn from seven district judicial circuits. Three of the judges must reside within twenty miles of the District of Columbia. Judges typically sit for one week at a time on a rotating basis. Their hearings are conducted "ex parte" (done by, for, or on application of and in the interest of one side only, or of an outside party) due to the need to protect classified national security information (U.S. Courts.gov 2020d).

Since 1984, U.S. bankruptcy courts have been located within each of the federal district courts to handle bankruptcy matters and bankruptcy cases. The courts are created under Article I of the Constitution and were established in 1978 (28 U.S.C. 1334). The decisions by bankruptcy judges are subject to appeal to the district court on appeal to the Bankruptcy Appeals Panel. Judges who serve on bankruptcy courts are appointed for terms of fourteen years by the U.S. Court of Appeals for the circuit in which the applicable district is located. The bankruptcy courts appoint a trustee to represent the interests of creditors and administer the cases (U.S. Courts .gov 2020b).

The Trademark Trial and Appeal Board (TTAB) hears and decides legal proceedings involving registration of trademarks, petitions to cancel trademark registration, and proceedings involving applications for concurrent use registrations of trademarks. The board also decides appeals from the trademark examining attorney's refusal to allow registration of trademarks. The board meets in Alexandria, Virginia, and hears hundreds of claims each year. The TTAB's twenty-six judges are appointed by the U.S. secretary of commerce based on a 2008 amendment specifying that the secretary of commerce is responsible for such appointments. Appeals of

TTAB decisions are heard by the U.S. District Court or by the U.S. Court of Appeals for the Federal Circuit (USPTO 2020b).

The U.S. Merit System Protection Board (MSPB) is an independent, quasi-judicial agency of the executive branch that oversees the federal merit system, a performance review system for civil servants that was enacted to reform the party-patronage system. It traces its history to the Civil Service Act of 1883. Its current system was established by the Civil Service Reform Act of 1978. The MSPB adjudicates individual employee appeals, conducts merit system studies, and reviews significant actions of the Office of Personnel Management (OPM). It reviews cases or claims of performance-based actions, reduction-in-force actions, improperly handled restorations, denials of within-grade increases, and denial or reduction in retirement benefits. It has its main offices in Washington, D.C., with regional offices in Atlanta, Chicago, Dallas, Denver, and New York.

The U.S. Alien Terrorist Removal Court was created by Congress as a provision within the Antiterrorism and Effective Death Penalty Act of 1996 (110 Stat. 1214). The chief justice of the Supreme Court is authorized to designate five U.S. district judges to review applications for removal of suspected alien terrorists from the United States and its territories. The judges are drawn from five different judicial circuits, and the chief justice may appoint the same judges to the Foreign Intelligence Surveillance Court. Under the 1996 law, the U.S. Attorney General drafts an application for removal of a suspected alien terrorist and submits it to the court. A judge then reviews the removal order. Upon granting a removal application, the court must hold a public hearing at which the accused may be represented by counsel, and the government bears the burden of proving the accused is an alien terrorist. Appeals of decisions of the U.S. Alien Terrorist Removal Court can be made to the U.S. Court of Appeals for the District of Columbia Circuit.

Appellate Jurisdiction Courts of Special Subject Matter

The following briefly describes eleven federal appellate courts established with jurisdiction to hear special subject matter cases.

The U.S. Court of Appeals for the Federal Circuit was established by Congress by the Federal Courts Improvement Act of October 1, 1982. That law merged the U.S. Court of Customs and Patent Appeals and the appellate division of the U.S. Court of Claims. The court is headquartered in Washington, D.C., and is comprised of twelve judges nominated by the president and confirmed by the Senate. It hears cases on appeal from the U.S. Court of Federal Claims, the Court of Appeals for Veteran Claims, the U.S. Trademark Trial and Appeal Court, the U.S. Patent Trial and Appeal Board, the Boards of Contract Appeals (for the Armed Service, Civilian, and Postal Service Boards), the U.S. Merit System Protection Board, and the U.S. International Trade Commission. Since the court has nationwide jurisdiction, it holds oral arguments outside of D.C. several times per year in federal and state courthouses, or even at law schools. Its twelve active circuit judges come from different circuits, but at least three must reside within fifty miles of D.C. At age sixty-five, a judge on this court may retire or elect to take senior status and remain on the bench.

The U.S. Court of Appeals for the Armed Forces is an Article I court that has appellate jurisdiction over members of the armed forces on active duty or other persons subject to the Uniform Code of Military Justice. Established by law in 1951, it is comprised of five civilian judges appointed for fifteen-year terms by the president and confirmed by the Senate. This court reviews decisions from intermediate appellate courts of the Army, Navy–Marine Corps, Coast Guard, and Air Force. In 1986, Congress enacted a law to enhance its effectiveness and stability, and in 1994, Congress gave the court its current name.

The U.S. Court of Appeals for Veterans Claims is a national court of record under Article I that has jurisdiction for judicial review of the Board of Veterans' Appeals of the Department of Veteran Affairs (VA). It provides veterans with an impartial forum to consider appeals from veterans when the VA rejects their claims of entitlement to benefits for service-connected disability, survivor benefits, education benefits, and waiver of indebtedness. It was established in 1988, and its name was changed to the current title in 1999. It has seven active judges with two additional part-time judges. The active judges serve for staggered, fifteen-year terms. They can retire at age sixty-five or elect to be senior judges. The court is headquartered in Washington, D.C., but it can and does meet elsewhere in the United States a limited number of times per year (U.S. Courts .gov 2020f).

The U.S. Foreign Intelligence Surveillance Court of Review (FISCR) was established in 1978 when Congress enacted the Foreign Intelligence Surveillance Act (50 U.S.C. 1801–1885). It sits in Washington, D.C., and is composed of a panel of three federal district court or appeals court judges designated by the chief justice of the Supreme Court. It conducts its work ex parte as required by statute to protect national security information (U.S. Courts.gov 2020d).

The U.S. Court of Military Commission Review (USMCR) was established as a direct result of the September 11, 2001, terrorist attacks on the United States. After that attack, Congress passed a joint resolution giving the President of the United States (POTUS) sweeping authority to use all necessary force against nations, organizations, or persons who committed or aided the attacks. President George W. Bush issued an executive order that led, among other actions, to the U.S. Secretary of Defense, then Donald Rumsfeld, to issue a military commission order that provided for a review panel of three military officers to review convictions of any person under the executive order. In 2004, Secretary of Defense Rumsfeld appointed four civilians to the panel. The Supreme Court ruled in *Hamdan v. Rumsfeld* (548 U.S. 557, 2006) that the military commission scheme violated the Uniform Code of Military Justice. In 2009,

President Bush signed a new Military Commission Act that established the Court of Military Commission Review, comprised of three military appellate judges or civilians of comparable qualification. The 2009 MCA was amended in 2011, 2017, and 2018 to modify some aspects of the appointment process. The president appoints all commission judges with the advice and consent of the U.S. Senate. In *Ortiz v. United States* (138 S.C. 2165, 2018), the Supreme Court held that judges on the CMCR could also serve as judges on the courts of criminal appeals. The CMCR hears oral arguments in the U.S. Court of Appeals in Washington, D.C.

The Armed Services Board of Contract Appeals (ASBCA) is the administrative tribunal for claims against the U.S. government for contract disputes with the Department of Defense or the National Aeronautics and Space Administration (41 U.S.C. 7105, 1978). First established in 1962, its provisions have since been amended on numerous occasions. It serves under the secretary of defense, who designates its twenty-four judges, and is headquartered in Falls Church, Virginia. The U.S. Court of Appeals for the Federal Circuit may exercise appellate review over the ASBCA's rulings (Armed Services Board of Contract Appeals 2020).

The Civilian Board of Contract Appeals (CBCA) was established in 1978 as an independent tribunal to hear and decide on contract disputes between government contractors and the General Services Administration (GSA), and several other civilian departments of the federal executive branch. It is headquartered in Washington, D.C. It is a consolidation of the boards of contract appeals previously established for the Departments of Agriculture, Energy, Housing and Urban Development, Interior, Labor, Transportation, and Veterans Affairs, as well as the GSA. It is comprised of fourteen administrative judges appointed by the administrator of the GSA.

The Postal Service Board of Contract Appeals is the independent tribunal that hears and decides appeals of contracts negotiated by the U.S. Postal Service or the Postal Regulatory Commission. Its first version was the Post Office Board of

Contract Appeals created in 1959. It was amended into its current form in 1978 and modified a bit more in 2007. It is headquartered in Washington, D.C., and has three judges (Postal Service Board of Contract Appeals 2020).

The agency now known as the Office of Dispute Resolution for Acquisition (ODRA) was established in 1978 by the Federal Aviation Administration (FAA) to hear and decide disputes between the agency and government contractors (41 U.S.C. 7101–7109). A part of the U.S. Department of Transportation, it holds its hearings in Washington, D.C., before judges from the General Services Administration.

The Board of Immigration Appeals (BIA) hears appeals from decisions by immigration judges of the Department of Homeland Security (DHS), from its constituent units of Immigration Control and Enforcement (ICE), U.S. Customs and Border Protection (USCBP), or United States Citizenship and Immigration Services (USCIS). As of 2009, it has fourteen board members. It has twenty-three appellate immigration judges and is headquartered in Falls Church, Virginia. It does not conduct courtroom proceedings, but rather does "paper review" of cases. It has nationwide jurisdiction and hears appeals from the decisions of any of the immigration judges (Board of Immigration Appeals 2020).

The Board of Veterans Appeals is the administrative tribunal of the Department of Veterans Affairs (DVA). First established in 1933, its operations and responsibilities have since been amended by law on numerous occasions over the years. It is comprised of as many members as is deemed necessary by the secretary of the Department of Veterans Affairs. Board members are appointed by the secretary of Veterans Affairs in accordance with provisions of the 1988 Veterans Judicial Review Act.

State and Local Judicial Systems

All fifty states have a state supreme court, although Oklahoma and Texas maintain two such courts, one for civil and one for criminal law cases. Most of the states have one or more intermediate courts of appeal below the state supreme court level (Montana, New Hampshire, and North Dakota do not have an intermediate court of appeals). These courts are typically named courts of appeals, although a few have various other names. Delaware, being one of the original states, called its intermediate courts the court of chancery and the Delaware Superior Court. Maine, admitted as a state in 1820, calls its supreme court "Superior Court," as does Rhode Island. Wyoming designates its courts of appeal as district courts. All states also have lower courts that are variously named superior courts, district courts, circuit courts, and courts of common pleas. All have established local courts, again variously named: county courts, municipal courts, justices of the peace courts, city courts, probate and/or family courts, magistrate courts, juvenile (or youth) courts, small-claims courts, town (or town and village) courts, problem-solving courts, land courts, housing courts, drug courts, tax courts, mayor's courts, and traffic courts.

The original thirteen colonies in 1776, when the Declaration of Independence was declared, became states upon ratification of the Constitution in 1788, when New Hampshire became the ninth state to ratify the Constitution. Those original thirteen states already had judicial court systems from their colonial periods and incorporated them into their new state constitutions, drafted by 1788. Most other states were gradually admitted to the union after some time as a territory, until their populations were sufficiently settled to warrant petition to Congress for admission to the union. Texas, however, came directly into the union in 1845 as a previously established Republic of Texas, with its own constitution and a state and local judicial system. When a new state was admitted to the union, it had to have a drafted and approved state constitution that specified its organization and structures—including its judicial system. States added after the original thirteen featured constitutions that were modeled roughly on the U.S. Constitution and tiered court systems. (See Table 5.1 for a list of the years in which states were admitted to the Union and rolled out their court systems.)

Court Systems in Each State

As the states grew in population and developed and diversified their economies, they typically amended their court systems into specific legal jurisdictions depending on geographic location or subject matter (e.g., traffic courts were created after the automobile became more common) (Buenger and De Muniz 2015; Jonakait 2008; Mays and Fidelie 2016; Neubauer and Meinhold 2009). Each state's judicial system is described briefly below.

Alabama

Alabama entered the Union in 1819 and has one of the oldest court systems in the country. Its court system is structured in the typical tiered fashion. It has a supreme court, two intermediate (or appellate) courts—one to hear civil appeals and one for criminal appeals—forty-one circuit courts of original trial jurisdiction, and lower courts, divided into sixty-seven geographic districts. Alabama has 273 municipal courts and sixty-eight probate courts. The court system was established in 1820 and reorganized in 1832. The reconstruction constitution, adopted in 1868, provided for judges to be elected by the people. The court of appeals, with three judges, was established to relieve the docket of the supreme court. In 1971, those judges were increased from three to five judges. In 1969, the court of civil appeals was created (Alabama Unified Judicial System 2010). Decisions by the Alabama Supreme Court are final unless appealed out of the state system on a challenge based on U.S. Constitutional grounds, in which case they are sent to the U.S. Eleventh Circuit Court of Appeals in Atlanta, Georgia (see Figure 5.1) (Alabama Unified Judicial System 2010).

Alaska

Alaska's court system is one of the newer such systems, given that Alaska and Hawaii were not admitted to the union until 1959 (see Table 5.1). Alaska has a state supreme court, a court of appeals, four district courts called the Alaska Superior Court and comprised of forty judgeships, and twenty-one Alaska district courts. Until statehood, Alaska's judicial system was part of the territorial justice system. Alaska has three supreme court justices and eight superior court judges. The state's district court system was established in 1968 and the court of appeals in 1980. Magistrates, who may be non-lawyers, serve as judicial officers in district courts that are limited in jurisdiction to hear small-claims and misdemeanor cases. Magistrates may hold preliminary hearings for more serious cases. Decisions by the Alaska Supreme Court are usually final, although challenged judgments occasionally reach the U.S. Court of Appeals for the Ninth Circuit (Courts.Alaska.gov 2020).

Arizona

Arizona was admitted to the union in 1912. It has a supreme court, two divisions of the Arizona Court of Appeals, and fifteen superior courts that are state trial courts of general jurisdiction, one for each county. At the local level of courts, Arizona has justices of the peace (county courts) and municipal courts (city trial courts and courts of limited jurisdiction). The state appellate courts have jurisdiction to review all cases appealed to them. In 1912, the new Arizona state legislature established police (municipal) courts for each of the state's incorporated cities and towns. In 1960, voters approved the Modern Court Amendment, which set up the state's current system and gave the Supreme Court of Arizona administrative supervision over Arizona's state courts. It also increased the number of supreme court justices from three to five and created the appeals court. In 1974, Arizona voters approved a merit system for the selection and retention of judges for both the supreme court and the appeals court. In 1992, state voters approved a system requiring public input to review judges' job performance. When a case is appealed out of the state system on a U.S. Constitutional challenge, the case is sent to the U.S. Court of Appeals for the Ninth Circuit (Arizona Courts.gov 2020).

Arkansas

Arkansas was admitted to the union in 1836. Prior to that date, it was governed as a territory and its courts were under the territorial court system. Under its state constitution, Arkansas has a supreme court, a court of appeals (an intermediate appellate court), and twenty-three circuit courts. For its local level courts, Arkansas has district courts (formerly called municipal courts) and Arkansas city courts. The current Arkansas Supreme Court is comprised of a chief justice and six associate justices who are elected statewide for eight-year terms of office. The court of appeals has a chief justice and eleven judges who are elected circuit-wide for eight-year terms of office. The Arkansas Circuit judges have 121 judges in twenty-eight circuits and are elected for six-year terms and handle criminal, civil, domestic relations, probate, and juvenile cases. There are sixteen state district courts with twenty-five judges who are elected to four-year terms. At the local level, there are seventy-seven local district courts comprised of ninety judges who are elected to four-year terms. Cases that are appealed out of the state system go to the Eighth U.S. Circuit Court of Appeals (Arkansas Courts.gov 2020).

California

California, with a population of 40 million, is the largest state in the union based on population, and has the largest state court system in the United States. California was admitted into the union in 1850. It had an ideologically very conservative judicial system in its early years, when it had many Know Nothing Party–associated justices and the state's justices often upheld highly discriminatory laws against Asians (land laws, segregated schools, and a host of municipal ordinances aimed at Chinese immigrants). By the 1950s, however, the attorney general and then state governor, Earl Warren, went on to serve as the most liberal chief justice in U.S. Supreme Court history, and today California government, and its courts, are generally considered among the nation's most liberal (or progressive).

The general trial courts in California are named superior courts. There are fifty-eight superior courts, one in each of the state's counties, and they hear both civil and criminal cases, as well as cases related to family law, probate, mental health and juvenile matters, and traffic law. There are roughly 1,700 superior court judges in California, and they annually hear about 5 million cases. California has six courts of appeal. There are 106 appellate judge positions in the state that handle about 21,000 cases annually. The California Supreme Court is headed by a chief justice and has six associate justices. Any case appealed out of the state system is heard at the U.S. Court of Appeals for the Ninth Circuit, located in San Francisco. California has four U.S. district courts located within it (Central, Eastern, Northern, and Southern) that have original jurisdiction over federal cases (Courts.California.gov 2020).

Colorado

The state judicial system in Colorado, which joined the union in 1876, is comprised of a supreme court, a court of appeals, twenty-two Colorado district courts, and Colorado county courts. Colorado's district trial courts hear civil cases of any amount, as well as cases related to domestic, criminal, juvenile, probate, and mental health matters. County courts handle civil cases under $25,000, misdemeanor criminal cases, traffic cases, felony complaints that then may be sent to district courts, issue domestic protection orders, and hear small claims. There are also seven water courts that have exclusive jurisdiction over water rights in each major river basin in Colorado. The state's supreme court consists of seven justices who serve for ten-year terms. The chief justice is selected by the associate justices and can serve in that capacity for many years, as long as a majority of those justices support them. The chief justice serves as the executive head of the state's judicial system and appoints the chief judge for the court of appeals and for each of the state's twenty-two judicial districts. In 1966, voters in Colorado passed a constitutional amendment that established that state judges be appointed rather than elected. The amendment also established a nominating commission for each judicial district to interview applicants and recommend individuals for consideration and appointment by the governor. The commissions recommend three nominees for each position on the supreme court and the court of appeals, and two for each county or district court. District nominating commissions have seven citizen members and are overseen by a nonvoting justice of the supreme court. Members of the commissions serve for six-year terms. Judges begin service after appointment and after two years must stand for retention in the next general election. All Colorado judges must retire at age seventy-two. State supreme court decisions are final, unless appealed on U.S. Constitutional grounds to the U.S. Court of Appeals for the Tenth Circuit, which is headquartered in Denver (Courts .State.Colorado 2020).

Connecticut

Founded as one of the original thirteen states in 1788, Connecticut's judicial system has a supreme court, an appellate court, thirteen superior courts (districts), and fifty-four probate courts. The supreme court was created in 1784, and in 1806 the number of seats on the court increased from five to nine. In 1818, the state constitution was amended to establish an independent judiciary. In 1982, voters approved a constitutional amendment to create the intermediate appellate court with nine judges. As of 1982, the supreme court has a chief justice and six associate justices who are appointed by the governor with approval of the General Assembly; justices must retire at age seventy. The appellate court has nine judges. Superior courts have general jurisdiction and are organized into thirteen judicial districts. They hear civil cases, family matters, felony criminal cases, and oversee criminal arraignments for misde-meanors, felonies, and motor vehicle cases. The superior court has four trial divisions: civil, criminal, family, and housing. In 1978, the General Assembly created the superior courts, merg-ing courts of common pleas and juvenile courts. The judges of the state's fifty-four probate courts are elected on partisan ballot every four years. Cases appealed out of the state to the federal court system are sent to the U.S. Court of Appeals for the Second Circuit (Jud.Ct.Gov 2020).

Delaware

Another one of the original thirteen states, Delaware was estab-lished in 1787. Its court system consists of a supreme court, a court of chancery, three superior courts (one for each county), and four types of local courts: family court, court of common pleas, justice of the peace court, and alderman's courts. From the lowest level to the highest, justice of the peace courts are the entry court level for most Delaware citizens. They have jurisdiction over civil cases of less than $15,000, as well as misdemeanor cases and most motor vehicle cases (excluding any constituting a felony offense). Justice of the peace cases are appealed to the courts of common Pleas. Alderman's courts are small local courts in Delaware authorized by some town or municipal charters to adjudicate civil misdemeanor mat-ters and traffic and parking offenses. Cases heard in alderman's courts are also appealed to the courts of common pleas. Courts of common pleas have jurisdiction in civil cases up to $75,000, all misdemeanor criminal cases except certain drug-related, and traffic offenses. Appeals of judgments from common plea courts are sent to superior courts. Family courts have jurisdic-tion over family and juvenile matters. Appeals of family court rulings go directly to the state's supreme court. Criminal cases in Delaware go to superior court.

Superior courts have general jurisdiction over civil and criminal cases except for equity cases. They have exclusive jurisdiction on felonies and most drug cases. Superior courts hear cases on appeal from the courts of common pleas, family courts in criminal cases, and from administrative agencies. In 2010, a business court was established within the superior courts. Appeals from superior courts go to the State supreme court. A court of chancery was first set in 1792 to hear all cases relating to equity: corporate issues, trusts, estates, fiduciary matters, land purchases, and commercial contractual matters. In 1831, the chancery court had one chancellor appointed by the governor for life. In 1897, that changed to an appointment for twelve-year terms. Vice-chancellor positions were added in 1939, 1961, 1984, and 1989. Since 1951, the state supreme court has consisted of five justices. That same year, the chief justice of the Delaware Supreme Court was given administrative authority over state courts. The Delaware system uses an assisted appointment methodology (also known as the Missouri Plan, some modification of which is used in thirty state systems), in which the governor appoints justices with the help of a judicial commission. Cases appealed out of the Delaware system go to the Federal Court of Appeals for the Third Circuit (see Figure 5.1) (Courts.Delaware.gov 2020).

Florida

The Florida territory was acquired by the Louisiana Purchase in 1803. Its government, including the courts, was governed as a territorial government until 1845, when Florida was admitted into the union as a state. Florida's courts are structured with a Florida Supreme Court, five district courts, twenty circuit courts, and sixty-seven county courts (one for each county). In 1851, the Florida constitution established a supreme court consisting of a chief justice and two associate justices appointed by the governor. The size of the court and the process by which justices were appointed underwent several changes over the ensuing century, but in 1940, the state constitution was amended to bring the court to its current number of seven justices. Florida maintains five district courts, created in 1957, as intermediate courts of appeal. The judges are appointed by the governor from nominating commissions, and thereafter are subject to retention elections every six years.

Florida's circuit courts are trial courts of original jurisdiction that handle civil cases over $15,000, felony criminal cases, and appeals from the county courts.

Florida's county courts have jurisdiction over misdemeanor criminal cases, county, and municipal ordinances, and civil cases under $15,000. In 1973, the constitution was amended to establish its current unified court system. Appeals out of the state system are heard by the Federal Circuit Court of Appeals for the Eleventh Circuit (State of Florida.com 2020).

Georgia

One of the original thirteen states, Georgia's court system was established in 1788. It is comprised of a supreme court, a court of appeals, forty-nine superior courts (in judicial circuits), state courts, and local courts designated as magistrate courts, juvenile courts, probate courts, and municipal courts. The Georgia Supreme Court was established in 1845, and in 1983, it was expanded to nine seats. The court of appeals was established in 1906 with twelve judges, and in 2016 increased to the current fifteen. Georgia's forty-nine judicial circuits feature anywhere from two to nineteen judges, depending on the size of the jurisdiction's population. County courts have limited jurisdiction, consisting of one or more of the following: magistrate court, probate court, juvenile court, or municipal court. Georgia's Supreme Court and Court of Appeals judges are elected statewide for six-year terms. Superior court judges are elected circuit-wide for four-year terms, as are county court judges.

Superior courts are general trial courts and hear appeals from the lower courts. Probate courts are limited in jurisdiction to wills, estates, appointment of guardians, and the involuntary hospitalization of adults. There is at least one probate court for every county.

State courts are established by certain counties and are courts of limited jurisdiction (misdemeanors and minor civil actions). Magistrate courts can hear claims of less than $15,000, issue distress warrants, trials over municipal ordinance violations, deposit account fraud, issue arrest and search warrants, and hold preliminary hearings for higher courts. Municipal courts are established by incorporated cities and hold hearings over ordinance violations, issue criminal warrants, misdemeanor shoplifting, and marijuana cases. There are 368 such courts in the state. Juvenile courts hear cases for persons seventeen years old or younger. Business courts are established within superior courts and hear equity cases. Judges are selected by a variety of means: assisted appointments for higher-level courts, and a mix of partisan or nonpartisan elections for lower-level courts. Appeals out of the state system are sent to the U.S. Circuit Court of Appeals for the Eleventh Circuit (Ballotpedia.org, "Courts in Georgia" 2020; Georgia Courts.gov 2020).

Hawaii

The State of Hawaii was the last one admitted to the union, in 1959. It has a state supreme court, an intermediate court of appeals, four circuit courts, four family courts (in circuits), and Hawaii state district courts (including small-claims court). It also has a Hawaii State Land Court and a Hawaii Tax Appeal Court. Hawaii's state supreme court decides questions of law from all state courts heard on appeal by a writ of certiorari and transfer from the intermediate court of appeals. The court also hears complaints regarding state elections; makes rules and practices for all state courts; and licenses, regulates, and disciplines lawyers and state judges. It has a chief justice and four associate justices nominated by the governor from the State Judicial Selection Commission and who serve for ten-year terms. They are held to a retention election after one year and must retire at the age of seventy. The intermediate court of appeals hears appeals from all trial courts and some state agencies. It is comprised of six judges who sit in three-judge panels. Jury trials are held in the circuit courts with jurisdiction over probate, guardianship, criminal felony cases, and civil cases more than $40,000. They share concurrent jurisdiction with district courts in civil nonjury trials between $10,000 and $40,000. District courts are courts of limited jurisdiction over traffic, misdemeanor criminal cases, small claims (less than $5,000), temporary restraining orders, and appeals from administrative decisions of motor vehicle registration. The family court provides resolution in all matters involving families and children, including delinquency, abuse and neglect, termination of parental rights, adoption, guardianship, detentions, divorce, child support, paternity claims, child custody, domestic violence matters, and civil commitment cases. Land courts are assigned by the chief justice to judges of the First Circuit Court. The tax appeals court hears appeals on real property taxation, are courts of record, and decide all questions of fact and law without intervention of a jury. For cases appealed out of the state court system, Hawaii's cases are sent to the U.S. Circuit Court of Appeals for the Ninth Circuit, which hears cases in San Francisco, California (Courts.State.Hawaii 2020).

Idaho

Idaho was admitted to the union in 1890. Its constitution establishes a unified court system comprised of a supreme court, a court of appeals, district courts established in seven judicial districts, a drug court, and a mental health court. The state supreme court has a chief justice and four associate justices, serving for staggered, six-year terms after nonpartisan, statewide elections. The court of appeals has a chief justice and three associate justices who serve staggered six-year terms after nonpartisan, statewide elections. The district courts, in seven districts, are comprised of forty-one judges who serve four-year terms after nonpartisan elections in their respective districts. Since 1999, judges in Idaho have been required to retire at age sixty-five. They have original jurisdiction over personal injury, civil claims, contract and property disputes, felonies, and appellate jurisdiction over magistrate courts, state agencies, and boards or small-claims departments. Idaho's legal system includes eighty-seven magistrate judges who are appointed by magistrate commissions; after eighteen months they stand for retention election for four-year terms in countywide elections. Magistrate judges hear civil actions under $10,000, traffic, small claims (under $4,000 with nonjury trials), probate matters, juvenile corrections, child protective proceedings, and misdemeanor criminal cases. These judges may be nonlawyers and are authorized to issue arrest warrants, search, and seizure orders, and hold preliminary probable cause hearings on felony complaints and domestic relations. Any cases appealed out of the Idaho system are sent to the U.S. Circuit Court of Appeals for the Ninth Circuit (Idaho.gov 2020).

Illinois

Illinois entered the union in 1890, prior to which it was governed by the territorial court system. Its constitution establishes a supreme court, appellate courts (in five districts), and circuit courts, created in twenty-four judicial circuits. The supreme court in Illinois has seven justices—a chief justice and six associate justices. It oversees the administration of the court system, hears cases on appeal from lower courts, and has mandatory jurisdiction over capital (death penalty) criminal cases and cases challenging the constitutionality of a state law. The justices are elected for ten-year terms. The appellate court has forty-four judges in five districts, ranging in number from six to nine judges. They are elected to ten-year terms. There are twenty-four circuit judges elected for six-year terms and who may be retained for an additional six-year term. They are elected in circuit-wide elections. Judicial circuit judges have general jurisdiction over civil and criminal matters, both felonies and misdemeanors. They are the state court system's general trial courts. They hear matters of revenue, mandamus, prohibition, habeas corpus, and review administrative decisions of state agencies. There is a special court of claims that decides monetary claims against the Illinois government, but it is better characterized as part of the legislative branch. Illinois has a courts commission comprised of one supreme court justice, two appellate justices, two circuit judges, and two citizens. If the commission finds that a judge has engaged in misconduct, it may remove them from office, order suspension without pay, or censure, or reprimand any member of the state judiciary. Cases appealed out of the Illinois system are sent to the U.S. Circuit Court of Appeals for the Seventh Circuit (Illinois Courts.gov 2020).

Indiana

Indiana was admitted to the union in 1816. The state constitution established a unified court system comprised of a supreme court, courts of appeals (in five districts), a tax court, ninety-one circuit courts, superior courts (in 177 divisions), and city and town courts. The Indiana Supreme Court was established in 1816 but was modified in 1970 by the most complete rewriting of the state constitution since 1851. The supreme court in Indiana is comprised of a chief justice and four associate justices chosen by a "merit selection" system with citizen input to the seven-member Judicial Nominating Commission. Judges are appointed by the governor. The commission selects the chief justice to serve for a five-year term. After initial appointment and two years of service, the justice must be elected in a statewide retention election to then serve for ten years. A justice must retire at age seventy-five, after facing a retention election every ten years prior to that age.

The Indiana Court of Appeals is comprised of a chief justice and fourteen associate justices. The court selects its chief justice, who serves for three years. All justices are nominated by the Judicial Nominating Commission, appointed by the governor, and face a nonpartisan retention election every ten years. The appeals court hears cases in three-judge panels. The Indiana Tax Court was created in 1986. It has exclusive jurisdiction over cases arising from tax laws and hears appeals from the Indiana Department of State Revenue or the Indiana Board of Tax Review. Indiana's trial courts are one of two levels: the Indiana circuit courts, with one in every county, has 102 judges. The Indiana superior courts have general jurisdiction for small claims and minor offenses and feature 196 judges who face election every six years. Courts of limited jurisdiction are municipal courts created by cities and towns and preside over violations of city ordinances, misdemeanors, and traffic matters. Cases that are appealed out of the Indiana state court system are sent to the U.S. Circuit Court of Appeals for the Eighth Circuit (Ballotpedia.org, "Courts in Indiana" 2020; Indiana.gov 2020).

Iowa

The state judicial system in Iowa, which entered the union as a state in 1846, includes a supreme court, a court of appeals, and eight district courts. Iowa's supreme court is the state's highest appellate court, comprised of a chief justice and six associate justices. They have the sole authority to admit persons as attorneys in courts in Iowa, supervise all state courts, their judicial officers and court employees. The justices are appointed by the governor from a list of nominees of the State Judicial Nominating Commission and serve for one year before coming up for election to serve eight-year terms. All judges in Iowa must retire at age seventy-two. The members of the Iowa Supreme Court select their own chief justice.

Iowa district courts are general jurisdiction trial courts overseeing civil cases of any amount, felony criminal cases, domestic relations cases, family law cases, and the supervision over state administrative issues. District judges are appointed by the governor from a list of nominees of the State Nominating Commission and serve for six-year terms. Juvenile judges have jurisdiction over juvenile matters, and probate judges have limited jurisdiction over probate cases. Magistrate judges serve their home counties and preside over simple misdemeanors, local infractions, and small claims. District associate justices have the same jurisdiction as magistrate judges, over their districts, but also have the authority to hear more serious misdemeanors, civil suits up to $10,000, and certain specified juvenile cases. Cases that are appealed out of the state system to federal courts are sent to the U.S. Circuit Court of Appeals for the Eighth Circuit (Iowa Courts.gov 2020).

Kansas

Established as a state in 1861, Kansas's constitution established a supreme court, a court of appeals, thirty-one district courts, and municipal courts. In 1972, the state gave the Kansas Supreme Court administrative authority over all courts in the state. The supreme court hears cases on appeal from the court of appeals and has original jurisdiction in a few cases. Since 1958, the supreme court has been a seven-member body, with justices selected via a merit-based nomination process that culminates with governmental appointments. After one year, newly installed judges face election every six years. The Kansas Court of Appeals is comprised of fourteen justices on three-judge panels that hear appeals from the district courts for both civil and criminal cases.

The chief justice is the most senior justice and has general administrative supervision over all state courts. Chief justices are selected by the members of the court itself. Appeals court judges are appointed by the governor with consent of the Kansas Senate. They serve four-year terms and are retained for successive terms by public vote. The thirty-one district courts have

163 judges and are the state's general trial courts with original jurisdiction over all civil and criminal cases. Each district covers from one to seven counties. Kansas municipal courts are trial courts for cases involving violations of city ordinances. The Office of Judicial Administration implements the rules and procedures of the supreme court as they apply to the operation and administration of the judicial branch. Cases that are appealed from the state to the federal court system are sent to the U.S. Circuit Court of Appeals for the Tenth Circuit (Kansas Courts.org 2020).

Kentucky

Kentucky entered the union in 1792. Its court system was extensively revised in 1975 with the passage of a new constitution that unified its court system. It has a supreme court of seven justices elected from seven districts in nonpartisan elections who serve for eight-year terms. The court selects the chief justice. It hears cases on appeal from the court of appeals, but cases regarding the death penalty, life imprisonment, or imprisonment of twenty years or more are sent automatically for review by the supreme court rather than to the court of appeals. The supreme court establishes rules of conduct for judges and attorneys in the state system. The court of appeals was also established in 1975 and has fourteen justices elected two each from seven districts for eight-year terms and in nonpartisan elections. They hear appeals from the circuit courts. The circuit courts are the state's courts of original jurisdiction; they consider cases of capital offense, felonies, land disputes, probate, civil lawsuits over $5,000, and issue injunctions. They also hear appeals from the district courts. There are fifty-seven circuits with one or more judges, and ninety-five judges in all. District courts are courts of limited jurisdiction hearing misdemeanor criminal cases, violations of municipal ordinances, traffic cases, small claims (under $2,500), juvenile cases, civil cases under $5,000, and some family court proceedings. They are elected in nonpartisan elections for four-year terms. Appeals from Kentucky are sent to the U.S. Circuit Court of Appeals for the Sixth Circuit (Ballotpedia.org, "Courts in Kentucky" 2020; Kentucky Courts.gov 2020).

Louisiana

Louisiana became a state in 1812. The state has a complex court system that still reflects its French and Spanish colonial heritage (with a parish structure, for example, and more court levels than most states). Since reorganizing in 1982, Louisiana's legal system features a supreme court, five circuit courts of appeals, and forty-two district courts. Among its courts of limited jurisdiction are four juvenile courts, one family court, 390 justice of the peace courts, mayor's courts, city courts, and three parish courts (See Figure 5.3).

The supreme court in Louisiana consists of seven judges elected for ten-year terms by partisan election. The court is the state's final court of appeals and hears cases appealed from the court of appeals (comprised of fifty-three judges who sit in three-judge panels and are also elected to ten-year terms by partisan election). There are 230 judges in the state's forty-two district courts, which has at least one judge per parish (called counties in other states). Judges in each district elect a chief judge for that district. District courts serve as the state's main trial courts. There are four juvenile courts comprised of fifteen judges who hear cases involving persons under the age of seventeen, delinquency cases, adoptions, support cases, and neglect cases. There is one family court with four judges that sits in East Baton Rouge Parish. The state also has approximately 390 justices of the peace courts that hear civil cases under $5,000, small-claims cases (up to $2,000), traffic, misdemeanor criminal cases, and hold preliminary hearings that are nonjury trial cases. The state also includes 250 mayor's courts and forty-six city courts each of which can hear civil cases of less than $15,000 and whose judges serve for six-year terms. City courts have been established to replace justice of the peace and mayor's courts. There are three parish courts that have jurisdiction to hear civil cases up to $10,000, misdemeanor criminal cases with the authority to impose fines of $1,000 or less and jail sentences of six months of less. All judicial elections in the state are by partisan election. Appeals from the Louisiana Supreme Court are sent to the U.S. Circuit Court of Appeals for the Fifth Circuit (Ballotpedia.org, "Courts in Louisiana" 2020; Louisiana.gov 2020).

Maine

Maine became a state in 1820. It has a supreme court of seven justices who are appointed by the governor with approval of the Senate. They hear cases on appeal from the superior courts. The chief justice is the head of the judicial branch in Maine. In 1929, the superior court system was established in Maine, and it remains the only type of court in the state to hold jury trials. There are seventeen justices that hold court in regular intervals in Maine's sixteen counties. Judges are appointed to seven-year terms by the governor with consent of the Senate. Appeals from superior courts go to the supreme court (there is no intermediate court of appeals in Maine). In 1978, an administrative court was established to hear appeals from administrative agencies, and in 1990, several specialized courts were organized within the Maine court system: problem-solving courts: family division; Juvenile Drug Treatment Program; and the Adult Drug Court Program. Maine has thirteen district courts, created in 1961, with thirty-six judges. In 1820, a probate court was established with jurisdiction over wills, trusts, adoptions, name changes, and appointment of guardians. It is the only court within Maine to which judges are elected to four-year terms by partisan election (Ballotpedia.org, "Courts in Maine" 2020; Courts.Maine.gov 2020).

Maryland

Maryland was one of the original thirteen states, established in 1788. Maryland's highest court is the court of appeals. Its intermediate-level appellate court is the court of special appeals. Its main trial courts of general jurisdiction are the Maryland circuit courts, established in eight judicial circuits. Its lower courts of limited jurisdiction are the district courts. The district court system was established in 1971. District courts hear cases in thirty-four locations in twelve districts with at least one judge in every county (and the City of Baltimore, which has a city/county government). They do not hold jury trials. Judges handle civil and criminal cases; claims up to $30,000, domestic violence, landlord–tenant disputes, traffic cases, and misdemeanor criminal cases. The circuit courts are the state's trial courts of general jurisdiction. They handle felonies, family and juvenile matters, and appeals from district and orphan's courts and administrative agencies. Within the state's circuit court system, its chief justice is simply the judge with the most seniority. Circuit court judges are elected for fifteen-year terms. The court of special appeals is the intermediate appellate court, established in 1966. It has fifteen judges that typically hear appeal cases in three-judge panels. They are appointed by the governor with consent of the Senate for ten-year terms. The state's final court of appeals is the court of appeals. It hears cases related to the death penalty, legislative redistricting, the removal of certain state officials for misconduct, and other questions of law. The court of appeals has a chief justice and six associate justices appointed by the governor with consent of the Senate to ten-year terms. The state also has an orphan's court to handle wills, estates, and other probate matters. In 1989, the Office of Administrative Hearings was established to hear administrative law cases. Appeals out of the Maryland state system are sent to the U.S. Circuit Court of Appeals for the Fourth Circuit (Courts.State.Maryland 2020).

Massachusetts

Massachusetts was another of the original thirteen states, established in 1788. It has a supreme judicial court, an appeals court, and seven trial courts with special jurisdictions. All judges in the state are appointed by the governor and serve until the mandatory retirement age of seventy. The Massachusetts Supreme Judicial Court is the highest appellate court in the state and the oldest in continuous existence in the United States (it was established in 1692 when Massachusetts was a colony). In 1781, the supreme court was expanded to five justices, and in 1873 the court expanded to seven justices led by a chief justice.

First established in 1972, the appeals court is today comprised of a chief justice and twenty-four associate justices. They hear appeals in three-judge panels. The superior courts have exclusive jurisdiction over first-degree murder cases but also hear cases involving civil actions over $25,000, labor disputes, and all other types of criminal cases. The court is comprised of a chief justice and eighty-one associate justices. Courts of specialized or limited jurisdiction include district courts (one chief justice and 157 associate judges), the Boston Municipal Court (one chief justice and twenty-nine associate judges), the housing court (chief justice and nine associate judges), the land court (chief justice and six associate justices), juvenile court (chief justice and forty-nine associate justices), and a probate/family court (chief justice and fifty associate justices). Cases appealed out of the Massachusetts state court system go to the U.S. Circuit Court of Appeals for the Fourth Circuit (Massachusetts.gov 2020).

Michigan

Michigan entered the union in 1837. Its court system consists of a supreme court, a court of appeals, circuit courts, and three lower-level courts of limited jurisdiction: the district courts, the probate courts, and the court of claims, plus twelve special subject-matter courts, the Native American tribal courts. Established in 1805, the Michigan Supreme Court is the court of final appeal. It has a chief justice and six associate justices who hear cases on appeal from the Michigan Court of Appeals. Judges on the supreme court are elected for eight-year terms in nonpartisan elections. The court of appeals is the intermediate appellate court. In 1963, it was created with nine judges, but since 2012, it has had twenty-four judges who are elected from four districts in nonpartisan elections for six-year terms. The chief justice of the court of appeals is selected by the supreme court. The court of appeals typically hears cases in three-judge panels. The circuit court is the general trial court of the state, organized into fifty-seven courts. Judges are elected for six-year terms. The Michigan Court of Claims is a specified court within the Michigan Court of Appeals and has statewide, limited jurisdiction and is comprised of the chief justice and four associate judges. The district courts (also known as the people's courts) are the general jurisdiction trial courts. There are one hundred district courts in the state, and the judges are elected for six-year terms. The probate court has seventy-eight probate judges who are elected for six-year-terms, and they hear cases on all types of probate matters. Since 1996, Michigan has also established twelve Native American tribal courts to hear cases involving Native Americans in the state on jurisdictional matters that operate in a manner similar to that of the district courts. Any case that is appealed out of the Michigan court system on U.S. Constitutional grounds is sent to the U.S. Circuit Court of Appeals for the Sixth Circuit (Ballotpedia.org, "Courts in Michigan" 2020; Courts.Michigan.gov 2020).

Minnesota

Minnesota entered the union in 1858. Its court system includes a supreme court, a court of appeals, ten district courts, a tax court, and the Minnesota Workers Compensation Court of Appeals. The Minnesota Supreme Court has a chief justice and six associate justices. They hear all cases on appeal from the court of appeals. In 2005, the state created a new governance structure call the Judicial Council to administer policy for the judicial branch and on which the chief justice is the head. The chief justice is appointed by the governor. Judges are elected on statewide, nonpartisan elections and serve for six-year terms. Vacancies are filled by appointment of the governor with consent of the Senate. Justices must retire at age seventy. The court of appeals is the intermediate appellate court. It was established in 1983 and has a chief justice (appointed by the governor for a three-year term) and eighteen associate justices. They typically hear cases in three-judge panels. The judges are elected in statewide, nonpartisan elections for six-year terms; but midterm vacancies are appointed by the governor with consent of the Senate. Judges must retire at age seventy. District courts are the general jurisdiction, original trial courts for the state; they include nearly three hundred judgeships across ten districts. Judges in the district court system, which was created in 1858, are elected by district in nonpartisan elections for six-year terms. In 2011, the state established the Minnesota Workers' Compensation Court of Appeals. It has a chief justice and four associate judges who are appointed by the governor, confirmed by the Senate, and serve for six-year terms. Cases appealed out of Minnesota go to the U.S. Circuit Court of Appeals for the Eighth Circuit (Minnesota Courts.gov 2020).

Mississippi

Mississippi joined the union in 1817. It has a two-tiered appellate court system with a supreme court as the final court of appeals, and a court of appeals as an intermediate-level appellate court. The supreme court has nine justices elected from three districts in staggered, nonpartisan elections for eight-year terms. The court of appeals was created in 1995. It has ten judges elected from five districts in staggered, nonpartisan elections to terms of eight years. The Mississippi circuit courts are the state's general jurisdiction trial courts. They are divided into twenty-two circuits and have fifty-seven judges, ranging in districts from one to four judges depending on population size. The judges are elected in nonpartisan elections and serve four-year terms. The state has several limited-jurisdiction courts at the county or municipal levels. The chancery courts are in twenty districts with fifty-two judges, ranging from one to four per district and are elected for four-year terms in nonpartisan elections. There are twenty-two county courts with thirty judges, also elected in nonpartisan elections to four-year terms. Justice courts have limited jurisdiction with civil cases under $3,500, misdemeanor criminal cases, and traffic offenses. There are eighty-two such courts with 197 judges. They are the sole courts of the state in which judges are elected by partisan elections to four-year terms. As of 2018, Mississippi has forty courts called intervention courts that deal with drug and alcohol addiction matters. The state has 237 municipal courts that hear misdemeanor cases and traffic cases. Their terms vary by municipal charter. Finally, there are twenty-two counties that have established youth courts that deal with persons under the age of eighteen. In counties that have no youth court, such cases are sent to the chancery courts. Cases that are appealed out of the state system are sent to the U.S. Circuit Court of Appeals for the Fifth Circuit (Courts.Mississippi.gov 2020).

Missouri

Missouri became a state in 1821. Its constitution establishes a supreme court as the appellate court of last resort (final appeal). There are three courts of appeals as intermediate appellate courts in three districts. The state's general jurisdiction trial courts are the circuit courts and number forty-five. Courts of limited jurisdiction are the municipal courts. The state's supreme court has seven judges selected by the Missouri Plan (an appellate judicial commission nominates judges, the governor appoints, and after one year the judge stands for a retention election). They serve for twelve-year terms and must retire at age seventy. The intermediate appellate court, the court of appeals, is divided into three districts. Appeals court judges are also selected by the Missouri Plan, and also must retire at age seventy. Circuit courts are the state's courts of general jurisdiction and are organized into forty-five districts. There are 140 circuit judges and about 260 associate judges that preside over small-claims courts, municipal courts, family courts, probate cases, and juvenile cases. Since 2001, Missouri has also maintained problem-solving courts that handle drug-related cases for either juvenile or adult offenders. Cases appealed out of the Missouri judicial system are sent to the U.S. Circuit Court of Appeals for the Eighth Circuit (Courts .Missouri.gov 2020).

Montana

Montana, which became a state in 1889, has only one appellate court—the Montana Supreme Court. The state's general jurisdiction trial courts are the district courts, comprised of fifty-six courts organized in twenty-two judicial districts. Under the district courts are courts of limited jurisdiction: the justice courts, the city courts, and the municipal courts. The state also has four courts of specific or limited subject-matter jurisdiction: youth courts, worker's compensation court, water court, and the asbestos claims court. They are separate dockets used by some inferior courts.

The Montana Supreme Court was originally established in 1889 with three justices but expanded to seven justices (a chief justice and six associate justices) in 1972. Justices are elected in statewide, nonpartisan elections for terms of eight years, but for midterm vacancies, they are appointed using the Missouri Plan system. District courts were also created in 1889; their operations and responsibilities were modified by the 1972 constitution and amended again in 2001. There are forty-five district judges who are elected in their respective districts by nonpartisan election for six-year terms. Montana also maintains several courts of limited jurisdiction: sixty-one justice courts, eighty-four city courts, and six municipal courts. For these courts, judges are elected for six-year terms in nonpartisan elections. Cases that are appealed out of the state system go to the U.S. Circuit Court of Appeals for the Ninth Circuit (Courts.Montana.gov 2020).

Nebraska

Nebraska, which became a state in 1867, has a four-tier system of courts established by its constitution. It has a supreme court, an intermediate appeals court called the Nebraska Court of Appeals, twelve district courts of general jurisdiction, and courts of limited jurisdiction consisting of ninety-three county courts, the juvenile court, the workers' compensation court, problem-solving courts, and drug courts. The supreme court has a chief justice and six associate justices appointed by the governor from a list selected by the Judicial Nominating Commission. The chief justice nominees are selected statewide, the six associate justices from one of six districts. All courts in the state operate under the supervision of the supreme court.

The court of appeals was established by passage of a constitutional amendment of 1990. It consists of six justices appointed by the governor from nominations by the Judicial Nominating Commission. A chief justice is selected for two-year, renewable terms. The Nominating Commission uses the same six districts as for the supreme court. The court of appeals also sits in Lincoln, but the court also travels to other cities to hear appeals, typically in the form of three-judge panels. The district courts are the state's general jurisdiction trial courts, organized in twelve districts that encompass the state's ninety-three counties. Cases appealed from district courts go to the court of appeals. County courts are courts of limited jurisdiction, for example, in civil matters, hearing cases for up to $57,000. There are three separate juvenile courts hearing cases relating to juvenile matters (under the age of eighteen). Montana also maintains a workers' compensation claims court. Cases appealed out of Nebraska go to the U.S. Circuit Court of Appeals for the Eighth Circuit (Ballotpedia.org, "Courts in Nebraska" 2020; Supreme Court.Nebraska.gov 2020).

Nevada

Nevada entered the union in 1864. Its constitution establishes the typical four-tier judicial system. Its supreme court is the appellate court of last resort. It is comprised of a chief justice and six associate justices who are elected for six-year terms in nonpartisan, statewide elections. Any vacancies occurring mid-term are filled by gubernatorial appointment. The court hears appeals in three-judge panels. The court of appeals is the intermediate appellate court. It has a chief justice and two associate justices also elected statewide in nonpartisan elections for six-year terms. The state's general jurisdiction trial courts are its eleven district courts. District judges are elected district-wide to six-year terms in nonpartisan elections. The number of judges varies per district, but there are eighty-two judgeships in total in the system. Courts of limited jurisdiction include seventeen municipal courts, established by city charter, and forty Justice courts that are local courts elected in townships for six-year terms. Appeals out of the Nevada state system go to the U.S. Circuit Court of Appeals for the Ninth Circuit (Ballotpedia .org, "Courts in Nevada" 2020; Nevada.Courts.gov 2020).

New Hampshire

A state since 1788, New Hampshire has a supreme court comprised of a chief justice and four associate justices. It 1983, the state's unified court system was established, and the chief justices of the supreme court and the superior court were charged with overseeing the state's court system, advised by a twenty-four-member Judicial Council. Supreme court justices are appointed by the governor for life (i.e., for "good behavior") but must retire at age seventy. The superior courts are the state courts of general jurisdiction for both civil and criminal matters. They are organized into eleven courts comprised of a chief justice and twenty-eight associate justices. The circuit courts were created in 1963, but the structure of these courts was revised in 2011. There are now thirty-six courts in the state's thirty-four counties. These are courts of limited jurisdiction. Circuit court judges are appointed by the governor with consent of the Executive Council. In 2011, several specified subject-matter courts were established by the state: ten family courts in three counties; ten probate courts in ten counties, and drug and mental health courts. Cases appealed out of the New Hampshire state system are sent to the U.S. Circuit Court of Appeals for the First Circuit (Courts.New Hampshire.gov 2020).

New Jersey

New Jersey is also one of the original thirteen states, with its first constitution dating all the way back to 1787. Its court system overall handles roughly 7 million cases per year. Its system was amended to its current unified form in 1947. The state supreme court has a chief justice and six associate justices who are appointed by the governor and confirmed by the Senate for seven-year terms. Justices must retire at age seventy. The New Jersey Superior Court has thirty-three justices and includes an appellate division with fifteen courts that hear appeals in two- or three-judge panels. The state's superior court system also has a chancery division that hears equity, family, and probate cases. The superior court has one main trial court in each of the state's twenty-one counties. They are courts of general jurisdiction over both civil and criminal cases. Municipal courts in New Jersey have only limited jurisdiction. New Jersey also maintains two special subject-matter courts related to taxes and the Palisades Interstate Park System. Cases appealed to the federal appellate court system go to the U.S. Circuit Court of Appeals for the Third Circuit (New Jersey Courts.gov 2020).

New Mexico

New Mexico was established as a state in 1912. It has a supreme court as well as a court of appeals, thirteen district courts, and four courts of limited jurisdiction: magistrate, Bernalillo County Metropolitan Court, municipal courts, and probate court. The court system was unified in 1988 by a new constitution that changed judicial selection from partisan election to a hybrid (modified Missouri Plan) system of appointment by the governor followed by a retention election. In New Mexico, judges are required to obtain 57 percent or more of the votes to be retained. The supreme court has a chief justice and four associate justices and is the state's court of last resort. It meets in Santa Fe and has mandatory jurisdiction for death penalty cases, appeals from Public Regulatory Commission, removal of public officials, writs of habeas corpus, and challenging nominations. It has discretionary jurisdiction by writ of certiorari. The court of appeals has ten justices, meets in both Santa Fe and Albuquerque, and hears appeals in panels of three. They hear about nine hundred cases per year. It has mandatory jurisdiction over civil cases, non–death penalty criminal felony cases, juvenile cases, and discretionary appeal in interlocutory decisions and administrative appeal cases. New Mexico has eighty-four district court judgeships spread across thirteen districts. District courts are the state's general jurisdictional trial courts for torts, contracts, real property, estate, domestic relations, mental health, appeals from administrative agencies and from lower courts, and exclusive jurisdiction over juvenile cases.

New Mexico's court system also includes several lower courts of limited jurisdiction. The state's fifty-four magistrate courts, for example, hold jury trials to hear misdemeanor criminal complaints and civil cases under $10,000, preliminary hearings for felony cases, and judge-only hearings for misdemeanors and traffic cases. The Bernalillo County Metropolitan Court has nineteen judges and is a court of limited jurisdiction comparable to the magistrate courts. New Mexico also maintains municipal and probate courts with limited jurisdictions. Appeals out of the New Mexico state system to the U.S. appellate court system are sent to the U.S. Circuit Court of Appeals for the Tenth Circuit (New Mexico Courts .gov 2020).

New York

New York is one of the thirteen original states and so traces its court system to 1788. It has a complex court system (see Figure 5.2). In New York state, the highest court is not the supreme court—rather it is called the court of appeals. First established in 1847, the court of appeals' seven justices are appointed by the governor—with the consent of the state Senate—based on recommendations made by the state's Commission on Judicial Nominations. Judges on this court, which is New York's court of last resort and its highest appellate court, are subject to mandatory retirement when they reach seventy-six years of age.

The New York Supreme Court, meanwhile, is the state's court of original and general jurisdiction and primary trial court. It has two upper divisions that serve as the state's intermediate courts of appeal: the appellate division of supreme court (in four departments), and the appellate terms of supreme court (in two departments). They hear appeals from the supreme courts and from the superior courts. The Supreme Court of the State of New York is akin to the major trial courts in other states at the county level. There are sixty-two supreme courts in New York, one for each county. Their judges are elected for fourteen-year terms in partisan elections and must retire at age seventy-six. New York also has superior courts of general jurisdiction—one in each of the state's sixty-two counties. They are not to be confused with the state's fifty-seven county courts outside of New York City that handle misdemeanors and civil cases under $25,000. Below them are several different courts of limited jurisdiction. There are two district courts (one in Nassau County with fourteen judges and one in Suffolk County with thirteen judges). They hear civil cases under $15,000 and misdemeanor criminal cases. There are numerous city courts (outside New York City) that are also of limited jurisdiction (e.g., under $15,000 in civil cases) and which have judgeships that are filled through popular elections. The state is also home to thirteen hundred town and village courts (also sometimes known as justice courts) presided over by approximately twenty-two hundred judges who are elected for four-year terms. Other specialized limited jurisdiction courts by subject matter are the court of claims, the family court, and the surrogate court (which handles probate matters). In addition, there are the Civil Court for the City of New York and the Criminal Court of the City of New York. Cases that are appealed outside the state of New York to the federal system go to the U.S. Circuit Court of Appeals for the Second Circuit (Ballotpedia.org 2020, "Courts in New York"; Courts.New York.gov 2020).

North Carolina

One of the original thirteen states, North Carolina traces its court system to 1789. The state has a tiered court structure, with a supreme court at the top followed by the court of appeals, superior courts (in forty-six districts), and district courts (in forty-five districts). The court system was established in 1977 into various judicial districts. It was amended in 2004 to have nonpartisan elections, and again in 2018 to return to partisan elections. The supreme court is the state's highest and final court of appeals and has original jurisdiction in death penalty cases. Its chief justice and six associate justices are elected to eight-year terms in statewide elections. Midterm vacancies are filled by gubernatorial appointment. The court of appeals is the intermediate appellate court and has fifteen judges that hear cases in three-judge panels. They hear appeals from the superior and district courts and certain administrative agencies. The judges are elected to eight-year terms in partisan statewide elections. The superior courts are the courts of general jurisdiction trial courts in civil and criminal matters (civil cases over $25,000). Restructured in 2018, superior courts include ninety-seven judgeships in forty-eight districts with five divisions. Superior court judges are also elected to eight-year terms in district elections. District courts are courts of limited jurisdiction organized in forty-one districts. They hear civil and criminal cases, and magistrate matters, and hear cases in some cities and towns when authorized by the General Assembly. Civil cases may have a jury, but child custody cases are judge-only. In criminal cases, they hear misdemeanor cases with no jury, such as in juvenile matters (under sixteen), and juvenile delinquency (under eighteen), cases of alleged abuse, neglect, and dependency. Magistrate courts are small-claims courts (under $10,000), and handle landlord evictions, vehicle mechanics' liens, and can issue warrants for arrests. North Carolina cases that are appealed out of the state are sent to the U.S. Circuit Court of Appeals for the Fourth Circuit (Ballotpedia.org, "Courts in North Carolina" 2020; North Carolina Courts.gov 2020).

North Dakota

North Dakota became a state in 1889. It has a three-tiered judicial system: a supreme court, district courts (in seven judicial districts), and municipal courts. The supreme court is the state's appellate court; it consists of five justices elected to ten-year terms in statewide, nonpartisan elections staggered every two years. Vacancies are filled by gubernatorial appointment. The justices themselves select their chief justice, who has a term of five years. The state's trial courts of general jurisdiction are the district courts, of which there is one in each of the fifty-three counties. These courts also hear juvenile matters and serve as appellate courts for certain administrative agencies. The district court judges are elected for six-year terms in district-wide, nonpartisan elections. Vacancies may be filled by gubernatorial appointment with nominees from the Judicial Nominating Committee or by special election. Appointed judges serve two years until the next general election, at which time they are filled by election for the remainder of any term.

The state's courts of limited jurisdiction are the municipal courts, which serve the state's incorporated municipalities. The municipal system contains seventy-five judgeships in ninety municipal courts. Municipal judgeships, which feature four-year terms, are determined via popular election. In 1911, a juvenile court was established in North Dakota as a subset of district courts to hear cases involving youth under the age of eighteen. In 2016, the state established a domestic violence court that began hearing cases in 2018. Cases from North Dakota that are appealed to the federal system are sent to the U.S. Circuit Court of Appeals for the Eighth Circuit (North Dakota Courts.gov 2020).

Ohio

Ohio was admitted to the union in 1803. It has a supreme court, district courts of appeals (in twelve districts), the court of claims, courts of common pleas, municipal courts, county courts, and mayor's courts. The supreme court is the court of last resort; it hears appeals from twelve district courts and has mandatory jurisdiction in the following: 1) death penalty cases; 2) if a U.S. Constitution or Ohio Constitutional question is raised; or 3) in cases where two or more courts of appeals issued conflicting legal opinions. The supreme court has a chief justice and six associate justices; all justices on the court are elected to six-year terms, in statewide, nonpartisan elections.

The courts of appeals are established in each of twelve appellate districts, with a varied number of judges depending on the district's population and caseloads. They are elected for six-year terms in even-numbered years, and each district has a minimum number of four judges. Vacancies are filled by gubernatorial appointment. Court of claims has original jurisdiction over all civil actions, and over decisions of the state's attorney general on claims allowed under the Victims of Crime Act. Typically, one judge hears cases, but three-judge panels may be held when a novel or complex issue of law or fact arises. The courts of common pleas are the state's main trial courts, and one can be found in each of Ohio's eighty-eight counties. They are organized into separate divisions: general, domestic violence, juvenile, and probate. Court of claims judges are elected for six-year terms by nonpartisan ballot. The general division courts hear all felony cases and civil cases of more than $15,000 and have appellate jurisdiction over some state agencies. Domestic relations divisions hear cases for divorce, annulment, legal separations, spousal support, and parental rights. The juvenile division hears cases involving youth under eighteen for criminal complaints, paternity, child abuse, non-support, and delinquency cases. The probate division was established in 1851 and hears all probate matters. Courts of limited jurisdiction include municipal courts (established in 1901) and county courts (in 1907). These courts hear cases of civil disputes of less than $15,000 as well as misdemeanor criminal cases. They also hold preliminary hearings for felony cases. Their judges are elected to six-year terms on nonpartisan ballots. Ohio also features "special subject" courts, called mayor's courts. These courts consider alcohol- and drug-related cases, local ordinances cases, and noncriminal traffic law cases. Any case appealed out of the Ohio state court system goes to the U.S. Circuit Court of Appeals for the Sixth Circuit (Supreme Court.Ohio.gov 2020).

Oklahoma

Oklahoma's court system was established when the territory entered the union in 1907. Some aspects of the state's court system are unique, with elements that can only be found in neighboring Texas. The state has two appellate courts of last resort: the supreme court, whose nine justices hear civil appeals, and the court of criminal appeals, whose five justices hear criminal appeals. The supreme court also serves as overall administrator of the judicial branch of the state. Judges to both courts are by gubernatorial appointments from a list supplied by the Judicial Nominating Commission. They are appointed for life but must win reelection (a retention election) every six years. There is also an intermediate court of civil appeals comprised of twelve judges organized into four divisions. The state's general jurisdiction trial courts are seventy-seven district courts, one in each of the state's counties, organized into twenty-six judicial districts. Those judges are election in district-wide, nonpartisan elections and serve four-year terms. Oklahoma's courts of limited jurisdiction are its municipal courts. For two cities, Oklahoma City and Tulsa, the operations of the municipal courts are specified for cities with two hundred thousand or more in population. For cities under two hundred thousand, municipal courts are not "courts of record," which are courts in which all testimony is recorded and can be reviewed by an appellate court. Oklahoma has two special courts: a Worker's Compensation Commission with four judges, and a court of tax review comprised of three-judge panels from the district court system. Two Independent courts operate in Oklahoma: a court on the judiciary, with nine judges from the district court system and five from the appellate division who hear cases to remove justices accused of misconduct or incompetence; and a court of impeachment, which is set up to hear impeachment cases of executive branch officials. Cases appealed out of the Oklahoma state system go to the U.S. Circuit Court of Appeals for the Tenth Circuit (Ballotpedia.org, "Courts in Oklahoma" 2020; CourtFacts.org 2020).

Oregon

In 1998—140 years after first achieving statehood—Oregon amended its court system into the unified system it follows today. As in most states, the highest appellate court of last resort or final appeal is the supreme court. It is comprised of a chief justice and six associate justices who are elected on statewide, nonpartisan ballots for six-year terms, although vacancies that occur midterm are filled by the governor. Oregon's supreme court hears mandatory appeals in death penalty cases and appeals from the tax court of appeals and is the administrative head of the Oregon Justice Department.

The court of appeals is the intermediate appellate court, with a chief justice and twelve associate justices organized into four panels to hear appeals from the circuit courts. Its judges are elected to six-year terms on nonpartisan ballots, but midterm vacancies are appointed by the governor. The state's trial courts of general jurisdiction are the circuit courts, of which there are 173 justices in twenty-seven judicial circuits, and at least one for each of the state's thirty-six counties. These judges are elected to six-year terms on nonpartisan ballots in countywide elections. The Oregon State Tax Court is a court of special jurisdiction related to taxation issues and has two divisions: the regular division, with one judge, and the magistrate division with three judges. Oregon also has several courts of limited jurisdiction: municipal courts, county courts (in seven eastern counties), and justice courts. Appeals out of the Oregon state system are sent to the U.S. Circuit Court of Appeals for the Ninth Circuit (Ballotpedia.org, "Courts in Oregon" 2020; Courts.Oregon.gov 2020).

Pennsylvania

Pennsylvania is one of the original thirteen states, and its constitution was established in 1787. It has a supreme court, superior courts of Pennsylvania in three districts, the commonwealth court of Pennsylvania, courts of common pleas in sixty judicial districts, and magisterial district courts. The supreme court has a chief justice and six associate justices. They may retire at age seventy, and the mandatory retirement age is seventy-eight. They are elected in statewide partisan elections, but vacancies are filled by gubernatorial appointment. The superior court is an intermediate appellate court established in 1895, and it hears both civil and criminal appeals from the courts of common pleas. It has fifteen judges elected for ten-year terms in statewide, partisan elections. The commonwealth court was established in 1968 and has nine judges elected to ten-year terms. They hear cases in three-judge panels. The president-judge (equivalent to chief justice) of the commonwealth court is selected by colleagues for a five-year term. The court meets in Harrisburg, Philadelphia, and Pittsburgh. The commonwealth courts hear disputes regarding civil matters in cases concerning banking, insurance, utility regulations, labor practices, elections, land use cases, taxes, and workers' compensation. The courts of common pleas are the general jurisdiction trial courts for both civil and criminal matters in Pennsylvania. There are courts for sixty-seven counties organized into sixty judicial courts (several counties with smaller populations are bundled together into districts). Judges on the bench for the courts of common pleas are selected by partisan election for ten-year terms, although vacancies due to death, illness, or retirement are filled by the governor, with nominations subject to Senate confirmation. The state also has courts of limited jurisdiction called magisterial district courts. The cities of Pittsburgh and Philadelphia have each established municipal courts by their city charters. Cases appealed out of the Pennsylvania system are sent to the U.S. Circuit Court of Appeals for the Third Circuit (Ballotpedia.org, "Courts in Pennsylvania" 2020; Pennsylvania Courts 2020).

Rhode Island

Rhode Island was one of the original thirteen states, and its state constitution of 1790 created its judicial system. It has a supreme court, superior courts, and several different courts of limited jurisdiction, including district courts, family courts, workers' compensation courts, and traffic tribunals. The Rhode Island Supreme Court has a chief justice and four associate justices who hear appeals from the superior courts. The judges are selected by gubernatorial-assisted appointment and serve for life with no mandated retirement age. Superior courts are the major trial courts of the state with general jurisdiction in criminal matters (all felonies) and civil cases over $5,000. They are comprised of a chief justice and twenty-one associate justices and five magistrates. They are organized into four judicial circuits and are selected by a merit system. District courts have a chief justice and twelve associate justices and two magistrates.

They are courts of limited jurisdiction hearing misdemeanor cases and civil cases under $5,000; appeals of district court rulings go to superior court. Another minor court of limited jurisdiction in Rhode Island is the family court, with a chief judge, eleven associate judges, and nine magistrates. They hear cases concerning domestic relations, juvenile offenders, and domestic violence. Appeals from the family court go to the supreme court. The state's workers' compensation court has a chief judge and nine associate judges. They hear all workers' compensation claim cases, with appeals of rulings going to the supreme court. Finally, the state has a traffic tribunal court of limited jurisdiction made up of a chief magistrate, two associate judges, and five magistrates. It hears all noncriminal traffic cases. Appeals from it are sent to the appropriate district court. Court rulings that are appealed out of the Rhode Island system go to the U.S. Circuit Court of Appeals for the First Circuit (Ballotpedia.org, "Courts in Rhode Island" 2020; Courts.Rhode Island .gov 2020).

South Carolina

One of the original thirteen states, South Carolina established its constitution and thus its early court system in 1788. It has a supreme court established in 1895 that is comprised of a chief justice and four associate justices who are appointed by the General Assembly, the state legislature's lower house. The South Carolina Supreme Court is the appellate court of last resort. In 1983, the state established the court of appeals as an intermediate appellate court comprised of a chief justice and eight associate justices appointed by the General Assembly for six-year terms. They hear cases in three-judge panels.

The circuit courts are the state's trial courts of general jurisdiction. They have limited appellate jurisdiction over cases from lower courts. They are organized into sixteen judicial circuits and hear civil cases in the court of common pleas and criminal cases in the court of general sessions. They are comprised of forty-six judges, elected by the General Assembly for six-year, staggered terms, and preside over cases on a rotating basis. The state has four courts of limited jurisdiction, including family courts and probate courts (each with fifty-seven judges placed in the same districts as the circuit courts). Magistrate courts deal with minor crimes punishable by less than thirty days' jail time, or fines less than $500. Municipal courts deal with city ordinance violations. Finally, South Carolina's legal system includes a court of special jurisdiction called the master-in-equity court that hears nonjury cases referred by circuit court judges. Appeals out of the South Carolina system are sent to the U.S. Circuit Court of Appeals for the Fourth Circuit (Ballotpedia.org, "Courts in South Carolina" 2020; South Carolina Courts.org 2020).

South Dakota

South Dakota was established as a state in 1889. It has a supreme court, with both circuit courts and magistrate courts installed in seven regions or circuits. The South Dakota Supreme Court is the highest court; this appellate court is comprised of a chief justice and four associate justices appointed by the governor, one justice each from five geographic districts. Three years after appointment they run in a nonpartisan, retention election, and again every eight years thereafter. The members of the court select their own chief justice.

South Dakota's circuit courts are the trial courts of general jurisdiction. There are forty-one judges overseeing cases in sixty-six counties divided into seven circuits. Circuit judges are elected to eight-year terms in nonpartisan elections, or for midterm vacancies, appointed by the governor. The supreme court appoints one judge in each circuit to act as the presiding circuit judge. South Dakota's magistrate courts are courts of limited jurisdiction hearing misdemeanor criminal cases and civil cases under $10,000. They are divided into the seven circuits, and each court has one full-time magistrate, with extra

judges appointed by the magistrate to serve specific counties and municipalities. When a case is appealed out of the
South Dakota state system, it goes to the U.S. Circuit Court
of Appeals for the Eighth Circuit (Ballotpedia.org, "Courts in
South Dakota" 2020; Unified Judicial System, South Dakota
.gov 2020).

Tennessee

Tennessee became a state in 1796. It has a supreme court, two
intermediate appellate courts, and six trial courts of varied
jurisdiction. The supreme court, as the court of final appeals,
was established in 1870. It has a chief justice and four associate justices appointed by the governor followed by a retention
election. They serve for eight-year terms. The retention election
system was challenged and upheld as constitutional in 1973, in
Higgins v. Dunn, and is known as the Tennessee Plan.

The court of appeals, set in 1925, is the state's intermediate
appellate court. It has twelve judges who hear cases in three-
judge panels. They are appointed by the governor, confirmed
by the General Assembly, and face retention elections. The
general trial courts, which serve the state's ninety-five counties,
are organized into thirty-one judicial districts, within which
each district has a chancery court (reflecting the English-court
tradition) and a probate court. Judges are elected to eight-year
terms in partisan elections. They also hear appeals from lower-
level courts. Criminal courts are in thirteen of the thirty-one
judicial circuits; they are presided over by judges elected to
eight-year terms on partisan ballots. Tennessee also maintains
several lower trial courts of limited jurisdiction. The general
session courts are found in each county. The juvenile and family courts number ninety-eight courts with 109 judges and
forty-five magistrates. Magistrates are court officials who may
not be lawyers. They assist judges and can hear cases in matters
of limited jurisdiction or hold preliminary hearings for cases
before such matters go to judges. There are special probate

courts in two Tennessee counties: Davidson and Shelby, whose judges are elected to eight-year terms. Municipal courts vary from city to city, but generally hear cases involving city ordinances. A case that is appealed out of the Tennessee court system is sent to the U.S. Circuit Court of Appeals for the Sixth Circuit (Ballotpedia.org, "Courts in Tennessee" 2020; Tennessee Courts.gov 2020).

Texas

Texas came into the union in 1846 without having spent time as a territory, so it never established territorial courts. Texas is the only state besides Oklahoma with an appellate court of last resort or final appeal divided into two courts by subject matter. The Texas Supreme Court was first established in 1846, the same year Texas joined the United States. It has a chief justice and eight associate justices who are elected on partisan ballots for six-year, renewable terms, although they may also be appointed by the governor in the event of vacancies on the court due to illness, death, retirement, or other circumstances.

In 1876, Texas established its court of criminal appeals, positions for which are filled in the same manner as the state's supreme court. Texas also maintains fourteen intermediate Courts of Appeals with jurisdiction to hear both civil and criminal matters on appeal from district courts or county courts. Each appellate court has jurisdiction over a specific geographic region, and each has a chief justice and at least two associate justices, but the total number in each appellate court varies, depending on the population and caseloads of their respective region. There are eighty justices in all who hear cases in three-judge panels. They are elected on partisan ballots for six-year, renewable terms.

The state's general jurisdiction, original trial courts are the district courts. Each county in Texas has at least one district court, although in sparsely populated counties, one district court may be served by a single district court and populous urban counties may be served by several district courts. The state's 254 counties have 448 district court judges who are elected in larger urban counties by partisan ballot for four-year terms. The larger urban districts have the one district court as the constitutionally stipulated district court, and the other district courts are statutory county courts. Texas's court system also includes statutory probate courts in ten of the fifteen largest metropolitan areas.

There are two types of courts of limited jurisdiction in Texas. Justice courts are one per county, with from one to eight justices of the peace (JPs) in county-designated precincts. JP's may issue search warrants, and some serve as coroners in counties with no medical examiner. They also preside over small-claims matters. Their terms of office vary by county charter stipulation. The other courts of limited jurisdiction in Texas are municipal courts, again having at least one per incorporated city, although larger cities are served by multiple municipal courts. They have exclusive jurisdiction over city ordinances, and in some cities, concurrent jurisdiction with justices of the peace. Municipal court judges are either elected or appointed (usually by the mayor) depending on the city charter. Verdicts appealed from the Texas court system go to the U.S. Circuit Court of Appeals for the Fifth Circuit (Ballotpedia.org, "Courts in Texas" 2020; Texas Courts.gov 2020).

Utah

Utah entered the union as a state in 1894. Since 1987, when the state's court system was revised, Utah has used a judicial appointment system in which the governor selects judges from a list submitted by a special advisory commission. After serving a three-year term, the appointed judges must then run in a retention election for either four- or six-year terms, depending on the seat.

The supreme court is the state's court of last resort. It has a chief justice—chosen by the members of the court—and four associate justices. The term of office for justices to the court is ten years. The court of appeals is the intermediate appellate court for the state of Utah. It has seven justices who serve for six-year terms. Like the supreme court, it meets in Salt Lake City. The state's trial courts of general jurisdiction are the eight district courts, whose seventy-one judges serve for four-year terms. There are two courts of limited jurisdiction: juvenile courts, which hear all juvenile-related cases, and justice courts, which deal with misdemeanors and small-claims civil cases. Cases that are appealed out of the supreme court to the federal level are sent to the U.S. Circuit Court of Appeals for the Tenth Circuit (Ballotpedia.org, "Courts in Utah" 2020; Utah Government 2020).

Vermont

Vermont was established as a state in 1791. It has a supreme court, superior courts organized into five divisions, and a Judicial Bureau. Being a smaller state both geographically and in population, Vermont's court system is relatively simple. The supreme court, the appellate court of last resort, traces back to 1777, but its current configuration was established in 2010, when the court system was unified. The 2010 reorganization established the uniform system of judicial selection: a merit selection system with assisted appointment by the governor, from a list provided by a Judicial Nominating Commission, confirmed by the Senate, with retention elections by the Vermont General Assembly at the end of each six-year term. The supreme court has a chief justice and four associate justices. The superior courts are the state's trial courts of general jurisdiction. There are fourteen courts, one in each county, divided into five divisions: civil, criminal, environmental, family, and probate. It also has a Judicial Bureau with statewide jurisdiction over civil matters and municipal ordinances. The courts of limited jurisdiction are the district courts, which have a total of seventeen judges. There is one judge in each county, except

Chittenden County (the state's most populous). Chittenden has six judges. Judges can retire at age seventy, and the mandatory retirement is age ninety. Any case appealed out of the Vermont state system goes to the U.S. Circuit Court of Appeals for the Second Circuit (Ballotpedia.org, "Courts in Vermont" 2020; Vermont Judiciary 2020).

Virginia

Virginia is one of the original thirteen states, and it ratified its state constitution in 1788. It has a supreme court, court of appeals, circuit courts (120 courts in thirty-one judicial circuits), general district courts (in thirty-two districts), and juvenile and domestic relations district courts (also in thirty-two districts). Judges in the Virginia system are elected by both houses of the Virginia General Assembly for varying terms depending on the level of court. Interim appointments are gubernatorial appointments for the appellate-level courts, and by the circuit court for lower courts in the circuit district. There are also magistrates who are appointed by the executive secretary of the supreme court. Magistrates can issue adult arrest warrants, search warrants, emergency protective orders, emergency medical health orders, and bail hearings.

The supreme court has a chief justice and six associate justices. It is the state's appellate court of last resort. Justices serve for twelve-year terms. The court of appeals is the intermediate appellate court, whose eleven judges serve for eight-year terms. Circuit courts are the general jurisdiction trial courts. The circuit court system is comprised of 120 courts organized into thirty-one circuits. The judges serve for eight-year terms. The general district courts, established in thirty-two districts, are courts of limited jurisdiction. Circuit court judges serve six-year terms, with interim appointments by the circuit court in which they are located. There are also thirty-two juvenile and domestic relations district courts in the same corresponding districts as the general district courts. They also serve for six-year terms. The state also has a Judicial Inquiry and Review Commission of seven members appointed for four-year terms by the General Assembly who supervise judge discipline. A case that is appealed out of the Virginia system is sent to the U.S. Circuit Court of Appeals for the Fourth Circuit (Courts.Virginia 2020).

Washington

Washington became a state in 1889. It has a four-tier court structure: a supreme court, a court of appeals (in three divisions), superior courts (thirty-nine, one in each county), and thirty-nine district courts and municipal courts of limited jurisdiction. Judges in the state are elected to either four- or six-year terms, depending on the level of the court, except interim vacancies are appointed (gubernatorial or by the city mayor, depending on the level of the court). The supreme court is the appellate court of last resort. It meets in Olympia and has a chief justice and eight associate justices who are elected to six-year terms staggered so that three are elected every two years. The mandatory retirement age is seventy-five. The court of appeals is the intermediate appellate court. It meets in three divisions (Tacoma, Seattle, and Spokane). The appellate judges are elected in statewide, nonpartisan elections for six-year terms.

Superior courts are the general trial courts of both civil and criminal jurisdiction, and are appellate courts for lower-level (district or municipal) courts. There are thirty-nine superior courts (one in each county). Judges are elected to four-year terms. There are two types of courts of limited jurisdiction. District courts, with one in each of the thirty-nine counties, have judges who hear misdemeanor cases, civil cases of less than $100,000, and small-claims suits. The judges are elected by district for four-year terms. Municipal courts are also of limited jurisdiction but can hear no civil cases. They hear noncriminal traffic cases and misdemeanors occurring in city limits. They are either elected to four-year terms in city elections or are appointed by the mayor in some cities, according to the city's charter. Appeals out of the Washington court system go to the U.S. Circuit Court of Appeals for the Ninth Circuit (Ballotpedia.org, "Courts in Washington" 2020; Courts.Washington.gov 2020).

West Virginia

West Virginia was split off from Virginia and established as a state in 1863, at the height of the Civil War. It has a supreme court, thirty-one circuit courts, and two lower courts of limited jurisdiction: family courts and magistrate courts. The court system was first organized by the Constitution of 1863 and modified subsequently in 1872, 1880, 1974, and 2002. Judges in West Virginia are elected in nonpartisan elections. Vacancies on the bench are filled by the governor, but appointees must then run for election in the next general election.

The supreme court is the state's appellate court; it has a chief justice and four associate justices who are elected statewide in nonpartisan elections for twelve-year terms, although many on the court were initially appointed. The circuit courts are the general jurisdiction trial courts for West Virginia, but they also hear appeals from the lower courts (family, magistrate) and from administrative agencies. The state's fifty-five counties are divided into thirty-one circuits. There are seventy-five judgeships spread across the thirty-one districts. Judges are elected in district-wide, nonpartisan elections for eight-year terms. The state has forty-seven judges serving in twenty-seven family courts, which were established by the state in 2002. Family court judges are elected to eight-year terms or are appointed by the governor to fill vacancies until the next election. Magistrate courts are courts of limited jurisdiction. There are 158 magistrates, at least two in each of the fifty-five counties. They hear civil cases of less than $10,000, misdemeanor criminal cases, hold preliminary hearings in felony cases, issue warrants (arrest and search), and can issue protective orders for domestic violence. They are elected in nonpartisan elections to four-year terms. Interim vacancies are appointed by the chief circuit judge of the circuit in which they are located. Interim judges serve until the next election. Decisions appealed to the federal system go to the U.S. Circuit Court of Appeals for the Fourth Circuit (Courts.West Virginia.gov 2020).

Wisconsin

Wisconsin entered the union in 1848. The state court system enshrined in the constitution approved that same year has since undergone modification in 1978 and 2002. The supreme court is the appellate court of last resort in Wisconsin. It features a chief justice and six associate justices and meets in the state capitol of Madison. Judges are elected in statewide, nonpartisan elections for ten-year terms, with midterm vacancies filled by gubernatorial appointment. The court of appeals is the state's intermediate appellate court. Established in 1978, the court of appeals features sixteen justices in four districts (Milwaukee, Waukesha, Wausau, and Madison). Since 2015, the chief justice of the court of appeals is appointed by the supreme court for a two-year term. Justices are elected in statewide, nonpartisan elections for six-year terms.

The circuit courts are the state's trial courts of general jurisdiction. First created in 1848, the current system was established in 1978. As of 2020, when twelve new positions were added, Wisconsin has 261 judgeships spread across the state's seventy-two counties. The judges are elected countywide in nonpartisan elections for six-year terms. Milwaukee County has forty-seven judgeships alone, but thirty counties with smaller populations have only one judge each, and some of Wisconsin's smallest counties share a judge. Circuit courts in Wisconsin hear civil and criminal cases, as well as appeals from the municipal courts.

The state's courts of limited jurisdiction are municipal court judges, of which there are 240 judges in 237 courts, many serving part-time. Madison and Milwaukee, Wisconsin's two biggest cities, have several municipal judges. There are sixty-seven municipal judges who are in smaller population municipalities that share justices. They are elected in municipal elections. Cases that are appealed out of the Wisconsin state system go to the U.S. Circuit Court of Appeals for the Seventh Circuit (Ballotpedia.org, "Courts in Wisconsin" 2020; Wisconsin.Courts.gov 2020).

Wyoming

Wyoming was established as a state in 1890. The state with the smallest population in the country, it has a correspondingly simple court system. It has a supreme court, district courts in nine districts, and circuit courts and municipal courts that have limited jurisdictions. Since its establishment in 1890, Wyoming's court system has undergone two major revisions, in 1957 and then again in 1971, when Wyoming approved a new state constitution. The 1971 constitution set the mandatory retirement age for judges at seventy.

The supreme court is the state's appellate court and sits in Cheyenne. It has five justices appointed by the governor. The district courts are the trial courts of general jurisdiction and are organized into nine judicial districts that preside over the state's twenty-three counties. District court judges are appointed by the governor to four-year terms from a candidate list maintained by the Judicial Nominating Commission, and they face retention elections after one year. The circuit courts hear civil cases of $50,000 or less and misdemeanor criminal cases. Circuit court judges in Wyoming serve for four-year terms. The lowest-level courts of limited jurisdiction are the municipal courts, established in all incorporated cities. They can impose fines up to $750 or jail time up to six months. The various municipalities set their terms for municipal courts in the city charter, and judges at this level are typically appointed by the mayor with consent of the municipal council. Cases appealed out of the Wyoming state system go to the U.S. Circuit Court of Appeals for the Tenth Circuit (Courts.Wyoming 2020).

Bibliography

Alabama Unified Judicial System Structure. 2010. "A History of the Alabama Judicial System, 1820–1991." http://judicial.alabama.gov/docs/judicial_history.pdf. Accessed August 7, 2020.

Arizona Courts.gov. 2020. https://www.azcourts.gov/AZCourts. Accessed August 7, 2020.

Arkansas Courts.gov. 2020. https://www.arcourts.gov/sites/default/files/Arkansas-Court-Structure.pdf. Accessed August 7, 2020.

Armed Services Board of Contract Appeals. 2020. "About the Board," https://www.asbca.mil. Accessed August 6, 2020.

Bach, Amy. 2010. *Ordinary Justice: How America Holds Court.* New York: Henry Holt.

Ballotpedia.org. 2020. "Courts in Georgia." https://ballotpedia.org/Courts_in_Georgia. Accessed August 9, 2020.

Ballotpedia.org. 2020. "Courts in Indiana." https://ballotpedia.org/Courts_in_Indiana. Accessed August 9, 2020.

Ballotpedia.org. 2020. "Courts in Kentucky." https://ballotpedia.org/Courts_in_Kentucky. Accessed August 10, 2020.

Ballotpedia.org. 2020. "Courts in Louisiana." https://ballotpedia.org/Courts_in_Louisiana. Accessed August 10, 2020.

Ballotpedia.org. 2020. "Courts in Maine." https://ballotpedia.org/Courts_in_Maine. Accessed August 10, 2020.

Ballotpedia.org. 2020. "Courts in Michigan." https://ballotpedia.org/Courts_in_Michigan. Accessed August 10, 2020.

Ballotpedia.org. 2020. "Courts in Nebraska." https://
ballotpedia.org/Courts_in_Nebraska. Accessed August 11,
2020.

Ballotpedia.org. 2020. "Courts in Nevada." https://
ballotpedia.org/Courts_in_Nevada. Accessed August 12,
2020.

Ballotpedia.org. 2020. "Courts in New York." https://ballotpedia
.org/Courts_in_New_York. Accessed August 12, 2020.

Ballotpedia.org. 2020. "Courts in North Carolina." https://
www.ballotpedia.org/Courts_in_North_Carolina. Accessed
August 12, 2020.

Ballotpedia.org. 2020. "Courts in Oklahoma." https://www
.ballotpedia.org/Courts_in_Oklahoma. Accessed August 13,
2020.

Ballotpedia.org. 2020. "Courts in Oregon." https://www
.ballotpedia.org/Courts_in_Oregon. Accessed August 13,
2020.

Ballotpedia.org. 2020. "Courts in Pennsylvania." https://
www.ballotpedia.org/Courts_in_Pennsylvania. Accessed
August 13, 2020.

Ballotpedia.org. 2020. "Courts in Rhode Island." https://
www.ballotpedia.org/Courts_in_Rhode_Island. Accessed
August 13, 2020.

Ballotpedia.org. 2020. "Courts in South Carolina." https://
www.ballotpedia.org/Courts_in_South_Carolina. Accessed
August 13, 2020.

Ballotpedia.org. 2020. "Courts in South Dakota." https://
ballotpedia.org/Courts_in_South_Dakota. Accessed
August 13, 2020.

Ballotpedia.org. 2020. "Courts in Tennessee." https://ballotpedia
.org/Courts_in_Tennessee. Accessed August 13, 2020.

Ballotpedia.org. 2020. "Courts in Texas." https://ballotpedia
.org/Courts_in_Texas. Accessed August 13, 2020.

Ballotpedia.org. 2020. "Courts in Utah." https://ballotpedia .org/Courts_in_Utah. Accessed August 14, 2020.

Ballotpedia.org. 2020. "Courts in Vermont." https:// ballotpedia.org/Courts_in_Vermont. Accessed August 14, 2020.

Ballotpedia.org. 2020. "Courts in Washington." https://ballotpedia .org/Courts_in_Washington. Accessed August 14, 2020.

Ballotpedia.org. 2020. "Courts in Wisconsin." https://ballotpedia .org/Courts_in_Wisconsin. Accessed August 14, 2020.

Barton, Benjamin. 2010. *The Lawyer-Judge Bias in the American Legal System.* New York: Cambridge University Press.

Board of Immigration Appeals. 2020. "About the Board." https://www.justice.gov/eoir/board-of-immigration-appeals. Accessed August 6, 2020.

Board of Veterans Appeals. 2020. "About the Board." https:// www.bva.va.gov. Accessed August 6, 2020.

Buenger, Michael L., and Paul De Muniz. 2015. *American Judicial Power: The State Court Perspective.* Northampton, MA: Edward Elgar Publishing.

Carp, Robert, Kenneth Manning, and Ronald Stidham. 2016. *Judicial Process in America.* Washington, DC: Congressional Quarterly Press.

Civilian Board of Contract Appeals. 2020. "About the Board." https://www.cbca.gov/board/index.html. Accessed August 6, 2020.

Corley, Pamela, Artemus Ward, and Wendy Martinek. 2015. *American Judicial Process: Myth and Reality in Law and Courts.* New York: Routledge.

CourtFacts.org. 2020. "Oklahoma Court System." https:// courtfacts.org/courtsystem. Accessed August 13, 2020.

Court of Military Commission Review. 2020. "About Us." https://www.mc.mil/AboutUs/OrganizationOverview.aspx. Accessed August 6, 2020.

Courts.Alaska.gov. 2020. "Court System Information." http://
www.courts.alaska.gov/main/ctinfo.htm#trial. Accessed
August 7, 2020.

Courts.California.gov. 2020. "About California Courts." https://
www.courts.ca.gov/2113.htm. Accessed August 9, 2020.

Courts.Delaware.gov. 2020. "An Overview of the Delaware
Court System." https://courts.delaware.gov/overview.aspx.
Accessed August 9, 2020.

Courts.Maine.gov. 2020. https://www.courts.maine.gov
/about. Accessed August 10, 2020.

Courts.Michigan.gov. 2020. "Michigan Courts." https://www
.courts.michigan.gov/About. Accessed August 10, 2020.

Courts.Mississippi.gov. 2020. "About the Courts." https://
courts.ms.gov/aboutcourts/aboutthecourts.php. Accessed
August 11, 2020.

Courts.Missouri.gov. 2020. https://www.courts.mo.gov
/government/judicial-branch. Accessed August 11, 2020.

Courts.Montana.gov. 2020. "Montana Courts." https://
courts.mt.gov/Courts. Accessed August 11, 2020.

Courts.New Hampshire.gov. 2020. https://www.courts.state
.nh.us. Accessed August 12, 2020.

Courts.New York.gov. 2020. "The Courts." https://www
.nycourts.gov/courts. Accessed August 12, 2020.

Courts.Oregon.gov. 2020. "About the Oregon Judicial
Department." https://www.courts.oregon.gov/about.
Accessed August 13, 2020.

Courts.Rhode Island.gov. 2020. https://www.courts.ri.gov
/Pages/Courts.aspx. Accessed August 13, 2020.

Courts.State.Colorado. 2020. "Colorado's State Court
System. https://www.courts.state.co.us/Courts/Index.cfm.
Accessed August 9, 2020.

Courts.State.Hawaii. 2020. https://www.courts.state.hi.us.
Accessed August 9, 2020.

Courts.State.Maryland. 2020. "Maryland Courts." https://
www.courts.state.md.us. Accessed August 10, 2020.

Courts.Virginia. 2020. https://www.va.gov/courts/orgchart
/jud_system.pdf. Accessed August 14, 2020.

Courts.Washington.gov. 2020. https://www.courts.wa.gov.
Accessed August 14, 2020.

CourtsWest Virginia. 2020. https://www.courtswv.gov/.
Accessed August 14, 2020.

Courts.Wyoming. 2020. "About the Courts." https://www.courts
.state.wy.us/about-the-courts. Accessed August 14, 2020.

Crowe, Justin. 2012. *Building the Judiciary: Law, Courts, and
the Politics of Institutional Development.* Princeton, NJ:
Princeton University Press.

Federal Judicial Circuit.gov. 2020. "Alien Terrorist Removal
Court, 1996–Present." https://www.fjc.gov/history/courts
/alien-terrorist-removal-court-1996-present. Accessed
August 5, 2020.

Georgia Courts.gov. 2020. https://www.georgia.courts.gov/.
Accessed August 9, 2020.

History.com. 2009. "Treaty of Paris." https://www.history
.com/topics/american-revolution/treaty-of-paris. Accessed
August 1, 2020.

Howard, J. Woodford, Jr. 2014. *Courts of Appeals in the Federal
Judicial System.* Princeton: Princeton University Press.

Idaho.gov. 2020. "Overview of the Idaho Court System."
https://isc.idaho.gov/overview.pdf. Accessed August 9, 2020.

Illinois Courts.gov. 2020. http://www.illinoiscourts.gov/.
Accessed August 9, 2020.

Indiana.gov, Judiciary. 2020. https://www.in.gov
/judiciary/2794.htm. Accessed August 9, 2020.

Iowa Courts.gov. 2020. https://www.iowacourts.gov/.
Accessed August 9, 2020.

Jonakait, Randolph. 2008. *The American Jury System.* New Haven, CT: Yale University Press.

Jud.Ct.Gov. 2020. https://jud.ct.gov/. Accessed August 9, 2020.

Kansas Courts.org. 2020. "About the Courts." https://www .kscourts.org/About-the-Courts. Accessed August 9, 2020.

Kentucky Courts.gov. 2020. https://kycourts.gov/pages/index .aspx. Accessed August 10, 2020.

Koelling, Peter M., ed. 2016. *The Improvement of the Administration of Justice.* Washington, DC: American Bar Association.

Kubicek, Theodore. 2006. *Adversarial Justice: America's Court System on Trial.* New York: Algora Publishing.

Landis, James, and Felix Frankfurter. 2017 (republishing the 1928 volume). *The Business of the Supreme Court.* New York: Routledge.

Law.jrank.org. 2020. "Colonial Period: Local Courts and Magistrates." https://law.jrank.org/pages/11879/Colonial -Period-Local-Courts-Magistrates. Accessed July 21, 2020.

Library of Congress. 2011. "The Articles of Confederation: The First Constitution of the United States." https://www .articlesofconfederation.com. Accessed July 21, 2020.

Louisiana.gov. 2020. https://www.louisiana.gov/government /judicial-branch. Accessed August 10, 2020.

Marcus, Maeva, ed. 1992. *Origins of the Federal Judiciary: Essays on the Judiciary Act of 1789.* New York: Oxford University Press.

Martin, James. 2011. "The Articles of Confederation: The First Constitution of the United States." September 18, 2011. https://blogs.loc.gov/law/2011. Accessed July 21, 2020.

Massachusetts.gov. 2020. "Massachusetts Court System." https://www.mass.gov/orgs/massachusetts-court-system. Accessed August 10, 2020.

Mays, G. Larry, and Laura Woods Fidelie. 2016. *American Courts and the Judicial Process.* New York: Oxford University Press.

Merit System Protection Board. 2020. "About MSPB." https://www.mspb.gov/about/about.htm. Accessed August 5, 2020.

Minnesota Courts.gov. 2020. "About the Courts." https://www.mncourts.gov/about-the-courts.aspx.

National Constitutional Center. 2019. "Packing the Supreme Court Explained." Scott Bomboy. https://constitutioncenter.org/blog/packing-the-supreme-court-explained. Accessed August 2, 2020.

Neubauer, David, and Stephen Meinhold. 2009. *Judicial Process: Law, Courts, and Politics in the United States.* Boston: Cengage.

Nevada Courts.gov. 2020. https://nvcourts.gov/Supreme/Court_Information/About_the_Nevada_Judiciary. Accessed August 12, 2020.

New Jersey Courts.gov. 2020. "New Jersey Court System." https://www.njcourts.gov/courts. Accessed August 12, 2020.

New Mexico Courts.gov. 2020. https://www.nm.courts.gov/about-the-courts.aspx. Accessed August 12, 2020.

North Carolina Courts.gov. 2020. https://www.nccourts.gov/structure-of-the-courts. Accessed August 12, 2020.

North Dakota Courts.gov. 2020. https://www.ndcourts.gov. Accessed August 12, 2020.

Office of Dispute Resolution for Acquisition. 2020. "About ODRA." https://www.faa.gov/about. Accessed August 6, 2020.

Pennsylvania Courts. 2020. "Courts." http://www.pacourts.us/courts. Accessed August 13, 2020.

Posner, Richard. 2017. *The Federal Judiciary: Strengths and Weaknesses.* Cambridge, MA: Harvard University Press.

Postal Service Board of Contract Appeals. 2020. "About USPS, judicial." https://about.usps.com/who/judicial. Accessed August 6, 2020.

Ragsdale, Bruce, ed. 2013. *Debates on the Federal Judiciary: A Documentary History*, Vol 1: 1787–1875.Washington, DC: Federal Judiciary Center.

Rosen, Jeffrey. 2007. *The Supreme Court: The Personalities and Rivalries That Defined America.* Online: Griffin Publishing.

Scheb, John M., II, and Hemant Sharma. 2015. *An Introduction to the American Legal System*, 4th ed. Albany, NY: West/Thomson Learning.

Shugerman, Jed H. 2012. *The People's Courts: Pursuing Judicial Independence in America.* Cambridge, MA: Harvard University Press.

South Carolina Courts.org. 2020. https://www.sccourts.org/Overview-SC-Judicial-System.cfm. Accessed August 13, 2020.

State of Florida.com. 2020. "Florida Courts." https://www.stateofflorida.com/florida-courts. Accessed August 9, 2020.

Supreme Court.Nebraska.gov. 2020. https://www.nebraska.gov/government/judicial. Accessed August 11, 2020.

Supreme Court.Ohio.gov. 2020. https://www.supremecourt.ohio.gov/. Accessed December 20, 2021.

Surrency, Erwin. 1956. "The Courts in the American Colonies." *American Journal of Legal History,* Vol. 11, No. 3 (July): 253–276. Accessed July 21, 2020.

Surrency, Erwin. 2002. *History of the Federal Courts.* Dobbs Ferry, NY: Oceana Publications.

Tennessee Courts.gov. 2020. "Courts." https://www.tncourts.gov/courts. Accessed August 13, 2020.

Texas Courts.gov. 2020. "About Texas Courts." https://www.txcourts.gov/about-texas-courts. Accessed August 13, 2020.

Unified Judicial System, South Dakota.gov. https://ujs.sd.gov. Accessed August 13, 2020.

United States International Trade Commission (USITC). 2020. "About the ITC." https://www.usitc.gov/about-court. Accessed August 4, 2020.

United States Patent and Trademark Office (USPTO). 2020a. "The PTAB." https://www.uspto.gov/learning-and-resources/newsletter/inventors-eye/patent-trial-and-appeal-board. Accessed August 4, 2020.

United States Patent and Trademark Office (USPTO). 2020b. "Trademark Trial and Appeal Board." https://www.uspto .gov/about-us/organizational-offices/trademark-trial-and -appeal-board. Accessed August 5, 2020.

U.S. Courts.gov. 2020. "About Federal Courts." https://www .uscourts.gov/about-federal-courts/court-role-and-structure. Accessed August 4, 2020.

U.S. Courts.gov. 2020. "Bankruptcy Cases." https://www. uscourts.gov/about-federal-courts/types-cases/bankruptcy -cases. Accessed August 5, 2020.

U.S. Courts.gov. 2020. "The Court of International Trade." https://www.cit.uscourts.gov/about-court. Accessed December 20, 2021.

U.S. Courts.gov. 2020. "FISCR." https://www.fisc.uscourts .gov/FISCR. Accessed August 5, 2020.

U.S. Courts.gov. 2020. "Judges & Judgeships." https://www .uscourts.gov/JudgesandJudgeships/FederalJudgeships.aspx. Accessed August 4, 2020.

U.S. Courts.gov. 2020. "United States Court of Appeals for Veterans Claims." https://www.usa.gov.federal-agencies /court-of-appeals-for-the-federal-circuit. Accessed December 20, 2021.

U.S. Courts.gov. 2020. "The U.S. Court of Appeals for the Federal Circuit." https://cafc.uscourts.gov/the-court/court -jurisdiction. Accessed August 5, 2020.

U.S. Courts.gov. 2020. "U.S. Court of Federal Claims." https://www.uscfc.uscourts.gov/. Accessed August 5, 2020.

U.S. Courts.gov. 2020. "U.S. Foreign Intelligence Surveillance Court." https://fisc.uscourts.gov/FISCR. Accessed August 5, 2020.

U.S. Tax Court.gov. 2020. "About the Court." https://www .ustaxcourt.gov/about-the-court. Accessed August 4, 2020.

Utah.Government.gov. 2020. https://www.utah.gov
/government/judicial.html. Accessed August 14, 2020.

Van Cleve, Nicole G. 2016. *Crook County: Racism and
Injustice in America's Largest Criminal Court.* Stanford, CA:
Stanford University Press.

Vermont Judiciary. 2020. https://www.vermontjudiciary.org
/Court-Divisions. Accessed August 14, 2020.

Washington, D.C.: Federal Judicial Center. https://www
.usa.gov/federal-agencies/federal-judicial-center. Accessed
December 20, 2021.

Wheeler, Russell R., and Cynthia Harrison. 2006. *Creating
the Federal Judicial System*, 3rd ed. Washington, DC:
Federal Judicial Center.

Wisconsin.Courts.gov. 2020. https://www.wicourts.gov
/courts/overview.htm. Accessed August 14, 2020.

2 Problems, Controversies, and Solutions

Introduction

The American judicial system is an integral part of its government and politics. Since adoption of the U.S. Constitution in 1789, America's government has been divided into three coequal branches—executive (presidency), legislative (Congress), and judicial (led by the Supreme Court). The U.S. government also operates at three levels—federal, state, and local. This tripartite division of power and authority was crafted by America's Founding Fathers to establish a complex system of checks and balances designed to keep any one branch from becoming too powerful. While that division works as intended to limit the power of government, historically it also has led to a number of associated and often unintended clashes, problems, and controversies between and within these branches. Some of those problems arise from the complexity that the tripartite division of power entails. Other problems arise from the complexity of American society as it has evolved since the late eighteenth century. This chapter discusses some of the most pressing or enduring problems and controversies, as well as some proposed solutions or responses to these issues.

As the Article III branch of government, the various courts in the judicial system are designed to be a check on the other two branches of government. Deriving from the English tradition

The Lady Justice statue is depicted as blindfolded Justitia, with balance scales and sword. In judicial practice, however, justice is often not blind to bias and prejudice. (Stevanovicigor/Dreamstime.com)

of common law and an adversarial approach to litigation, the American judicial system's emphasis on the role of judges and lawyers has been a source of controversy since the inception of America's bold experiment in self-governance. Given that the very nature of American democracy is to reflect the society that it governs, it is not surprising that many of the problems facing the judicial system reflect the complex and sometimes wrenching cultural, demographic, and economic changes that have transformed America over nearly two and a half centuries.

Problem 1: The Bewildering Complexity of the American Judicial System

Regarding the national level of government, Section 1 of Article III of the U.S. Constitution states rather succinctly that "The judicial power of the United States shall be vested in one Supreme Court, and in such inferior Courts as the Congress may from time to time ordain and establish. The Judges, both of the supreme and such inferior Courts, shall hold their Offices during good Behavior, and shall, at stated Times, receive for their Services, a Compensation, which shall not be diminished during their Continuance in Office." The simplicity of the wording in Section 1 does not define or elaborate on what is meant by "good behavior." Neither does it specify the process by which a judge who does not exhibit good behavior may be removed from office. It delineates the authority of the U.S. Congress to "ordain and establish" inferior courts without specifying any details as to the number or jurisdiction of such inferior courts. The process by which the U.S. Congress carried out that authority contributes to the overall complexity of the American judicial system.

Among the first acts of the new Congress was passage of the Judiciary Act of 1789. It was enacted in response to the constitutional grant of authority to ordain and establish inferior courts. The Act of 1789 elaborated on the number of justices and on the jurisdiction of the U.S. Supreme Court and the circuit court. The Act of 1789 was amended and the number of justices and circuits was changed in ten subsequent judiciary acts passed between 1801 and 1925. These assorted judiciary acts established the primary structural organization and hierarchy of the federal judiciary into what we know today: a U.S. Supreme Court, thirteen circuit courts, and ninety-four district courts. These legislative acts not only established today's federal court system, it placed limits on the capacity of the U.S. Supreme Court to review lower-court decisions. Federalism is a system of government that divides authority and power into three separate levels, each with its own base of power. It thus constrains the federal courts and provides strong pressure either to adopt hard-edged categorical rules and tests or to defer to the political process to address and resolve problems brought to the federal courts for adjudication. Several critics have suggested reforms, for example, to reduce the impact of the judicial philosophy of "originalism" (i.e., a strict adherence to the original language and meaning of the Constitution) (Coan 2019; Koelling 2016; Mays and Fidelie 2016; Posner 2017).

To a certain extent, the increasing complexity of the federal judiciary is an unintended consequence of the attempt by the U.S. Congress to address the growing size—in terms of both population and geographic territory—of the United States. As the country added and settled territories in the west—territories that ultimately became states—Congress recognized the need to establish, extend, and expand court systems in these regions. It added to and amended the geographic jurisdiction of what ultimately became ninety-four district courts and thirteen circuit courts that were established or amended in 1891, 1893, 1911, 1948, 1963, 1981, and 1982.

During this same era of geographic expansion and settlement, the federal court system was expanded to accommodate a number of federal courts of special subject-matter jurisdiction, including the U.S. Court of Federal Claims (1855), the U.S. Court of Customs and Patent Appeals (1909), the Commerce Court (1910), the U.S. Tax Court (1924), the U.S. Court of

Appeals for the Armed Forces (1951), the Bankruptcy Appellate Panel (1978), the U.S. Merit Systems Protection Board (1979), the U.S. Court of Appeals for Veterans Claims (1980), the U.S. Court of International Trade (1980), and most recently, the U.S. Alien Terrorist Removal Court (1996). These courts were established to ensure that the judges sitting on their respective benches had the special subject-matter expertise to deal with the complex legal issues with which they dealt. However, the sheer number of such courts contributes to the complexity of the judicial system.

As the United States acquired new territories, Congress also established territorial courts. These are exemplified today by the territorial courts of American Samoa, Guam, Northern Mariana Islands, Panama Canal Zone, Puerto Rico, and the U.S. Virgin Islands. Congress likewise established special courts of limited jurisdiction and duration, such as the U.S. Court of Private Land Claims (1890–1904), the U.S. Court for China (1906–1943), the U.S. Court for Berlin (1955–1990), and the U.S. District Court for the Canal Zone (1982). Congress further exacerbated the complexity of the federal judiciary by establishing appellate boards and commission of limited jurisdiction for special subject matter, such as the U.S. Court of Military Commission Review, the Civilian Board of Contract Appeals, the Armed Services Board of Contract Appeals, the Office of Dispute Resolution for Acquisition, the Board of Immigration Appeals, and the Board of Veterans Appeals. While each of these boards, commissions, and courts were tailored to address particular complex legal issues, their proliferation made the court system as a whole appear increasingly opaque and mazelike to many ordinary Americans (Corley, Ward, and Martinek 2015; Koelling 2016; Mays and Fidelie 2016; Neubauer and Meinhold 2009; Posner 2017).

The bewildering complexity of the judicial system is further exacerbated by the fact that a host of different types of courts also exist at the state and local levels. Those court organizations, established and codified by state constitutions upon achieving statehood, have also changed over time so that state and local court structures and jurisdictions can keep up with the evolving needs of state and local citizens. But the combination of local, state, and federal court systems—and the ways in which they interact with one another—has resulted in additional obstacles and uncertainties for people seeking to navigate America's courts (Barton 2010; Buenger and De Muniz 2015; Kubicek 2005; Neubauer and Meinhold 2009).

For example, some states and local systems use different names for the same kinds of courts or have courts with the same name that perform different functions or have different responsibilities. Different jurisdictional authority granted to the bewildering number of courts at the state and local levels is undoubtedly confusing to citizens as well.

Even so, all states have some commonalities in the way they organize their judicial systems. Every state, for example, has a tiered system of courts, varying in number from three to four tiers. Every state has a court of final appeal, but the number may vary from one to two such highest courts, and these courts are called by different names as well, depending on the state. Most states name their highest court the supreme court, for example, but Maryland calls its highest court the court of appeals, which is the name assigned in most states to identify their intermediate-level appellate court(s). There is far more variety in the titles and jurisdictions of state intermediate courts of appeal. These courts vary in number in most states from one to six, although Texas has fourteen such intermediate appellate courts. They are typically named district courts or court of special appeals. In several states, however, the title of district court refers to a trial court of general jurisdiction rather than to an appellate court.

States also have different approaches in organizing and managing their courts of original and general jurisdiction. Original jurisdiction means simply that that court is the first court to hear a case. General jurisdiction means that court can hear cases pertaining to both civil and criminal law. They are a state's primary trial courts and handle the bulk of judicial action in a state. Within the various states, they are called such names as chancery court, circuit court, commonwealth court, court of common pleas, court of general sessions, district courts, and superior courts. All such courts can hear both civil and criminal cases and usually have original jurisdiction for any felony criminal matter. In civil cases, there is considerable variation in the financial amount at issue in the civil dispute, but all have a floor above which the case must be heard at that level. There is also variation in the length of prison time they can impose (most often, any penalty in excess of a year must be heard at the general trial court level). There is also considerable variation in the amount of fines they can impose. Generally, the higher the level of a state's economy, the higher the level of fines they may impose, ranging from $15,000 or more in the less economically developed states to as high as $50,000 for the wealthier states.

The greatest variety in nomenclature and jurisdictional authority is found among courts of limited jurisdiction, which comprise one or two tiers in various states. Again, sometimes confusion is caused by naming courts of limited jurisdiction in some states by the same name used for higher-level courts in other states. A bewildering number of names are used to refer to courts of limited jurisdiction: administrative court, alderman's courts, asbestos claims court, chancery court, city court, common pleas courts, county courts, district courts, domestic relations courts, drug courts, equity courts, family courts, intervention courts, justice of the peace courts, juvenile court, magistrate's court, master-in-equity court, mayor's courts, mental health courts, municipal courts, Native American trial court, parish courts, probate courts, problem-solving courts, small-claims courts, surrogate courts, tax courts, water courts, workers' compensation courts, and youth courts (Buenger and De Muniz 2015; Jonakait 2008; Mays and Fidelie 2016; Neubauer and Meinhold 2009).

American states also fill their judgeships in a wide range of ways. These methods are often broadly similar but include important differences in detail, ranging from how judges are seated to how long their terms last to how long they can serve in a judicial capacity before being subjected to mandatory retirement. Considerable variety can also be found in how judges are selected for state and local courts. Higher-level, appellate court judges are more commonly appointed to the bench. Lower-level courts, particularly courts of limited jurisdiction, tend to be elected. The states vary considerably in the length of terms of office for the courts, with the general trend being that higher-level court judges are appointed for life or for longer terms (e.g., from eight years to as long as fifteen-year terms), whereas general jurisdiction trial court judges and judges serving on the bench of courts of limited jurisdiction typically are elected or appointed to terms ranging from six to eight years.

One "reform" solution that is being used more often, now in some thirty states, is some variation of what is known as the Missouri Plan or the Tennessee Plan, two different names for basically the same approach. States using these approaches have established nominating commissions that are typically nonpartisan (meaning free from political affiliation or bias) to review the qualifications of potential nominees to courts. This system is most often used for appellate courts or for original trial courts of general jurisdiction. After an initial appointment, most often made by the governor but in some states by the state legislature, the appointed justice serves for a limited time (typically one to two years) before facing a retention election in which the judge runs unopposed and voters simply choose to keep the judge on the bench or, very rarely, vote to reject the judge. If the latter occurs, the process for filling the court seat begins anew (Buenger and De Muniz 2015; Koelling 2016). Critics, however, allege that this appointment/retention system or process contributes to a sort of lawyer-judge bias that favors the perspectives and views of the legal profession. This sort of bias can have a far-reaching and negative effect on American law and may negatively impact the legislative-judicial relationships and the oversight of the judiciary (Barton 2010; Buenger and De Muniz 2015).

Most often the overall administration of the state court system is assigned to the state's supreme court. Several states, however, have established agencies like a court on the judiciary or an office of judicial administration to supervise the court system (Koelling 2016; Mays and Fidelie 2016).

Another approach to reforming the complexity of the judicial system is to reduce its maze of technical and procedural rules by employing technological innovations designed to simplify the legal process and streamline complex civil and criminal procedures. Technology can make the system of justice faster and thereby control costs (Barton and Bibas 2017).

Problem 2: Judicial Ethics

Judicial ethics are supposed to keep judges and other officers of the court (prosecutors and defense attorneys) honest and to keep them from letting personal biases or beliefs influence their interpretations of the law. However, some critics argue that today's court system is rife with examples of cases in which lawyers and judges appear to care more about winning or simply the settlement of cases than about the rule of law. The pressure to settle criminal cases without going to court is often strong for public defenders, who are defense counsel employed by a state to provide defense to people who cannot afford to hire their own defense attorney. The heavy caseloads of courts may induce prosecutors and judges alike to pursue out-of-court settlements that reward mediocre legal representation and that bypass due process (a course of formal proceedings carried out with established rules and principles) (Bach 2010). Especially in civil court cases, the financial, personal, and professional pressures that appellate court judges face can threaten judicial ethics and the supposed independence of the courts (Schudson 2018).

Legal proceedings also can sometimes deteriorate into situations where prosecutors or defense attorneys become more caught up in "winning" than in delivering justice or getting the best legal deal for a client. Legal experts have also expressed growing concern that the personal ideology and political beliefs of judges—rather than the law—are increasingly influencing their rulings, especially at the higher-level courts (Epstein, Landes, and Posner 2013).

Other critics note that local court systems are also susceptible to unconstitutional, illegal, and unethical conduct by judges, by other court officers, and by private attorneys in the legal system. They claim that such courts can become almost "systemic criminal enterprises" akin to the mafia's behavior, in the way they use judicial power, influence, fear, and intimidation to manipulate the machinery of courts, especially family courts (Morrison 2018). In state and local courts where judges are elected, often for shorter terms (typically two-, four-, to six-year terms), judicial electoral politics can impact how interest groups influence the outcomes of judicial election that in turn effect judicial shaping of public policy (Baum, Klein, and Streb 2017).

Judicial canons or codes of ethics are not self-enforcing. To work, they depend on judges (and indeed, other court officers) to voluntarily comply with and uphold legal and ethical codes of conduct. When the system of self-enforcement fails and corrupt, inept, unqualified, or unethical judges are selected or elected to the bench, the rule of law suffers.

Problem 3: Screening of Federal Judicial Nominees

To guard against the appointment of unqualified judges, nominees to the federal court have traditionally gone through a screening and rating process by the American Bar Association. The Standing Committee on the Federal Judiciary (FJC) of the American Bar Association provided the Senate Judiciary Committee with peer evaluations of the professional qualifications of every judicial nominee to an Article III appointment. Those include nominees to the U.S. Supreme Court, the circuit court of appeals, district courts (including territorial district courts), and the court of international trade. The ABA's goal in the process is to encourage the selection of the best-qualified persons for the federal judiciary—especially given that those are lifetime appointments. The FJC restricts its evaluation to issues bearing on the professional qualifications of candidates and does not consider a nominee's philosophy or judicial ideology. The peer-review process is structured to achieve impartial evaluations of the integrity, professional competence, and judicial temperament of nominees for the federal judiciary. The FJC rates the individual nominee as well qualified, qualified, or not qualified (American Bar Association.org 2020a, b).

Prior to the Trump administration, nominees who were rated not qualified generally withdrew from the process or had their nominations withdrawn by the administration. With the arrival of the Trump administration in January 2017, however, the FJC's ratings were cast aside. Instead, the Trump administration decided to rely on the evaluations of the Federalist Society for Law and Public Policy. Founded in 1982, the Federalist Society is an organization of conservatives and libertarians that claim to advocate for an interpretation of the Constitution that relies on strict adherence to the text of the document and its original intent rather than a more flexible interpretation recognizing the evolution of American society and values over time. The Federalist Society's recommendations are all about the judicial philosophy or ideology of the nominee, not about their professional qualifications. In other words, the Federalist Society takes the exact opposite approach of the American Bar Association's FJC in evaluating potential candidates (Federalist Society.org 2020). Together with the Heritage Foundation, a powerful American conservative think tank based in Washington, D.C., the Federalist Society successfully lobbied the Republican-controlled U.S. Senate to approve Trump administration judicial nominees rated only "qualified" or even "not qualified" by the ABA's FJC. Democrats and many legal experts asserted that those nominations showed that during Trump's presidency, Republicans were more interested in reshaping the federal courts with conservative appointments than in making sure that judgeships went to strong, well-qualified candidates. Some of the Trump administration's most controversial nominees with "unqualified" ratings from the FJC were seated only after straight partisan votes in the Senate's Judiciary Committee's recommendations and on the floor vote in the U.S. Senate. Several had little to no prior judicial experience, and a few were only a few years out of law school. All of them, however, had powerful links to conservative Republican politics (Heritage Foundation.org. 2020).

The second structural device designed to cope with federal court judges charged with ethical failures is the impeachment process. All Article III judges are subject to impeachment. Since 1803, the impeachment and removal process for federal judges has been used fifteen times. Eight federal judges have been impeached in the U.S. House of Representatives, convicted by the U.S. Senate, and removed from office. Five judges were impeached but not removed. In one case, the impeachment was dismissed in the U.S. Senate before any trial was held. Four other judges were tried and acquitted by the U.S. Senate. The other two judges resigned their office after impeachment but before a Senate trial was held (see Table 5.3) (Ballotpedia.org 2020a; Brennan Center.org 2020; Federal Judicial Center.gov 2020).

The solutions proposed or used for state and local judicial systems to deal with violations of judicial ethics have likewise been twofold: devices to address the character and qualifications of persons before they are seated as judges, and responses to alleged ethical transgressions by state or local judges already on the bench. For screening prior to appointment, thirty states use a form of the Judicial Nominating Committee in conjunction with a Missouri Plan (or Tennessee Plan) system of appointment. Both those plans use a retention election following appointment to the bench, whether by the governor or by the state's legislature. For instances of alleged misconduct after election or appointment to a judicial office, most states authorize the state's supreme court to administer the system. Three states have a different structure, however. Minnesota maintains a State Judicial Council to administer policy for the judicial branch. Oklahoma has established two independent courts to deal with those matters: a court on the judiciary, which deals with judges, and a court of impeachment, which deals with the impeachment of executive branch officials. Finally, the state of Virginia has a Judicial Inquiry and Review Commission that supervises judge discipline.

Problem 4: Forced Arbitration Agreements

Legal scholar Bruce Gibney has highlighted a rapidly growing problem that he describes as the "privatization" of justice—the use of forced or mandatory arbitration in legal cases (Gibney 2019). Forced or mandatory arbitration is a clause inserted into a contract that requires the parties (e.g., an employee or a consumer buying a certain product or service) to resolve any legal disputes through an arbitration process. Mandatory employment arbitration procedures are unilaterally developed (by the employer) and forced on employees by the employer, who make signing the contract a condition of being hired for the job. In forced arbitration, the employers define the process and select the arbitration provider. Forced or mandatory arbitration effectively binds the parties to resolve disputes outside the courts, usually to the advantage of the employer (Colvin 2017; Oregon State Bar.org 2020). As such, an estimated 60 million nonunionized American workers are barred from access to courts. Studies have shown that employees are less likely to win arbitration cases of this type, and when they do win, they receive a lower amount in the damages that are awarded.

According to Gibney, the rise of forced or mandatory arbitration has left growing numbers of nonunionized employees and consumers at the mercy of arbitrary power. Forced or mandatory arbitration should not be confused with labor arbitration, in which the union and the employers jointly agree to arbitrate disputes; jointly design the arbitration procedures, including the agreement in a contract arrived at by joint negotiation; and in which both sides select the arbitration provider.

The use of mandatory arbitration has expanded exponentially since 1990, spurred by several U.S. Supreme Court decisions. In 1992, only about 2 percent of nonunionized employees were bound by mandatory arbitration clauses. As of 2021, that number exceeds 55 percent. A 2017 study found that 53.9 percent of private-sector employers have established mandatory arbitration procedures, and 55.2 percent of employees are subject to mandatory arbitration procedures (Colvin 2017). They have also become commonly employed in many other areas of American life. For example, many consumers who purchase a cell phone or subscribe to a service provider are not aware that they are signing an agreement that has a mandatory arbitration clause in it.

The dramatic expansion in the use of mandatory arbitration began with the decision of the U.S. Supreme Court in *Gilmer v. Interstate/Johnson Lane* (1991). The *Gilmer* ruling upheld the enforceability of mandatory arbitration agreements. The use of the procedure by employers and producers of products and services greatly expanded after two subsequent decisions: *AT&T Mobility LLC v. Concepcion, et al.* (2011), and *American Express Co. v. Italian Colors Restaurants* (2013). These two decisions upheld the legality of the arbitration clauses to cover class-action waivers in those agreements (Colvin 2017).

Since the use of mandatory arbitration has been upheld so firmly by the U.S. Supreme Court, it is likely to become even more commonplace in the future. After all, the economic incentives all favor employers, product manufacturers, and service providers over ordinary nonunionized workers and purchasers of a product or service (Ware and Rau 2018).

Problem 5: Gender Bias in the Judicial System

Gender bias in the judicial system, as is the case of gender bias elsewhere in American society, has been often and well documented in research studies. Until fairly recently, women were dramatically underrepresented on the bench across both federal and state judicial systems. While there has been improvement in that regard, women in the legal profession still report pervasive bias in many sectors of the American court system. They report gender-based difficulties in getting hired, in receiving fair performance evaluations, in getting mentoring, in receiving high-quality assignments, in accessing networking opportunities, in getting paid fairly, and in getting promoted. Women of color report the highest level of experiencing bias of any group (Williams et al. 2018).

Advocates for women's rights (and for racial/religious/LGBTQ equality) contend that American's court system pays more attention to women's issues and rights when they are more heavily represented on the bench (Hirshman 2016; National Association of Women Judges 2010; Toobin 2008, 2013; Tushnet 2008; Wainwright 2019). Studies have found that women are heavily underrepresented on state supreme courts around much of the country (Berry 2016; National Center for Lesbian Rights 2010; National Center for State Courts 2020; NOW Legal Defense and Education Fund 2001; The Gavel Gap 2016).

Notable steps have been taken in some states like Georgia, New Mexico, Oklahoma, Pennsylvania, Texas, and Washington, however, to address persistent gender bias in the judiciary. Several states have established task forces and special commissions to address gender bias in their court systems. These commissions and task forces have advocated for increased representation of women in jury pools, more women judges, and greater gender diversity in law enforcement (National Center for State Courts 2020; Smith 2017).

Problem 6: Increasing Partisanship of the U.S. Courts and Judicial Systems

Political parties and interest groups influence the nomination and election of judges, who in turn shape public policies with their legal rulings. Judicial campaign activities, voting behavior, and judicial policymaking are thus closely intertwined (Baum, Klein, and Streb 2017; Buenger and De Muniz 2015). From colonial times to the present day, political parties and advocacy groups have recognized that the legal authority that judges wield can make them important factors in how government and the policies it pursues are crafted and implemented.

Judges in the federal system are all lifetime appointments by the president (with the advice and consent of the U.S. Senate). Lifelong appointment has long been viewed as a key to ensuring judicial independence from political factors and public passions concerning specific cases, but lifetime tenure does not prevent partisan political considerations from influencing the initial selection of judges, or the rulings that judges hand down. Interest groups across the political ideological spectrum (e.g., the ACLU on the liberal side, the American Bar Association on the centrist side, and groups like the Federalist Society and the Heritage Foundation on the conservative side) influence which judges are nominated and confirmed, with progressive voices having greater influence over selections when Democrats control the White House and Senate and conservative groups enjoying greater influence when Republicans hold those positions. The strident nature of partisanship in that nomination and confirmation process has been evident since the 1980s, critics allege as increasingly obvious in its use and impact on Supreme Court decisions. For example, two decisions of the Supreme Court handed down on partisan alignment are hugely impactful. In *Bush v. Gore*, 2000, the Supreme Court effectively handed the presidency to Bush on controversial legal grounds, despite Gore having won the popular vote by several million votes. In *Citizens United*, 2010, the court upheld the unlimited campaign contributions corporations could make (mostly to Republican candidates) through independent expenditure-only organizations commonly called Super PACs. It is especially noteworthy that the Trump administration essentially shifted the evaluation of potential nominees from the nonpartisan (or at least, less partisan) American Bar Association to the blatantly partisan Federalist Society and the Heritage Foundation.

At the state level, a much wider variety of methods of judicial selection are used. Some states select all or most of their judges in partisan elections (Alabama, Arkansas, Connecticut, Illinois, Louisiana, Pennsylvania, Tennessee, and Texas). Thirteen states use officially nonpartisan elections to select all or most of their judges: Idaho, Kentucky, Michigan, Minnesota, Missouri, Montana, Nevada, North Carolina, North Dakota, Ohio, Oklahoma, Washington, and West Virginia. In several of those states, however, voters know without a partisan designation on the ballot which candidates each of the major parties want to win. According to a 2021 study by Denver University, twenty-nine states use some mixture of gubernatorial or legislative appointments from candidate lists supplied by a judicial nomination commission, followed by a retention election after a year or two, for some of their judges. Eleven states and the District of Columbia select their judges using a nomination commission for all judges: Alaska, Colorado, Connecticut, Delaware, D.C., Hawaii, Iowa, Maryland, Nebraska, Rhode Island, Vermont, and Wyoming. Nine states use the nominating commission for some of their judges (usually appellate or supreme court judges): Arizona, Florida, Indiana, Kansas, Missouri, New York, Oklahoma, South Dakota, and Tennessee. Eight states use a commission-based gubernatorial appointment process for filling vacancies that occur between elections: Alabama, Idaho, Kentucky, Montana, Nevada, New Mexico, North Dakota, and West Virginia. States using elections generally have judicial terms that range from four years to as high as fifteen years, depending on the level of the court.

In those states using elections to fill court seats, many campaigns and even some candidates have become much more blatantly politically partisan in recent decades. Even states using the appointment method are not immune from increased partisan influences, as parties and interest groups in those states simply shift their focus from the direct election

of judges to attempting to influence the judicial philosophical perspectives of the members of judicial nominating commissions. Although such commission/retention election state
systems are officially nonpartisan, voters (and commission-
recommending members) often know the partisan orientation
or conservative versus progressive ideological orientation of
prospective nominees.

There is no easy solution to the problem of increasing partisanship in judicial politics. Judges and courts are in fact political institutions. As American society has become increasingly
divided along partisan lines, so too have judges and courts.
While the use of nonpartisan elections or some modification
of the Missouri Plan may lessen the partisanship of the selection process, it does not eliminate partisanship altogether. The
effectiveness of any methodology for filling judgeships is still
subject to the attitudes, customs, norms, and perspectives of
decisionmakers and voters (Baum, Klein, and Streb 2017).

Problem 7: Inequity in the Judicial System—Racial and Ethnic

The criminal justice system in the United States is by far the
largest of any country in the world. As of mid-2020, approximately 1.8 million persons were incarcerated in federal, state,
and local prisons and jails. The U.S. rate of incarceration dwarfs
that of any other nation, and racial disparities pervade the U.S.
criminal justice system. Blacks are more often than whites to
be arrested, and once arrested, to be tried and convicted. Once
convicted, they are more likely to receive longer prison sentences for the same crimes committed by whites. Blacks are
nearly six times as likely to be incarcerated as whites; and Hispanics are three times more likely than non-Hispanic whites
to be incarcerated (see figure 5.5) (The Sentencing Project
2018). The sources of such disparities are so deep and systemic
that advocates for racial justice assert that the United States in
many ways has two criminal justice systems: one for white and

wealthy (or at least middle-class) people, and another for the poor and people of color. Numerous studies and reports have found that Americans who are white, affluent, and educated are much more likely to be able to secure strong and effective legal representation than minorities and poor people. Too often, courtroom professionals classify and deliberate the fate of Blacks and Latino defendants in ways in which racial abuse and due process violations are tolerated (Decker and Wright 2005; Free 2003; Herivel and Wright 2003; Van Cleve 2016). As one scholar of the American judicial system puts it, people of color, the poor, and minority defendants often confront a double standard when they enter the American court system:

> Those double standards are not, of course, explicit. On the face of it, the criminal law is color blind and class-blind. . . . The rhetoric of the criminal justice system sends a message that our society carefully protects everyone's constitutional rights, but in practice the rules assure that law enforcement will generally prevail over the rights of minorities and the poor. . . . The formal fairness obscures the systemic concerns that ought to be raised by the fact that the prison population is overwhelmingly poor and disproportionately black. (Cole 2010: 8–9)

The Sentencing Project, established in 1986, is a justice reform organization that has consistently documented racial disparities in the justice system in policing, in pretrial processing, in sentencing, and in post-prison collateral consequences, such as disenfranchisement, employment, and welfare services (The Sentencing Project.org 2018). A defendant's race and ethnicity impact decisions regarding bail, charging, plea bargaining, and sentencing (Bucerius and Tonry 2014). In a 2016 study, Blacks comprised 27 percent of persons who were arrested, double their percentage of the population. Mass incarceration begins with the disproportionate levels of police contact with Blacks. Blacks were 3 times more likely to be arrested for marijuana possession than whites, although usage rates of marijuana were comparable in 2016. Blacks were incarcerated in local jails at 3.5 times that of non-Hispanic whites in 2016 (Bureau of Justice Statistics 2018; Johnson 2017). Although Blacks and Latinos comprise 29 percent of the U.S. population, in 2018 they made up 57 percent of the prison population. Incarceration rates per 100,000 prisoners have been declining, however, since 2006 by 34 percent among all racial/ethnic groups. Black prisoners per 100,000 black adults, for example, declined from 2,261 in 2006 to 1,501 in 2018; Hispanics decreased from 1,073 for every 100,000 adults in 2006 to 797 in 2018; and white prisoners per 100,000 white adults decreased from 324 in 2006 to 268 in 2018, according to the Bureau of Justice Statistics (Pew Research Center 2020).

The Sentencing Project found such inequities in the biased use of discretion by prosecutors, and in an array of policies that disadvantage people of color in drug-related prosecutions. A variety of criminal justice system policies disadvantage the poor, including inadequately funded indigent defense programs, the reliance of the poor on overworked public defenders for legal representation, lower rates of release on parole, racial bias among correctional officers, and higher likelihoods of having their probation revoked for violations. The organization has also confirmed that judges are more likely to sentence people of color than whites to prison and jail, and to give them longer sentences, even after accounting for differences in crime severity and criminal history. The Sentencing Project found Black men are perceived as being more dangerous because of their race and socioeconomic characteristics. Moreover, criminal records follow people their entire lives, even decades after their have completed their sentences. Ex-convicts find it much more difficult to secure decent post-prison employment, and many of them face a life of disenfranchisement even after their release. In 2020, the Sentencing Project estimated that 5.2 million Americans—2.3 percent of the nation's voting-age population—were not allowed to vote in the 2020 elections because of prior felony convictions.

Several proposed solutions to the racial and ethnic bias problem have been suggested. These include: (1) revising policies and laws that have evidenced disparate racial impact, such as ending the war on drugs, (2) eliminating mandatory minimum sentences, (3) reducing the use of cash bail, (4) fully funding indigent defense agencies (public defenders offices), (5) adopting a policy requiring the use of racial impact statements, (6) developing and implementing training to reduce racial bias, and (7) addressing the issue of collateral consequences, such as denying the right to vote to an entire class of citizens that is counterproductive to effective reentry to society (Ghandnoosh 2015; The Sentencing Project.org 2018).

Problem 8: Lack of Minority Judges on the Bench

Closely related to the inequities in the judicial system is the stark fact that there is a pronounced lack of minority judges serving on the benches of local, state, and federal courts. The lack of minority judges contributes to something of a legitimacy crisis for America's courts among historically underrepresented groups—people of color, women, individuals who identify as LGBTQ, people with disabilities, and people belonging to minority religions (Root, Faleschini, and Oyenubi 2019; see also Root and Berger 2019; Johnson 2017; Washington 1994).

The lack of diversity is both descriptive and substantive. Descriptive diversity refers to the number of judges on the bench from minority backgrounds relative to the number of that minority group in the general population. In 2020, while about 73 percent of sitting federal judges are men, they comprise less than 50 percent of the U.S. population. Whereas 80 percent of judges are white, whites make up 76 percent of the population. The gender bias is evident in that while only 27 percent of sitting federal judges are women, women make up 51 percent of population. Where 6 percent of federal judges are Hispanic, Hispanics comprise more than 18.5 percent of the population. On the U.S. Supreme Court, it was not until

1967 that Justice Thurgood Marshall, the first Black justice, was appointed to the Supreme Court; and not until 1981 that the first woman, Justice Sandra Day O'Connor, was so appointed (Root, Faleschini, and Oyenubi 2019). And several studies have shown that federal judicial appointments have not kept pace with the increasingly diverse U.S. population (Chung et al. 2017; Root, Faleschini, and Oyenubi 2019; Strum 2010).

Political party affiliation plays a significant role in the appointment of non-white male federal judges. A 2016 Pew Research study found that more federal judicial appointments of judges from minority backgrounds have occurred under Democratic presidents than under Republican presidents. The study examined federal judicial appointments under every president from Truman to Obama. It found that Democratic presidents appointed three times as many Black judges as did Republican presidents (162 v. 49); more Hispanic judges (73 v. 51); and that since 1990, Democratic presidents have elevated thirty-two minority judges to a higher court versus only eight such judicial elevations by Republican presidents. President Obama appointed the most minority judges to the federal bench of any president during the period 1990 to 2016: 55 Blacks, 33 Hispanics, 17 Asians, and 4 others (as well as 198 whites) (Pew Research.org 2016).

Diversity within the federal judiciary declined under President Trump. During his single term in office, women accounted for 24 percent of his total nominees; by comparison, 42 percent of federal judicial nominees during President Obama's two terms were women. Similarly, only 16 percent of Trump's nominees were of Black, Asian, Hispanic, or other non-white race or ethnicity, well below the 36 percent of Obama nominees that fit into one of those categories (Gramlich 2021).

The lack of diversity is even starker on the federal circuit court of appeals according to data from a 2016 Pew Research study. For example, on the Seventh Circuit (serving Illinois, Indiana, and Wisconsin), there is not one judge of color, yet people of color make up one-third of the population of those states. On the Eighth Circuit Court of Appeals (serving the states of Arkansas, Iowa, Minnesota, Missouri, Nebraska, North Dakota, and South Dakota) there is only one female judge, yet women make up more than one-half of the circuit's population. On the Fifth Circuit Court of Appeal (Louisiana, Northern and Southern Districts of Mississippi, and Texas), 85 percent of its sitting judges are white (Pew Research.org 2016).

A similar picture emerges when examining state courts. Most Americans agree that racial and gender diversity is an important quality for judicial systems. A 2021 report on the racial diversity of the judiciary at the state level found that white judges make up more than 80 percent of state court judges at all levels. White judges make up more than 83 percent of trial court judges, 80 percent of appellate court judges, and 84.5 percent of state supreme court judges (Halton 2021).

Where there is a lack of diversity, a lack of substantive representation is also evident. Several studies have shown patterns in the ways judges of specific religions decide certain types of cases. For example, Jewish judges are more likely to decide cases in ways that protect minority religions, perhaps because they belong to a historically persecuted religion. In a similar fashion, Catholic and evangelical Christian judges tend to issue more conservative rulings in LGBTQ-rights cases and are more likely to rule against defendants in cases involving obscenity, a trend consistent with papal teachings and evangelical positions on those issues. Female judges have been found to be more likely than their male counterparts to rule in favor of plaintiffs in sexual harassment and employment discrimination cases. Women judges also have been found more likely to rule statutes unconstitutional if they violate the equal protection, due process, or freedom of association rights of LGBTQ-identifying people. Asian American judges have been found to rule more sympathetically in cases involving immigration or other types of discrimination, and Black judges have been found to be more sympathetic to defendants alleging violations of Fourth Amendment rights than have white judges

(American Progress.org 2019; see also Johnson 2017; Washington 1994).

A number of specific recommendations have been made to address diversity shortcomings in the American judicial system: (1) address the pipeline problem that currently blocks the career paths of minority background persons who could be judges; (2) make law school admissions programs fairer and more accessible to minorities; (3) ensure that students from underrepresented groups get into law school; (4) ensure the law school environments are inclusive and welcoming to students of color or minority status; (5) ensure that law students have equal access to professional opportunities; (6) prioritize diversity as stepping-stones for judgeships, for example, in the use of judicial clerkships and entry-level positions with prestigious law firms; (7) increase appointments to state supreme or appellate courts, election or appointment as states' attorneys general, and to appointment as U.S. attorneys; (8) prioritize judicial diversity in the nomination and appointment process; (9) address inequities in the ABA's judicial rating system; (10) require sitting judges and court staff to undergo implicit bias training; and (11) provide guidance for Blacks, Hispanics, females, and low-income Americans in navigating and changing discriminatory practices in the criminal and civil judicial systems (Center for American Progress 2019; Chung et al. 2017; Johnson 2017; Root, Faleschini, and Oyenubi 2019).

Problem 9: Oversight Relationships

The system of checks and balances that exists between the American government's three branches (executive, legislative, and judicial) includes Congressional oversight over the courts. Congressional oversight of the courts derives from two sections of Article I of the U.S. Constitution. Section 3 states that the U.S. Senate shall have sole power to try all impeachments, including impeachment of judges of the federal judiciary. This authority has only been exercised about a dozen times in the long history of the United States. Section 8 grants Congress the authority to "constitute Tribunals inferior to the Supreme Court." This section means Congress can establish new federal courts, as it has done, for example, in creating numerous special jurisdiction courts.

Those sections provide the constitutional basis for Congress to oversee the courts. Congress can impeach uncooperative judges. It can change the jurisdiction of district and appellate courts, and it can create and specify the jurisdiction of special federal courts. Congress can slash (or threaten to do so) the budgets of the courts or increase funding for their operations. More often, however, Congress has impacted the judicial system through indirect methods, such as blocking the appointment of ideologically unacceptable nominees to the federal judiciary. Historically, Congress has had to strike a balance in which it both exercises its oversight powers and respects historical norms of judicial independence (Geyh 2009; Gur-Arie and Wheeler 2020: 133–147; Hagedorn and LeMay 2019: 35–41). Meanwhile, the Supreme Court has the power of judicial review by which it can, and sometimes does, declare acts of Congress to be unconstitutional.

The Senate Judiciary Committee plays a particularly important role in America's court system. It is integral to the advice and consent process with respect to all judicial appointments to the federal courts. Given that federal judges have lifetime appointments, that is an important political power of Congress. It carries out this duty by calling and holding hearings, conducting congressional investigations, and requiring Department of Justice (DOJ) officials to appear before the committee to answer questions.

American government and politics have two conflicting values to maintain with respect to the judiciary. On the one hand is the value of judicial independence. On the other hand, there is an equally strong belief in the value of democratic accountability. Judicial independence has been a core political value since the founding era. However, the idea that judges should be democratically accountable means that the public, either directly or through their elected representatives, needs to have a voice in how the courts perform (Gur-Arie and Wheeler 2020). Judicial independence is largely promoted by granting federal judges secure tenure (i.e., lifetime appointment) and secure compensation (i.e., salaries that can't be cut) (Judiciary Act of September 24, 1789, 1 Stat. 73).

Administrative control over the federal courts was amended by the Administrative Office Act of November 6, 1939 (28 U.S.C. 444). By this law, Congress established the Administrative Office of the U.S. Courts. That office assumed responsibility from the Department of Justice over federal court budget and personnel administration. In addition, at the urging of Chief Justice Earl Warren in 1967, Congress created the Federal Judicial Center to provide judges and employees of the federal courts with orientation and continuing education resources to address difficult cases of management, complicated statutory schemes, and complex scientific and economic evidence that is often presented in court. The federal courts also adopted judicial codes of conduct comprised of seven "canons" that address such issues as the propriety of sitting judges serving on boards of private organizations, public speaking, and association with political parties.

Legislative oversight of America's state court systems, comprised of roughly 28,000 judges, varies in structure and approach. State judges, whether appointed or elected, serve for limited terms, ranging from four to fifteen years. Even appointed judges usually stand for some sort of "retention" election. As with federal judges, state judges have only rarely been impeached. Ten states do have a recall provision affording an additional means of removing judges from office: Arizona, California, Colorado, Georgia, Minnesota, Montana, Nevada, North Dakota, Virginia, and Wisconsin (Ballotpedia .org 2020b).

Administrative control over judges and state and local courts varies as well. Some states have established a court administrative body, and increasingly states have established commissions for nominating judges, screening their qualifications to serve, their judicial temperament, and so on. (See Table 5.2 for a listing of the number of states using various judicial-selection methods.)

Suggested reforms to address accountability issues with the judiciary have centered on some sort of structural device, the most common of which has been some variation of the Missouri Plan for the selection of judges, and the establishment of an administrative commission or agency with a degree of disciplinary mechanisms. Other reforms that have been imposed on judges include requirements for statistical reporting, education and training, disclosures of personal information that may lead to conflicts of interest (including personal financial holdings), and provisions that require judges to disqualify themselves from cases in which they have personal knowledge or a financial interest (Gur-Arie and Wheeler, 137–138; see also Barton and Bibas 2017; Howard 2014; Koelling 2016; Schudson 2018).

Problem 10: Public Defender Issues

A public defender represents "indigent" (poor) defendants in criminal cases. Public defender offices exist at the federal, state, and local levels. There are also specialized public defender offices in some states that provide legal services in death penalty cases. The extensive use of a formal office of public defender arose after the landmark U.S. Supreme Court decision in *Gideon v. Wainwright* (1963). In *Gideon,* the court applied the Sixth Amendment's right to counsel to the states (in this case, Florida) using the Fourteenth Amendment's Due Process Clause. The Court ruled unanimously in the *Gideon* case that the Sixth Amendment's right to counsel provision requires that the government provide legal counsel to indigent defendants in criminal cases—including misdemeanor and felony cases (Lewis 1989).

The term public defender applies to a lawyer who is appointed by a court to represent a defendant who cannot afford to hire a defense counsel. The term most often is used to describe a lawyer who works for a public defender's office, a government-funded agency that provides legal representation to indigent defendants. Some public defenders are lawyers in private practice who have agreed to represent indigent defendants on a contractual basis or on a case-by-case basis. Some law firms may keep on their staff a lawyer who will represent pro bono cases. Pro bono is a Latin phrase (shortened from pro bono publico) that refers to professional work done voluntarily and without payment to provide the skills of a professional service to those unable to afford them. A pro bono legal counsel may assist an individual or a group in a legal case by filing government application or petition. On occasion, in civil cases, a judge may determine that the loser should compensate a winning pro bono counsel.

Following the *Gideon* ruling, most states passed laws requiring the establishment of public defender offices. As the need for public defender lawyers increased, many states created special training programs for their public defenders to keep them current in criminal law procedures and practices (Lewis 1989). By 2007, forty-nine states and the District of Columbia had public defender offices (Maine being the only state without a public defender program), and twenty-two states created public defender programs to oversee the operations and policies of the 427 public defender offices located within those states. Most of these operations functioned under a central office that funded and administered all local (usually at the county-level) public defender offices. In the remaining twenty-seven states, public defender offices are county-based, administered at the local level, and funded by the county or a combination of county and state funds (Bureau of Justice Statistics 2010: 9).

Critics of public defender programs charge that the high levels of caseloads that such attorneys often are forced to take give them insufficient time to adequately defend their clients. As a result, overworked public defenders are often tempted to encourage their clients to simply plead guilty. Some defenders acknowledge that they do so to lessen their own workload; others argue that their clients often can obtain lighter sentences by negotiating a plea bargain as compared to going to trial, where they are likely to receive longer sentences if convicted. As a result of these combined factors, 90 to 95 percent of defendants do plead guilty—creating what one critic refers to as an "assembly-line" approach to justice that rewards mediocre advocacy and often simply bypasses due process (Bach 2010). Virtually everyone studying the public defender system agrees that it has too few attorneys carrying excessively heavy caseloads. Proposed reforms center on increased funding for the system, increased number of lawyers, increased support staff, and increased training. Public defender burnout is another worrisome issue, with state programs averaging an annual attrition rate of 10 percent according to one 2010 study (Bureau of Justice Statistics 2010: 1).

Problem 11: Juries in the Judicial System

The right to trial by jury is one of the fundamental rights established by the U.S. Constitution. It is, in fact, cited several times in the document. Section 2 of Article III states: "The Trial of all Crimes, except in Cases of Impeachment, shall be by Jury, and such Trial shall be held in the State where the said Crimes shall have been committed, but when not committed within any State, the Trial shall be at such Place or Places as the Congress may by Law have directed." The Fifth Amendment specifies rights in criminal cases and asserts: "No person shall be held to answer for a capital or otherwise infamous crime, unless on a presentment or indictment of a Grand Jury. . . ." The Sixth Amendment specifies the right to a fair trial and indicates requirements that must be met to ensure a fair trial, stating: "In all criminal prosecutions, the accused shall enjoy the right to a speedy and public trial, by an impartial jury of the State and district wherein the crime shall have been committed, which district shall have been previously ascertained by law, and to be informed of the nature and cause of the accusation; to be confronted with the witnesses against him, to have compulsory process for obtaining witnesses in his favor, and to have the Assistance of Counsel for his defence." The Seventh Amendment specifies rights that are guaranteed for civil cases, stating: "In Suits at common law, where the value in controversy shall exceed twenty dollars, the right of trial by jury shall be preserved, and no fact tried by a jury, shall be otherwise re-examined in any Court of the United States, than according to the rules of the common law."

The prominent mention of common law in these constitutional provisions is important. The right to a trial by jury was an integral part of English common law that was brought over to the colonies. Restrictions on jury trial rights inflamed the colonists and became one of the many reasons cited for the colonies' decision to fight for independence from the British crown (Hale 2016; Law.jrank.org 2020). The Declaration of Independence explicitly condemned England "For depriving us in many cases, of the benefits of Trial by Jury." The Founders firmly believed that providing a person accused of a crime with the right to a jury trial by his peers was an important safeguard against the actions of a biased, corrupt, or overzealous prosecutor or judge (Hale 2016). In both civil and criminal cases, juries play an important social role of legitimizing and affirming the fairness of the jury system (Jonakait 2008).

Juries have changed somewhat historically as to their role and characteristics. In England, juries were inquisitorial, with jurors directly asking questions of the parties to the conflict. In U.S. law, they are to be impartial and are not authorized to ask questions during trial proceedings. It is generally desired for juries to consist of persons who do not already know the circumstances and facts of the case. That is a characteristic that is often hard to assure when pretrial coverage of a case in the local or national media has been extensive. Pretrial publicity has on occasion been used to justify a change of venue for a notorious criminal case. If potential jurors affirm that they can keep an open mind about the case, they are allowed to serve on a jury.

There are three types of juries used in the American judicial system: criminal grand juries, criminal petit juries, and civil juries (U.S. Courts.gov 2020). The proceedings of a grand jury (meaning large, typically having sixteen to twenty-three members) are not public. They are convened to weigh whether there is enough evidence of probable cause that a person has committed a crime that warrants putting him or her on trial. Grand juries decide if there is enough evidence to issue an indictment against a person. Grand juries are typically impaneled to serve for four months and meet one day each week. A petit jury is a trial jury in a criminal case in which six to twelve jurors decide on the guilt or innocence of a defendant in a specific case. Their deliberations are private, and their decision is known as a verdict. Jurors are supposed to operate under the principle that a person is innocent until proven guilty beyond a reasonable doubt, and that conviction requires a unanimous decision of the jury (Hale 2016).

The right to a jury trial in all criminal cases in the federal judicial system is guaranteed in the Constitution. Most state constitutions grant the right to a trial by jury in criminal cases (whether felony or misdemeanor), but some have eliminated that right in cases punishable by fine only. In *Baldwin v. New York* (399 U.S. 66, 1970), the Supreme Court held that in cases where imprisonment is for six months or less, a trial by jury is not required. The Supreme Court has ruled further that a defendant has the right to a jury trial not only for the purpose of assessing guilt or innocence, but whenever any fact is used to increase a defendant's sentence beyond the maximum time allowed by statute or sentencing guidelines (i.e., to assess extenuating circumstances). These rights were upheld in two cases: *Apprendi v. New Jersey* (530 U.S. 466, 2000) and *Blakely v. Washington* (542 U.S. 296, 2004). These rulings invalidated state statutes that allowed sentencing enhancement based on a "preponderance of evidence" where enhancements could be decided by a judge alone. Moreover, in *Ramos v. Louisiana* (590 U.S. —, April 2020), the court held that for felony convictions, the jury's verdict for conviction must be unanimous.

For most criminal cases, which are tried in state or local level courts, a jury trial may be waived when both prosecutors and defendants agree to a plea bargain (Hale 2016). In those cases, a "bench trial" is held. A bench trial is held before a judge without a jury and usually proceeds more quickly since a jury need not be impaneled. Judges still must agree to any plea bargain agreement between counsel for the defense and the prosecutor; they have the option of rejecting the plea agreement and holding a trial if the terms of the agreement are not to their liking.

For civil cases, the right to a jury trial is stipulated by the Seventh Amendment, which "preserves" the right to a jury trial. The right to a jury trial in federal civil cases is based on a demand in the complaint brought by a plaintiff without regard to the defenses or counterclaims of a defendant. The right to a jury trial in civil cases does not extend to the states, except in a case where a state court is enforcing a federally created right. In civil law, alternative dispute resolution (or mandatory arbitration) has become increasingly common, to the point that it is difficult for consumers to purchase many products and services without waiving their right to a jury trial in the event of a dispute between the parties (American Bar Association.org 2020d; Edwards 1982; Ware and Rau 2018).

In most states, jury selection is done through voter registration and drivers' license lists. These resources are used to form a pool of prospective jurors, and to prequalify them by asking a series of questions about citizenship, disabilities, English-language comprehension, and whether there are any conditions that would excuse them from serving on a jury. Once qualified, a summons is issued. Juries of six to twelve individuals are selected from the jury pool, but the size of the jury varies from state to state and by the type of case being tried. In civil cases and misdemeanor criminal cases tried in courts of limited jurisdiction the most common number of jurors is six. In serious criminal cases where the accused face felony charges, twelve jurors are generally required. In misdemeanor cases and civil cases, states often provide for verdicts based on the agreement of three-fourths of the jurors. Alternate jurors are selected in some cases to take the place of jurors who may become ill during the trial. They hear the evidence but don't participate in the deliberations unless they replace an original juror.

Jury selection typically begins with the court clerks calling twelve people on the jury list. The judge makes a brief statement about the kind of case being tried and asks whether there is any reason the potential juror cannot serve, and the judge or the lawyers (for both sides of the case) ask questions as to their knowledge of the case or if they have had experiences that might cause them to be biased or unfair, a process known as *voir dire* (Latin, meaning to speak the truth). If either lawyer believes there is information that a prospective juror may be prejudiced about the case, the lawyer may ask the judge to dismiss that juror "for cause." Each lawyer may request the dismissal of an unlimited number of jurors for cause, but the judge determines if the dismissal for cause is allowed. In addition to challenges for cause, each lawyer has a specific number of preemptory challenges that permit a lawyer to excuse a potential juror without giving a reason for the decision. The number of such preemptory challenges is limited by the kind of suit being tried and cannot be based on the sex or race of a juror. When both sides agree on a jury, the jurors are sworn in by the court clerk to try the case. Any potential jurors in the pool not selected are excused (American Bar Association.org 2020c).

Jury selection in federal courts is stipulated in the Jury Selection and Service Act (28 U.S. 186, 1968). The law provides that all litigants in federal courts are entitled to trial by jury and have the right to grand and petit juries selected at random from a cross section of the community in the district or division where the court convenes, and that citizens have the obligation to serve as jurors when summoned for that purpose (Jonakait 2008).

Solutions to jury-based problems have been proposed, including abolishing the jury system for civil cases to clear up the backlog of cases and obtain a more efficient administration of justice. Other proposed reforms have included better instructions to juries, expanded use of administrative procedures and arbitration instead of jury trials, and the use of contempt power to enforce law rather than a trial by jury. Contempt power refers to the power of a public institution, such as courts or the Congress, to punish a person who shows contempt for the process, orders, or proceedings of that institution without use of a trial (Hale 2016; Jonakait 2008).

Problem 12: Structural Problems

Several scholars of the American judiciary emphasize structural problems with the nation's court system. For example, some critics have charged historical methods of selecting judges for the bench contribute to a lack of judicial diversity on the bench. Critics maintain that the lack of diversity enhances the "club-like legal culture" that places higher priority over the rules by which lawyers play the game than the rule of law (Bach 2010; Barton 2010; Coan 2019; Van Cleve 2016). State court systems that elect judges are critiqued as being too open to the influence of interest groups and political parties (Baum, Klein, and Streb 2017). Critics argue that the federalism structure of the American judicial system itself complicates justice, promoting the use of hard-edged categorical rules in the courts and leading some judges to push cases back into the political arena rather than deciding them in court (Coan 2019; Mays and Fidelie 2016; Melone and Karnes 2008). The structure of state courts in handling civil cases also promotes the overuse of arbitration (Gibney 2019). Meanwhile, critics contend that some laws, statutes, and regulations have become so complex that they hamstring effective regulatory oversight (Howard 2014).

Another group of scholars critique the selection of judges (whether by appointment in the federal courts or through judicial nominating commissions in many state court systems) that prioritize the judicial philosophy or ideology of the justices, whether conservative or liberal, over their legal qualifications. They less often propose a specific "reform" as a solution to the issue of ideological bias of judges. They more often simply point out the effects of ideology, and how the differing ideologies of the justices, particularly on the U.S. Supreme Court, tend to influence their legal decisions

Problem 13: Unqualified Judges

A final problem discussed in the literature on the American judicial system concerns the appointment of unqualified judges to important positions on the bench. Candidates for appointment to the federal bench must be nominated by a U.S. president and confirmed by the U.S. Senate. The Senate Judiciary Committee plays a leading role in the confirmation process; it holds hearings with the nominee about his or her judicial philosophy, legal experience, judicial temperament, and fitness for confirmation. A variety of organizations and interest groups submit ratings about judicial nominees and in some cases also appear before the Senate Judiciary Committee and argue their points about the fitness or lack thereof of the nominee to serve on the federal bench, which is after all, a lifetime appointment.

The oldest organization that rates judicial nominees is the American Bar Association (ABA), which was founded in 1878 and currently has about 400,000 members. Since 1923, the ABA is the accrediting body for U.S. law schools; that is, it provides a formal and independent, third-party recognition of their legitimacy. A voluntary bar association including both lawyers and law students, the ABA publishes model ethics rules, publishes the *ABA Journal,* and provides continuing education courses on a variety of subjects for lawyers and legal academicians. The ABA began rating nominees to the judiciary in 1956. It has a standing committee of fifteen members appointed by the ABA president to staggered terms of three years, and committee members are limited to two terms. In its evaluation of all nominees to an Article III judgeship, it rates each nominee in three areas: (1) integrity—the nominee's character and reputation in the legal community and their industry and diligence; (2) professional competence—the nominee's intellectual capacity, judgement, writing and analytical abilities, knowledge of the law, and breadth of professional experience, and (3) judicial temperament—their compassion, decisiveness, open-mindedness, courtesy, patience, freedom from bias, and commitment to equal justice under the law. The ABA then rates the nominee as either well qualified, qualified, or not qualified. The ABA does not examine or rate any nominee on their judicial philosophy. However, critics of the ABA, which is headquartered in Chicago, Illinois, charge that the organization does have a liberal bias (American Bar Association.org 2020a).

As of September 1, 2020, the ABA rated 267 of President Trump's nominees to the federal bench. It rated 188 as well qualified, seventy as qualified, and nine as not qualified—seven of whom were nonetheless confirmed by the U.S. Senate, which was controlled at the time by Trump's Republican Party. Since 1989, the ABA has rated a total of twenty-one nominees to the federal circuit court appellate bench as being not qualified, of which fifteen were nonetheless confirmed. Four of those twenty-one nominees were nominated by President Clinton, eight by President George W. Bush, and nine by President Trump (see Table 5.4) (Ballotpedia.org 2020c).

The Federalist Society (FS) was founded in 1982 and is a 501(c)(3) nonprofit organization. It is an organization of conservative and libertarian lawyers, legal academicians, and law students who advocate a textualist and originalist interpretation of the U.S. Constitution (i.e., a strict adherence to the original language and meaning of the Constitution). It has grown to become one of the most influential legal organizations in the United States, described as the de facto gatekeeper for conservative lawyers seeking government jobs and federal judgeships under Republican presidents (Hollis-Brusky 2015). The Federalist Society claims a membership of 70,000 and is headquartered in Washington, D.C. It has a student division, a lawyer's division, and a faculty division. It has 200 student chapters across the United States and sponsors highly influential legal conventions. FS publishes the *Harvard Journal of Law and Public Policy.* It is very well funded, with annual revenues in 2017 of more than $20 million. It is backed financially by the Olin Foundation, the Koch family foundation, Google, Chevron, Richard Mellon Scaife, and the Mercer family (Federalist Society.org 2020). Its ratings of nominees focuses on the judicial philosophy of the nominees, with higher ratings going to candidates that adhere to what the Federalist Society sees as an originalist interpretation of the U.S. Constitution (Avery and McLaughlin 2013; Hollis-Brusky 2015; Levin, DiSalvo, and Shapiro 2012; Politico.com 2019; Riehl 2007; and Teles 2008). After Trump became president in January 2017, his administration relied heavily on the recommendations of the Federalist Society for all open federal judgeships (267 in total for U.S. District Courts, U.S. Circuit Courts of Appeal, and three to the U.S. Supreme Court).

The American Constitution Society (ACS) was founded in 2001. It is also a 501(c)(3) nonprofit that is headquartered in Washington, D.C. It is the liberal legal philosophical answer to the Federalist Society. It is likewise a network of students, judges, and policymakers who share a similar legal vision— an interpretation of the U.S. Constitution as a living document, one that embodies core values that should be a force for improving the lives of all people. Members of ACS seek to revitalize and transform legal and policy debates in classrooms, courtrooms, legislatures, and the media. It describes itself as a diverse and dynamic network of progressives committed to justice. ACS has a more diffuse legal philosophy than the Federalist Society, and no natural donor base of big donors (American Constitution Society.org 2020; Ballotpedia.org 2020c; Politico.com 2019).

Judges to state and local courts are elected or appointed, and most of those appointed are screened to some extent as to their qualifications, typically by a judicial nominating commission. Although organized to be nonpartisan, these commissions have been accused of being under excessive influence of the bar association in their respective states, and by political party and interest groups advocating for a conservative or progressive legal philosophy. Their stated intention is to ensure that appointees to the bench are qualified. However, critics and some academic studies have contended that judges appointed with input from judicial nominating committees are not measurably more competent than those elected to the bench.

There is no easy solution to the problem of selecting unqualified judges. If appointing authorities (U.S. presidents, state governors, or state legislatures) and the legislative bodies that confirm nominees appointed by executives are willing to place judicial ideological considerations above criteria that emphasize integrity, professional competence, and judicial temperament, problems of selecting judges who are not qualified to serve on the bench will remain.

Bibliography

American Bar Association.org. 2020a. "About the ABA." https://www.americanbar.org/about_the_aba/. Accessed September 4, 2020.

American Bar Association.org. 2020b. "Groups, Committees and Federal Judicial Ratings." https://Americanbar.org /groups/committees/federal-judiciary/ratings. Accessed August 27, 2020.

American Bar Association.org. 2020c. "How Courts Work." https://www.americanbar.org/group/public-education /resources/law-related-education/how-courts-work. Accessed September 3, 2020.

American Bar Association.org. 2020d. "Dispute Resolution Process/Arbitration." https://www.americanbar.org/groups

/litigation/committees/alternative-dispute resolution. Accessed October 27, 2021.

American Constitution Society.org. 2020. "About ACS." https://www.acslaw.org/about-us. Accessed September 4, 2020.

American Progress.org. 2019. "Building a More Inclusive Federal Judiciary." https://www.americanprogress.org /issues/courts/reports/2019/10/03/475359/building -inclusive-federal-judiciary/. Accessed August 31, 2020.

Archives.gov. 2020. "The Declaration of Independence." https://www.archives.gov/founding-docs/declaration -transcript. Accessed September 3, 2020.

Avery, Michael, and Danielle McLaughlin. 2013. *The Federalist Society: How Conservatives Took the Law Back from Liberals.* Nashville, TN: Vanderbilt University Press.

Bach, Amy. 2010. *Ordinary Justice: How America Holds Court.* New York: Henry Holt.

Ballotpedia.org. 2020a. "Impeachment of Federal Judges." https://ballotpedia.org/Impeachment_of_federal_judges. Accessed August 27, 2020.

Ballotpedia.org. 2020b. "Laws Governing Recall." https:// ballotpedia.org/Laws_governing_recall. Accessed September 2, 2020.

Ballotpedia.org. 2020c. "ABA Ratings during the Trump Administration." https://ballotpedia.org/ABA_ratings _during_the_Trump_administration. Accessed September 4, 2020.

Barton, Benjamin. 2010. *The Lawyer-Judge Bias in the American Legal System.* New York: Cambridge University Press.

Barton, Benjamin, and Stephanos Bibas. 2017. *Debooting Justice: More Technology, Fewer Lawyers, and the Future of Law.* New York: Encounter Books.

Baum, Lawrence, David Klein, and Matthew Streb. 2017. *The Battle for the Court: Interest Groups, Judicial Elections, and Public Policy.* Charlottesville: University of Virginia Press.

Berry, Kate. 2016. *Building a Diverse Bench: A Guide for Judicial Nominating Commissions.* New York: The Brennan Center, New York University School of Law.

Brennan Center.org. 2020. "Beyond Impeachment," February 5, 2020, Michael Waldman, https://www.brennancenter.org /our-work/analysis-opinion/beyond-impeachment. Accessed December 20, 2021.

Bucerius, Sandra M., and Michael Tonry, eds. 2014. *The Oxford Handbook of Ethnicity, Crime, and Immigration.* New York: Oxford University Press.

Buenger, Michael, and Paul J. De Muniz. 2015. *American Judicial Power: The State Court Perspective.* Northampton, MA: Edward Elgar Publishing.

Burbank, Stephen B., and Barry Friedman, eds. 2002. *Judicial Independence at the Crossroads: An Interdisciplinary Approach.* Thousand Oaks, CA: Sage Publications.

Bureau of Justice Statistics.gov. 2020. "About BJS." NCJ 254789, https://bjs.ojp.gov/about. Accessed August 31, 2020.

Bureau of Justice Statistics.gov. 2018. "Criminal Victimization Rates." https://bjs.ojp.gov/library/publications/criminal -victimization. Accessed August 31, 2020.

Bureau of Justice Statistics.gov. 2010. "State Public Defender Programs, 2007." https://bjs.ojp.gov/library/publications /state-public-defender-programs-2007. Accessed September 2, 2020.

Canes-Wrone, Brandice, and Tom S. Clark. 2008. "Judicial Independence and Nonpartisan Elections." https:// biblioteca.cejamericas.org/bitstream/handle/2015/2258 /Judicial-Independence-and-Nonpartisan-Elections .pdf?sequence=1&isAllowed=y. Accessed August 30, 2020.

Carmon, Irin, and Shana Knizhnik. 2015. *The Notorious RBG: The Life and Times of Ruth Bader Ginsburg.* New York: Dey Street Books.

Carson, Clayborne. 1981. *In Struggle: SNCC and the Black Awakening of the 1960s.* Cambridge, MA: Harvard University Press.

Chung, Eric, et al. 2017. "A Portrait of Asian Americans in the Law." Yale Law School and Washington National Asian Pacific American Bar Association. https://static1 .squarespace.com/static/59556778e58c62c7db3fbe84/t /596cf0638419c2e5a0dc5766/1500311662008/170716 _PortraitProject_SinglePages.pdf. Accessed August 31, 2020.

Coan, Andrew. 2019. *Rationing the Constitution: How Judicial Capacity Shapes Supreme Court Decision-Making.* Cambridge, MA: Harvard University Press.

Cole, David. 2010. *No Equal Justice: Race and Class in the American Criminal Justice System.* New York: New Press.

Colvin, Alexander J. S. 2017. "The Growing Use of Mandatory Arbitration." Economic Policy Institute.org, https://www.epi.org/publication/the-growing-use-of -mandatory-arbitration/. Accessed August 28, 2020.

Corley, Pamela, Artemas Ward, and Wendy Martinek. 2015. *American Judicial Process: Myth and Reality in Law and Courts.* New York: Routledge.

Criminal.findlaw.com. 2020. "How Does a Grand Jury Work?" https://criminal.findlaw.com/criminal-procedure /how-does-a-grand-jury-work. Accessed September 3, 2020.

Decker, Scott H., and Kevin A. Wright, eds. 2005. *Criminology and Public Policy*, 2nd ed. Philadelphia: Temple University Press.

Douglas, Todd. 2017. *The Police in a Free Society: Safeguarding Rights While Enforcing the Law.* Santa Barbara, CA: Praeger.

Edwards, George. 1982. *The Politics of the Urban Frontier.* New York: Institute of Human Relations.

Epstein, Lee, William Landes, and Richard Posner. 2013. *The Behavior of Federal Judges: A Theoretical and Empirical Study of Rational Choice.* Cambridge, MA: Harvard University Press.

Federal Judicial Center.gov. 2019. "Biographical Directory of Article III Federal Judges, 1789-present." https://www .fjc.gov/history/judges/search/advanced-search. Accessed August 31, 2020.

Federal Judicial Center.gov. 2020. "Impeachments of Federal Judges." https://www.fjc.gov/history/judges/impeachments -federal-judges. Accessed August 27, 2020.

Federalist Society.org. 2020. "About Us." https://fedsoc.org /about-us. Accessed August 27, 2020.

Fogelson, Robert. 1977. *Big City Police.* Cambridge, MA: Harvard University Press.

Free, Marvin D., Jr. 2003. *Racial Issues in Criminal Justice: The Case of African Americans.* Westport, CT: Praeger.

The Gavel Gap. 2016. "Who Sits in Judgment on State Courts?" https://gavelgap.org/pdf/gavel-gap-report.pdf. Accessed August 28, 2020.

Geyh, Charles G. 2009. *When Courts and Congress Collide.* Ann Arbor: University of Michigan Press.

Ghandnoosh, Nazgol. 2015. "Black Lives Matter: Eliminating Racial Inequity in the Criminal Justice System." The Sentencing Project.org. https://www.sentencingproject.org /publications/black-lives-matter-eliminating-racial -inequity-in-the-criminal-justice-system. Accessed August 31, 2020.

Gibney, Bruce. 2019. *The Nonsense Factory: The Making and Breaking of the American Legal System.* New York and Boston: Hachette Books.

Ginsburg, Ruth Bader, with Mary Hartnett and Wendy W. Williams. 2016. *My Own Words.* New York: Simon and Schuster.

Gramlich, John. 2021. "How Trump Compares with Other Recent Presidents in Appointing Federal Judges." Pew Research Center, January 13. https://www.pewresearch.org /fact-tank/2021/01/13/how-trump-compares-with-other -recent-presidents-in-appointing-federal-judges/

Gur-Arie, Mira, and Russell Wheeler. 2020. "About the U.S. Courts: Judicial Independence."

Federal Judicial Center. https://www.fjc.gov/content/judicial -independence. Accessed September 1, 2020.

Hagedorn, Sara, and Michael C. LeMay. 2019. *The American Congress: A Reference Handbook.* Santa Barbara: ABC-CLIO.

Hale, Dennis 2016. *The Jury in America: Triumph and Decline.* Lawrence: University Press of Kansas.

Halton, Clay. 2021. "Racial Diversity in the Judiciary." https://www.investopedia.com/racial-diversity-in-the -judiciary-5114231, March 25. Accessed June 28, 2021.

Harvard.edu. 2020. "What Is Public Interest Law?" https://hls.harvard.edu/dept/opia/what-is-public-interest -law/public-interest-work-types/. Accessed October 27, 2021.

Heritage Foundation.org. 2020. "About Heritage." https:// www.heritage.org/about-heritage/mission. Accessed August 27, 2020.

Herivel, Tara, and Paul Wright, eds. 2003. *Prison Nation: The Warehousing of America's Poor.* New York: Routledge.

Heumann, Milton, and Lance Cassak. 2003. *Good Cop, Bad Cop: Racial Profiling and Competing Views of Justice in America.* New York: Peter Lang.

Hirshman, Linda. 2016. *Sisters in Law: How Sandra Day O'Connor and Ruth Bader Ginsburg Went to the Supreme Court and Changed the World.* New York: Harper Perennial.

Hollis-Brusky, Amanda. 2015. *Ideas with Consequences: The Federalist Society and the Conservative Counterrevolution.* New York: Oxford University Press.

Johnson, Anthony. 2017. *America's Corrupt and Discriminating Judicial System against Black, Hispanic, Female, and Low Income Americans.* New York: Scribner.

Jonakait, Randolph. 2008. *The American Jury System.* New Haven, CT: Yale University Press.

Kanefield, Teri. 2016. *Free to Be Ruth Bader Ginsburg: The Story of Women and Law.* New York: Amon Books.

Keck, Thomas M. 2004. *The Most Activist Court in History: The Road to Modern Judicial Conservatism.* Chicago: University of Chicago Press.

Koelling, Peter. 2016. *The Improvement of the Administration of Justice*, 8th ed. Washington, DC: American Bar Association.

Law.jrank.org. 2020. "Juries: The Jury System in America." https://law.jrank.org/pages/22534/Juries-Jury-System-in -America.html. Accessed September 3, 2020.

Lazarus, Edward. 2005. *Closed Chambers: The Rise, Fall, and Future of the Modern Supreme Court.* New York: Penguin Books.

LeMay, Michael. 2006. *Guarding the Gates: Immigration and National Security.* Westport, CT: Praeger Security International.

LeMay, Michael. 2009. *The Perennial Struggle: Race, Ethnicity, and Minority Group Relations in the United States*, 3rd ed. Upper Saddle River, NJ: Prentice-Hall.

LeMay, Michael, and Elliott Barkan, eds. 1999. *U.S. Immigration and Naturalization Laws and Issues: A Documentary History.* Westport, CT: Greenwood Press.

Levin, Martin, Danielle DiSalvo, and Martin Shapiro. 2012. *Building Coalitions, Making Policy: The Politics of the Clinton, Bush, and Obama Presidencies.* Baltimore: John Hopkins University Press.

Lewis, Anthony. 1989. *Gideon's Trumpet: How One Man, a Poor Prisoner, Took His Case to the Supreme Court and Changed the Law of the United States.* New York: Vintage Books.

Masotti, Louis H., ed. 1968. *Riots and Rebellion: Civil Violence in the Urban Community.* Beverly Hills, CA: Sage Publications.

Mays, G. Larry, and Laura Woods Fidelie. 2016. *American Courts and the Judicial Process.* New York: Oxford University Press.

McClain, Paula D., and J. Steward. 1995. *Can't We All Get Along? Racial and Ethnic Minorities in American Politics.* Boulder, CO: Westview Press.

Melone, Albert, and Allan Karnes. 2008. *The American Legal System: Perspectives, Politics, Processes, and Policies*, 2nd ed. Lanham, MD: Rowman and Littlefield.

Morrison, Christine. 2018. *Judicial Criminals: The Greatest Fraud upon American Society: United States Divorce Courts.* Scotts Valley, CA: Create Space Independent Publishing.

National Association of Women Judges. 2010. "Women and the Judiciary." C-SPAN video of the meeting of the NAWJ. https://www.c-span.org/video/?292480-1/national -association-women-judges-conference. Accessed September 17, 2021.

National Center for Lesbian Rights. 2010. "State by State Guide to Laws That Prohibit Discrimination against Transgender People," San Francisco and Washington, DC: National Center for Lesbian Rights. https://www.lgbtagingcenter.org/resources/pdfs /StateLawsThatProhibitDiscriminationAgainstTransPeople.pdf

National Center for State Courts. 2020. "Gender and Racial Fairness." https://www.ncsc.org/topics/access-and-fairness /gender-and-racial-fairness/resource-guide. Accessed August 28, 2020.

National Institute of Justice, U.S. Department of Justice. 1989. "Gender Bias Study of the Supreme Judicial Court,

Commonwealth of Massachusetts. Washington, DC: National Institute of Justice.

Neff, Abigail, and Sarah Wainwright, eds. 2019. *In Defense of Justice: The Great Dissents of Ruth Bader Ginsburg.* Fairhope, AL: Mockingbird Press.

Neubauer, David, and Stephen Meinhold. 2009. *Judicial Process: Law, Courts, and Politics in the United States.* Boston: Cengage Publishing.

Newton, Jim. 2006. *Justice for All: Earl Warren and the Nation He Made.* New York: Riverhead Books.

NOW Legal Defense and Education Fund. 2001. "Gender Fairness in the Courts: Action in the New Millennium." https://www.legalmomenturn.org/sites/default/files/reports/gender-fairness-in-courts-milenium.pdf. Accessed October 28, 2021.

Oregon State Bar.org. 2020. "Mandatory Arbitration." https://www.osbar.org/public/legalinfo/1216_MandatoryArbitration.htm. Accessed October 27, 2021.

Pew Research Center.org. 2016. "More Minority Judges Have Been Appointed under Democratic than Republican Presidents." https://www.pewresearch.org/fact-tank/2016/07/19/more-minority-federal-judges-have-been-appointed-under-Democratic-than-Republican-presidents. Accessed August 31, 2020.

Pew Research Center.org. 2020. "Black Imprisonment Rate in the U.S. Has Fallen by a Third Since 2006." https://www.pewresearch.org/fact-tank/2020/05-05/share-of-black-white-hispanic-americans-in-prison-2018. Accessed July 28, 2021.

Politico.com. 2019. "Why There Is No Liberal Federalist Society." https://www.politico.com/magazine/story/2019/01/23/why-there-is-no-liberal-federalist-society-2240331/. Accessed October 27, 2021.

Posner, Richard. 2017. *The Federal Judiciary: Strengths and Weaknesses.* Cambridge, MA: Harvard University Press.

Powe, Lucas. 2000. *The Warren Court and American Politics.* Cambridge, MA: Harvard University Press.

Reddick, Malia, Michael Nelson, and Rachel Paine Caufield. 2009. "Racial and Gender Diversity on State Courts, an AJS Study," *The Judges Journal,* Vol. 48, No. 3 (Summer): 28–32.

Riehl, Jonathan. 2007. *The Federalist Society and Movement Conservation: How a Fractious Coalition on the Right Is Changing Constitutional Law and the Way We Talk and Think about It.* Chapel Hill: University of North Carolina Press.

Robertiello, Gina, ed. 2017. *The Use and Abuse of Police Power in America: Historical Milestones and Current Controversies.* Santa Barbara, CA: ABC-CLIO.

Root, Danielle, Jack Faleschini, and Grace Oyenubi. 2019. "Building a More Inclusive Federal Judiciary." https://www.americanprogress.org/issues/courts/reports/2019/10/03/475359/building-inclusive-federal-judiciary. Accessed August 31, 2020.

Root, Danielle, and Sam Berger. 2019. "Structural Reforms to the Federal Judiciary: Restoring Independence and Fairness to the Courts." Center for American Progress. https://www.americanprogress.org/issustilles/courts/reports/2019/05/08/469504/structural-reforms-federal-judiciary. Accessed September 2, 2020.

Rosen, Jeffrey. 2007. *The Supreme Court: The Personalities and Rivalries That Defined America.* Santa Barbara, CA: Griffin Publishing.

Rosen, Jeffrey. 2019. *Conservations with RBG: Conversations with Ruth Bader Ginsburg on Life, Love, Liberty, and Law.* New York: Henry Holt.

Ruchelman, Leonard, ed. 1973. *Who Rules the Police?* New York: New York University Press.

Schudson, Charles B. 2018. *Independence Corrupted: How American Judges Make Their Decisions.* Madison: University of Wisconsin Press.

The Sentencing Project.org. 2018. "Report to the United Nations on Racial Disparities in the U.S. Criminal Justice System." https://www.sentencingproject.org/publications /un-report-on-racial-disparities/. Accessed October 27, 2021.

Shugerman, Jed H. 2012. *The People's Courts: Pursuing Judicial Independence in America.* Cambridge, MA: Harvard University Press.

Smith, Deborah. 2017. "Women and Girls in the Justice System." National Center for State Courts. https://www .ncsc.contentdm.oclc.org/digital/collection;accessfair /id/807. Accessed October 27, 2021.

Strum, Philippa. 2010. *Mendez v. Westminster: School Desegregation and Mexican-American Rights.* Lawrence: University Press of Kansas.

Teles, Steven. 2008. *The Rise of the Conservative Legal Movement: The Battle for Control of the Law.* Princeton, NJ: Princeton University Press.

Toobin, Jeffrey. 2008. *The Nine: Inside the Secret World of the Supreme Court.* New York: Anchor Books.

Toobin, Jeffrey. 2013. *The Oath: The Obama White House and the Supreme Court.* New York: Anchor Books.

Tushnet, Mark. 2008. *Dissent: Great Opposing Opinions and Landmark Supreme Court Cases.* Boston: Beacon Press.

U.S. Courts.gov. 2020. "Jury Service." https://www.uscourts .gov/services-forms/jury-service. Accessed September 3, 2020.

Van Cleve; Nicole. 2016. *Crook County: Racism and Injustice in America's Largest Criminal Court.* Stanford, CA: Stanford University Press.

Ware, Stephen, and Alan S. Rau. 2018. *Arbitration.* Eagan, MN: Foundation Press.

Washington, Linn. 1994. *Black Judges on Justice: Perspectives from the Bench.* New York: New Press.

Williams, Joan C., Martina Multhaup, Su Li, and Rachel Korn. 2018. *You Can't Change What You Can't See: Interrupting Racial and Gender Bias in the Legal Profession.* Chicago: American Bar Association. https://www.mcca .com/wp-content/uploads/2018/09/You-Can't-Change -What-You-Can't-See-Executive-Summary.pdf. Accessed October 27, 2021.

Zaia, Mary. 2018. *You Can't Spell Truth without Ruth: An Unauthorized Collection of Witty and Wise Quotes from the Queen of Supreme, Ruth Bader Ginsburg.* New York: Castle Point Books/St. Martin's Press.

3 Perspectives

Introduction

This chapter presents nine original essays on the American judicial system contributed by scholars from several disciplinary backgrounds, graduate students, and a former clerk of a county court system. Each of the essays provide insights into various facets of the American judicial system.

Remote Control: How Appellate Court Online Hearings Can Help Offset Judiciary Budget Cuts
Taraleigh Davis

State appellate courts, sometimes referred to as intermediate appellate courts (IAC), are a stepping-stone between the trial courts in a state and the court of last resort, known in most states as the state supreme court. The two primary functions of state appellate courts are "to review individual decisions of lower tribunals for error and to interpret and develop the law for general application in future cases filed in all levels of the legal system" (CCJSCA 2012). Most states have at least one intermediate appellate court. There are over ninety IACs in the United States, with jurisdictions that vary by state. The main reason for their establishment is to take some of the burden off the state's court of last resort by serving as the place where litigants can appeal adverse decisions from the state's trial courts.

Justice court gavel and the U.S. passport symbolize immigration court and legal issues for immigrants. Immigration court is one of several "specialty" courts established by Congress. (Zimmytws/Dreamstime.com)

Most IACs hear all cases; they do not have the discretion to ignore an appeal. Their mandatory jurisdiction leads them to often serve as an error-correction court. Instead of advocating for a client before a judge and jury, a lawyer appearing before an IAC finds themselves advocating before a panel of judges where oral argumentation is better viewed as a dialogue than as a presentation. Unlike trial courts, which issue decisions based on a single case, appellate courts often issue rulings that impact other cases.

Over time, the IAC's role has expanded to include being responsible for the definition and development of law. This expansion of their role, and the resulting increased workload of the IACs, garnered support from state legislatures for adding more judges and staff to the IAC system. IACs are committed to meet the increased demands while providing quality and timely jurisprudence.

Many IACs serve to recognize referendums passed by voters. In 2021, for example, the Michigan State Court of Appeals issued a precedent-setting decision that judges must not overrule protections granted to medical marijuana users by the voters in Michigan, who passed the Michigan Medical Marihuana Act in 2008. As a result of this decision, Michigan probation officers and judges can no longer ban medical marijuana use by an offender while on probation when that person is also a state-registered medical marijuana user. Despite voters' overwhelming approval of the law, it took twelve years for Michigan courts to recognize fully the law's protections (Laitner 2021).

Intermediate appellate courts have also issued rulings weighing in on public health during the COVID-19 pandemic, even in states that have not issued a mask mandate. In Florida, the state appellate court rejected a challenge to a Palm Beach County mask mandate for businesses and public places. "(Requiring) facial coverings to be worn in public is not primarily directed at treating a medical condition of the person wearing the mask or face shield," stated the court. "Instead, requiring individuals to cover their nose and mouth while out in public is intended to prevent the transmission from the wearer of the facial covering to others (with a secondary benefit being protection of the mask wearer). Requiring facial coverings in public settings is akin to the state's prohibiting individuals from smoking in enclosed indoor workplaces" (Saunders 2021).

In March 2020, the COVID-19 pandemic forced most state courts to close their physical, in-person courthouses. The pandemic impacted the court system in multiple ways. State appellate courts rescheduled oral arguments to a remote setting and sent judges and staff home to work remotely. Case conferencing—a meeting in which IAC judges discuss issues on appeal and assign who authors the opinion—also had to move to an online, remote format. In a survey done by the National Center for State Courts, appellate justices and judges reported that remote case conferences were efficient and effective. Advantages to remote conferencing included ease of scheduling and a good (i.e., more efficient) use of judicial time (Congressional Research Service 2020).

Courts were quick to adapt to remote oral arguments and conferencing. Does an online format restrict litigants from accessing justice? The IAC is unique regarding the concern for equitable access to justice in that the attorneys alone attend and argue before the panel of appellate judges. Conducting remote hearings has also made the judicial process even more transparent before the public. When state appellate courts moved to remote hearings, they also started streaming the oral arguments and archiving the videos on their website. As of February 2021, most state courts are still closed for in-person hearings except for cases of emergencies.

In 2020, many states had to implement budget cuts to mitigate the effects of the economic downturn caused by the COVID-19 pandemic. New York state, for example, had to cut its judicial budget by $300 million, and California implemented $200 million in judiciary budget cuts. However, the courts' transition to remote oral arguments and case conferencing may have uncovered a unique solution to state judicial budget crises across the country. With the technology infrastructure already in place, courts could consider employing remote hearings even when things return to "normal" in the judicial world. By using remote hearings for oral arguments and case conferencing even after courthouses open to the public, intermediate appellate courts can save money while also providing quality jurisprudence.

Bibliography

Congressional Research Service. 2020. "The Courts and COVID-19," March 30. https://crsreports.congress.gov /product.pdf/LSB/LSB10437

Laitner, Bill. 2021. "Michigan Appeals Court OKs Medical Marijuana for Those on Probation." *Detroit Free Press,* February 15. https://www.freep.com/story/news/local /michigan/oakland/2021/02/15/michigan-marijuana -medicine-probationers/6752623002. Accessed July 30, 2021.

Council of Chief Judges of the State Courts of Appeal (CCJSCA). 2012. "The Role of State Intermediate Appellate Courts: Principles for Adapting to Change November 2012." White paper produced by the Council of Chief Judges of the State Courts of Appeal.

Saunders, Jim. 2021. "Florida Appeals Court Upholds County Mask Mandate," January 28. https://www.news4jax.com /news/florida/2021/01/28/florida-appeals-court-upholds -county-mask-mandate/. Accessed July 30, 2021.

Taraleigh Davis is a PhD candidate, a teaching assistant, and the Political Science Student Association coordinator for the Department of Political Science, University of Wisconsin-Milwaukee.

"Let 'em Play, Ref": The Superabundance of Law in the United States
Troy W. Hinrichs

How many times over the years have sports fans—pick a sport—complained about the excessive interference of referees and umpires with the flow of games? The plaintive cry of "Let 'em play, ref!" echoes throughout the stadiums, bars, and living rooms of America's sports fans when a referee's decision to call a foul or a penalty affects the potential outcome of the game or negates a particularly athletic or exciting play. Fans understandably want, and pay to see, the athletic prowess of athletes, not the inner workings of the rules. However, rule books have grown over the last few decades as high schools, university athletic conferences and programs, and professional franchises and leagues have grown more concerned about game fairness, health and safety concerns, revenue, and gambling. Regardless of the reasons for expanding rules and regulations, sports fans know intuitively that penalty-filled games are not as enjoyable to watch. When sports were simpler, the rules were few and easily understood by the participants and fans. As sports have become more complex, the rules have become more arcane, and their sometimes seemingly arbitrary application have become sources of extreme frustration for fans, players, and coaches. Outcomes of games and seasons can hang in the balance of a referee's decision.

An analogous issue—with much more serious consequences and implications—has been at work in American society over the years. American laws and regulations have expanded greatly in recent decades. The Heritage Foundation estimates that there are over 5,000 federal criminal statutes plus 300,000 federal regulations that carry potential criminal penalties. The U.S. Census Bureau's 2017 Census of Governments records over 90,000 federal, state, and local government units, many with their own statutes, ordinances, and regulations—and enforcement mechanisms. Violators of these rules may be subject to potential criminal penalties. While traditional "street" criminals suffer the more visceral effects of this expanding empire of laws, Harvey Silverglate noted in *Three Felonies a Day* (2011) that even so called "white-collar" professionals and politicians can find themselves in legal trouble from unwitting violations of these ever-expanding codes. The problem is not one solely of social or racial justice but of excessive regulation that potentially affects all Americans and contributes to the erosion of our constitutional democracy and the rights and liberties it is meant to protect.

When society was relatively less complex, the rules were simple and easily understood. "Simple" does not always mean "fair" or "just," of course. Jim Crow laws—while easily understood—were racist and grossly unjust. Another way to facilitate injustice, though, is to make rules inscrutable and unknowable either through complexity or sheer volume.

Legal codes (also known as statutes) and administrative regulations have exploded over the previous few decades, and the substance of those laws has also increased in complexity. They have grown so much and so fast that knowing the rules in any given endeavor is nigh impossible. The Twitter feed @CrimeADay, run by defense attorney Mike Chase, documents daily the inanity and volume of the federal statutes and regulations. For example, it is a federal crime for a Department of Agriculture employee to reveal how a watermelon handler voted in a watermelon referendum. 7 USC §§4912(a) & 4908(c). The penalty is up to a $1,000 fine and/or a year in federal prison. In a society that prides itself on its self-identity of "freedom and justice for all," it is a growing reality that more and more otherwise law-abiding Americans may unwittingly find themselves afoul of the law and subject to all manner of criminal and civil penalties. Concomitant with this growth of law and regulation is the force of that ancient legal maxim: "Ignorance of the law is no excuse."

James Madison warned of this problem in Federalist No. 62 in 1788:

> It poisons the blessing of liberty itself. It will be of little avail to the people, that the laws are made by men of their own choice, if the laws be so voluminous that they cannot be read, or so incoherent that they cannot be understood; if they be repealed or revised before they are promulgated, or undergo such incessant changes that no man, who knows what the law is to-day, can guess what it will be

to-morrow. Law is defined to be a rule of action; but how can that be a rule, which is little known, and less fixed?

How does a society founded on due process, individual liberty, and self-governance find itself so bound by statutes and regulations? The quickest answer is that we as voters have failed to hold our lawmakers accountable for the laws and regulations they pass. We have fallen prey to the fallacy that criminal sanction is the best or even a good way to control our fellow Americans' bad behaviors or to engineer a just society. As we have learned from the costly War on Drugs, we can legislate morality, but we cannot make people moral by legislation. Laws drawn up with the beneficent motive to limit drug manufacture, sales, and use ended up costing us a lot more in the consequential effects of mass incarceration and people who have been forever tarnished with criminal records. Other injustices have been wrought by "strict liability" crimes. Strict liability crimes are those acts for which offenders are penalized even though they did not know they are breaking any laws. People can run afoul of the law and be jailed for unwitting criminal behavior like serving bacon-infused vodka in Oklahoma (Copeland and Mangual 2018). Strict liability offenses also remove any possibility of a "mistake of law defense."

How does American society free itself from this superabundance of law and regulation that restricts individual liberty while simultaneously empowering the various levels of government to insert themselves into almost every area of life? How do we go about revisiting and reforming these codes? The first place to start is for Americans to take the responsibilities of citizenship more seriously. Benjamin Franklin's famous statement that we formed "a Republic if you can keep it" is and always has been true. A free society depends on a vigilant citizenry. While "ignorance of the law is no excuse," ignorance of the lawmakers and the legislative process should be no excuse either. Crimes and criminal punishment should be reserved for those things that are intuitively wrong or at the very least given a *mens rea* requirement that the offender is proven to have known the behavior was criminal.

Law professor Bruno Leoni noted three dangers in what he termed "the resort to legislation" to resolve a society's problems. The obvious danger, such as during our Jim Crow period, is the use of law to deny minority rights. It often also denies people the right to come to their own solutions to issues as opposed to having those solutions forced on them by regulators and legislators who may be unfamiliar with the issues in addition to lacking expertise in a particular area. Lastly, Leoni notes that given the potential consequences of lawbreaking—especially of criminal laws—such as fines, incarceration, and the stigma of a criminal record, laws should be passed only after accurate assessments of the problems they purport to resolve. That last danger is especially timely given a growing acknowledgment that legislators often do not bother to read the laws being passed (Leoni 1961).

In the current environment, especially after the George Floyd killing, there is a renewed interest in reforming the American criminal justice system specifically and perhaps the legal system more broadly. As the Manhattan Institute notes in its ongoing project called "Over-criminalizing America," the U.S. Congress should revisit their codes of laws and regulations and mandate *mens rea* requirements for crimes, reduce or remove criminal penalties, and remove redundant or overly punitive laws and regulations. We fought a war for independence over the injustice of "taxation without representation." "Criminalization without representation" is no less unjust.

Bibliography

Chase, Mike. "A Crime a Day" [@CrimeaDay]. https://twitter.com/CrimeADay

Copeland, James R., and Rafael Mangual. 2018. "Overcriminalizing America." Manhattan Institute. https://www.manhattan-institute.org/overcrim

The Heritage Foundation. 2020. "Heritage Explains: Overcriminalization." https://www.heritage.org/crime-and -justice/heritage-explains/overcriminalization. Accessed July 29, 2021.

Leoni, Bruno. 1991. *Freedom and the Law*, 3rd ed. Indianapolis: Liberty Fund.

Rossiter, Clinton, ed. 2003. *The Federalist Papers by Hamilton, Madison, and Jay.* New York: Signet Classic (originally published in 1787).

Silverglate, Harvey. 2011. *Three Felonies a Day: How the Feds Target the Innocent.* New York: Encounter Books.

Troy W. Hinrichs is professor of criminal justice at California Baptist University in Riverside, California.

The Supreme Court, the Incorporation Doctrine, and the States
Timothy R. Johnson and Rachel Houston

"No state shall make or enforce any law which shall abridge the privileges or immunities of citizens of the United States; nor shall any state deprive any person of life, liberty, or property, without due process of law; nor deny to any person within its jurisdiction the equal protection of the laws."

Any read of Section 1 of the Fourteenth Amendment to the U.S. Constitution confirms that states may not abridge privileges or immunities of U.S. citizens, and they must afford to them due process and equal protection of laws. One interpretation of this section is that the Bill of Rights applies to state governments in the same way as it does to the federal government—meaning states may not encroach on the liberties explicated in the First through Eighth Amendments. The question is whether the deciding authority—the U.S. Supreme Court—has ever suggested such a literal interpretation of Section 1. The short answer is no; it has not done so. The longer answer—that the Court has only applied select liberties of the Bill of Rights to state governments—is the focus of this essay. Specifically, we explain the development of law concerning the incorporation (application to the states) of liberties outlined in the Bill of Rights, including the Court's inconsistent interpretation of these clauses.

We begin by noting that the Bill of Rights was originally applied only to the federal government. After all, it was a strong central government that the founders (and Revolutionary War-era citizens) most feared. That said, James Madison's first attempt at crafting the first Bill of Rights (with seventeen articles or amendments) included some, albeit limited, protection from state encroachment. As he wrote in Article 14, "No State shall violate the equal rights of conscience, or the freedom of the press, or the trial by jury in criminal cases." Unfortunately, this section was rejected by Congress, which may be an indication the members did not intend for the Bill of Rights to apply to the states. It is in this context that the Court decided *Barron v. Baltimore* (32 U.S. 243, 1833), an incorporation case (of sorts) decided thirty-five years prior to the ratification of the Fourteenth Amendment.

Barron focused on whether the takings clause of the Fifth Amendment (mandating fair compensation for taking private property for public use) applied to the states. The Court ruled that it did not. In his majority opinion, Chief Justice John Marshall wrote that the Constitution was ordained and established by the people of the United States for their own government. As such, the Fifth Amendment must be understood to restrain only the powers of the federal government and is not applicable to the states. If the states had wanted limits to safeguard liberty, Marshall reasoned, they would have applied limits themselves. In addition, had the framers intended limits to be placed on states, they would have expressed that intention. Finally, the unanimous Court decision pointed out that almost every state ratifying convention understood the amendment to limit the federal government and not the state governments. In short, the Fifth Amendment could not, and would not, be construed as limiting states. While *Barron* ostensibly applied only to the takings clause, the precedent was read by subsequent courts as applicable to other liberties.

Barron led the Court down a path of decisions that demonstrated exactly what U.S. society was like without the universal application of the Bill of Rights. A case in point was *Scott v. Sandford* (60 U.S., 393, 1857), among the most reviled decisions in the Court's history. In *Sandford*, Chief Justice Roger Taney argued that the Constitution does not grant federal citizenship to African Americans whose ancestors had been brought to the United States as slaves. In terms of the incorporation doctrine, he wrote that states may not grant citizenship, nor provide "the rights and privileges," secured in the Constitution.

With the North's Civil War victory, the Thirteenth, Fourteenth, and Fifteenth Amendments were ratified with the intent of providing protection for emancipated slaves (and all African Americans). The Fourteenth Amendment was the most general of the three, with its privileges or immunities, due process, and equal protection clauses.

In these three clauses of the Fourteenth Amendment attorneys saw an opportunity to ask the Supreme Court to apply the Bill of Rights to state governments. The first avenue they chose—the privileges or immunities clause—was a bold move considering what the Taney Court said in *Sandford*. And, indeed, this avenue was quickly closed in the *Slaughterhouse Cases* (83 U.S. 36, 1873). In an economic regulation case that focused on whether a state can control an entire industry (in this case, slaughterhouse operations in Louisiana), the Court ruled that the privileges or immunities clause could not be used to protect the rights of citizens to conduct business, because the right to one's livelihood or the right to be protected against a monopoly is not specified in the Constitution. More to the point, the Court gutted the privileges or immunities clause and indicated it would never use this clause to nationalize the Bill of Rights.

The door to incorporation seemed closed for the privileges or immunities clause, but the other two clauses were ripe for use to achieve this goal. In this spirit, attorneys turned next to the due process clause because, with a commensurate clause already in the Fifth Amendment, this path to incorporation seemed intuitive. The Court took up this argument in *Hurtado v. California* (110 U.S. 516, 1884). *Hurtado* was a criminal procedure case that focused on the right to have a grand jury determine whether to issue an indictment. The case arose because California's policy allowed prosecutors to use an information-charging document rather than a grand jury. The state used this latter method to bring Hurtado to trial, and he was found guilty of murder. Hurtado's lawyer argued he had a right to due process that applied to federal hearings under the Fifth Amendment and to states under the same clause found in the Fourteenth Amendment. The Court disagreed and argued precisely the opposite. In particular, the majority argued that because due process is explicitly contained in the Fifth Amendment, it applies only to this amendment. It reasoned that inclusion of the term "due process" in the Fourteenth Amendment could not be used as the path to incorporate the entire Bill of Rights.

Based on using Justice John M. Harlan's dissent in *Hurtado*, a majority took up the concept of "fundamental rights" in *Chicago, Burlington, and Quincy Railroad v. Chicago* (166 U.S. 226, 1897). In *Burlington*, the Court decided that just compensation for private property taken for public use (raised sixty-two years earlier in *Barron*) was a vital (fundamental) principle and therefore a liberty that must be protected against federal *and* state government encroachment. The Court held that states must honor the Bill of Rights requirement to pay owners just compensation. Thus, this federal liberty was now incorporated, or applied, to state governments.

Even with *Burlington* opening the door toward incorporation, the Court continued to eschew full incorporation. Instead, it embarked on a process of selective incorporation whereby liberties in the Bill of Rights are incorporated on a piecemeal basis. It fleshed out this concept in *Twining v. New Jersey* (211 U.S. 78, 1908) where the majority reiterated that some provisions of the Bill of Rights might be protected from state abridgment through the due process clause of the Fourteenth Amendment. Ironically, while it decided that the due process right against self-incrimination did not need to be protected against state encroachment, the majority admitted that some liberties are fundamental and inalienable—just not protection against self-incrimination.

The first meaningful step toward selective incorporation came in *Gitlow v. New York* (268 U.S. 652, 1925). Although the Court did not protect Gitlow's specific speech from state suppression, it did incorporate free speech generally. Unlike *Twining*, the Court finally addressed a specific right as fundamental rather than ignoring this concept. In other words, invoking selective incorporation, freedom of speech was the first fundamental right to be protected from state encroachment. From there, other rights were incorporated through the twentieth and into the twenty-first century. These included, for example: freedom of the press in *Near v. Minnesota* (283 U.S. 697, 1931), the free exercise of religion in *Cantwell v. Connecticut* (310 U.S. 296, 1940), the protection against evidence used at trial from illegal searches in *Mapp v. Ohio* (367 U.S. 643, 1961), the right to counsel in *Gideon v. Wainwright* (372 U.S. 335, 1963), and the right to keep and bear arms in *McDonald v. Chicago* (566 U.S. 742, 2009).

As recently as the last two terms, the Supreme Court has incorporated two more rights. Specifically, in *Timbs v. Indiana* (596 U.S. ___, 2019), it incorporated the Eighth Amendment protection against excessive bails and fines, while in *Ramos v. Louisiana* (590 U.S. ___, 2020), it incorporated the Sixth Amendment requirement that jury criminal convictions be unanimous. However, several liberties have yet to be incorporated to the states. These include the Third Amendment protection against quartering troops, the Fifth Amendment right to a grand jury, and the Seventh Amendment right to a jury trial in civil cases. These rights have not been incorporated because the law moves slowly and because a majority of the justices on the U.S. Supreme Court have never taken the stance that all of the Bill of Rights should be incorporated.

Despite the adherence to selective incorporation, some justices have held different views about whether, and how, the Bill of Rights should apply to the states. For instance, Justice John Marshall Harlan II (the grandson of former justice John Marshall Harlan I who dissented in *Hurtado*) and Justice Potter Stewart focused on whether (in terms of criminal cases) trials are fundamentally fair. For them, this meant that procedures should be fair for all litigants even if the procedures differed from what was laid out in the Bill of Rights. Perhaps the most radical approach to incorporation was held by Justices William O. Douglas and Hugo Black, who both advocated total incorporation of the Bill of Rights. Unfortunately, they never found three other votes to agree with their view (although they came close with Justices William Brennan and Thurgood Marshall).

In the end, the U.S. Supreme Court has taken the approach it takes with many areas of the law—a legally conservative one. This means it has moved slowly to incorporate liberties (after more than 200 years it still has not applied the full Bill of Rights to the states). Time will tell whether U.S. citizens will be protected from state encroachment of the remaining rights that have not yet been incorporated.

Timothy R. Johnson is the Morse-Alumni Distinguished Professor of Political Science, University of Minnesota; Rachel Houston is a PhD candidate, Department of Political Science, at the University of Minnesota.

There Are Reversals and Then There Are REVERSALS
Scott Merriman

The U.S. Supreme Court has reversed itself multiple times over the last century, but some reversals have loomed larger than others in prompting major changes to American society and law. Three reversals are worthy of specific note.

The Supreme Court directly reversed itself between 1896, when it issued its notorious *Plessy v. Ferguson* decision upholding "separate but equal" racial segregation in schools and other public spaces as constitutional, and 1954, when it overturned that decision and desegregated America's schools with its *Brown v. Board of Education* ruling.

The whole idea of equality of rights for Americans only really enters the U.S. Constitution in 1868 with the Fourteenth Amendment. Prior to that point, the word "equal" had only been used to refer to how one state was treated versus another in terms of votes. The relevant clause of the U.S. Constitution's Fourteenth Amendment is that "no state shall . . . deny to any person within its jurisdiction the equal protection of the laws." Passage of the Fourteenth Amendment had been sparked by the unequal treatment of post-Civil War southern governments toward African Americans, so its general aim was clear.

However, enforcing the provisions of the Fourteenth Amendment proved difficult. In case after case, the U.S. Supreme Court limited the federal government's power to enforce it, and former slaveholding states across the South were not interested in enforcing it. The Court's refusal to support the Fourteenth Amendment reaches its low point in 1896 with *Plessy v. Ferguson*. That case concerned a Louisiana law that mandated different coaches on streetcars for African Americans and whites. The text of the Fourteenth Amendment would seem to ban such laws as discriminatory. However, the Supreme Court held in an 8-1 decision that the separate treatment was allowed, as long as the coaches were "equal." This embrace of the notion of "separate but equal" was disastrous for African Americans. As whites were the ones in positions of power to interpret and define equality, the treatment was hardly ever equal. Furthermore, the decision held that the Supreme Court was not the one to mandate equality, and it dismissed African American claims that segregation was inherently unequal as a figment of their imaginations.

Fifty years later, the Supreme Court still generally had not spoken about equality, except in a few federal policies. During the 1950s, however, activists in the emerging civil rights movement worked to change that silence. The main issue being litigated was the right to attend integrated schools, as all the schools in the American South remained segregated. It was against that backdrop that the U.S. Supreme Court took up the case of *Brown v. Board of Education*. There the Supreme Court ruled that "separate but equal is inherently unequal," striking down segregation in education and putting the Court firmly on the side of equality.

A second reversal came in the policy area of busing of students following *Brown*. During the 1950s and 1960s, many whites moved out of the cities or sent their children to "segregation academies," which were all-white private schools. Thus, integration was thwarted. Some cities subsequently turned to a strategy of integrating schools by busing white students to historically black schools and vice versa. The Supreme Court at first allowed this in *Swann v. Charlotte-Mecklenburg Board of Education* (1971). However, violent opposition to these busing policies erupted in places as far north as Boston, and lawsuits against busing programs continued. In 1974, the federal government passed the General Provisions Act, which prohibited federal funds being spent on busing. The U.S. Supreme Court then issued a ruling in *Milliken v. Bradley* (1974) prohibiting inter-district busing. This decision gave white families the option of avoiding school integration by simply moving outside of the district. In the wake of these two blows to integration, many whites who lived in integrated cities in the South sent their children to all-white private schools—which in turn diminished support for public school funding.

A final momentous reversal by the Supreme Court came in the area of LGBTQ rights. As late as the 1980s, the Supreme Court treated LGBTQ individuals with disdain. In the case of *Bowers v. Hardwick* (1986), for example, the Court upheld a law (the law was being tested in the abstract and no one had been charged under it) that suggested that people engaging in sodomy could be put in prison for twenty years. The majority opinion in *Bowers* held that there was no right to engage in homosexual conduct, and a concurring opinion described homosexual behavior as having always been immoral. However, less than thirty years later, the Supreme Court ruled by a narrow 5-4 margin in *Obergefell v. Hodges* (2015) that the right to marry could not be denied based on the sex of the plaintiffs. This decision gave LGBTQ Americans the same right to marry as other Americans.

Of these reversals, the most important was *Brown v. Board*. This is not to denigrate the low level of rights that LGBTQ individuals had before the line of cases that ended in *Obergefell*. However, if one is to compare the level of oppression that African Americans had before *Brown* versus the level LGBTQ individuals had before *Obergefell*, *Brown* changed more. *Brown* also gave LGBTQ individuals hope, and African Americans had no such case.

Scott Merriman is a professor in the Department of History at Troy University. He is the author of twelve books, including Religion and the Law in America *(2007),* Religion and the States *(2009), and* When Religion and Secular Interests Collide *(2020).*

The Judicial System from a Clerk's Perspective
Dennis McKinney

The U.S. judicial system is one of the cornerstones of our democracy. The Founding Fathers saw fit to instill foundational principles such as "innocent until proven guilty" and the "right to be tried by a jury of your peers." That being said, each state has its own rules and laws when it comes to selecting judges, punishment for different levels of crime, rules concerning access to judges by litigants, civil law procedures, and laws concerning jury selection.

This essay examines the American court system from the perspective of a judge's clerk. When I started working as a bailiff in Colorado in 1983 and a few months later as a clerk (there is no longer a bailiff position assigned to courtrooms in Colorado), computers were just beginning to be used in the judicial department. Most work was done using forms that had to be completed by hand. It took the judicial system some time to become computer savvy (some judges took even longer), but by the time I retired in 2016, almost everything was being done by computer entry, with very few paper forms being required.

Judge's clerks are usually required to have a high school education or GED (general education development) certification. Many clerks are college graduates (some judges even require that), while some judges prefer law clerks (law school graduates or interns). The clerk is responsible for scheduling cases (the court's docket), data entry of court cases such as minute orders (a small narrative of what happened in each case during a hearing), entering fines, printing bench warrants, preparing paperwork for incarceration of defendants, and many other details required to keep the chambers and courtroom running smoothly.

The judge and their clerks have a special relationship. There is a trust that must be maintained between all individuals on the judge's staff in and out of the chambers (the private offices of a judge and their staff). Many unwritten rules are put in place to protect not only the judge but also the staff.

First and foremost is the confidentiality agreement, meaning that anything said between a judge and clerk remains confidential and is not to leave the confines of the chambers. This is important because a clerk may be tasked with typing an order in a case, meaning the clerk will be the first person to see a decision on an important issue before the court that must remain confidential until released to all litigants simultaneously.

Second, a clerk is the frontline barrier between the judge and attorneys or pro se litigants (litigants not represented by a lawyer). Communication without all parties present, whether on the record or off, is called ex-parte communication. If this isn't addressed in law school, an attorney quickly learns that a clerk is very protective and will not let them talk to the judge without all parties present. However, pro se litigants sometimes have a difficult time grasping this concept. There have been cases where a judge will actually go on record in the courtroom, explain the reason for the ex-parte rule, and secure a statement from the pro se litigant to state that they understand it and will abide by it.

In my opinion, something that is never taught in law school is the rule of contempt of clerk. A person, whether attorney or pro se litigant, never wants to say or do something to a judge's clerk that will land them in the proverbial doghouse of the clerk because it could also impact their relationship with the judge that employs that clerk. Veteran attorneys know this rule very well because most of them, at one time or another, have broken it. Remember the relationship between the judge and clerk is special, so being in the clerk's doghouse could conceivably be detrimental to the attorney's client.

During my years as a clerk, I was amazed at some of the things I observed in the courtroom. Although the courtroom is a very serious place and decorum must be maintained, there is still the occasion where something humorous will take place. One judge was in court advising a defendant of charges filed against him. The judge was reading the probable cause affidavit out loud when he started laughing uncontrollably. The defendant, who was planning on burglarizing a bar after-hours, had gone into the restroom and climbed on a urinal to hide in the ceiling. He got caught when a patron came in and found the defendant's feet dangling from the ceiling. The judge got this image in his mind and could not stop laughing. He had to recess court three times before he could get through the advisement.

Judges have heard all of the excuses that people can come up with to explain running afoul of the law. When a defendant in a criminal case pleads guilty, they must state in court what they did. In DUI (driving under the influence) cases, a judge will ask the defendant how much he had to drink. No matter how high the defendant's blood alcohol content was, in the majority of cases the standard response is two beers. One judge got so tired of hearing that response that when one defendant insisted that he had only consumed two beers, the judge reached under the bench, pulled out two empty 24-ounce beer cans, and asked the defendant "two beers like these?"

I spent the last eighteen years of my career as jury commissioner. I was responsible for sending out summons, checking in jurors on the day of their service, sending them to courtrooms, and crediting them and paying them for their service if they were eligible for payment. Jury service laws differ significantly from state to state, but the excuses people try to use to avoid serving on juries are the same across the country, and judges have heard them all. It always amazed me, and still does, why people dislike appearing for jury duty. Many people may have to report to the courthouse, but actually only about 25 percent serve as jurors. The rest sit in a room a couple of hours and are sent home or to work. I would tell people that answering a jury duty summons was like going to the dentist; you never want to go but sooner or later you have to.

I enjoyed my career in the judicial system. Every day was met with different challenges and observations. I feel blessed that I was able to observe the process firsthand.

Dennis McKinney is a medically retired Air Force Veteran who has a bachelor's degree in communications and a bachelor's degree in sociology from the University of Colorado. He worked for the judicial branch from 1983 to 2016.

Congressional Oversight of the Federal Judiciary
Mark C. Miller

Should Congress exert oversight control over the federal courts and federal judges? This question is fundamental to our understanding of the relationship between the legislative and judicial branches in the U.S. federal government's separation of powers system. As two independent and coequal branches of the federal government, how much and what type of control should the Congress have over the federal judiciary?

Congressional oversight over federal executive branch agencies is quite common. Since Congress delegates to federal agencies the responsibility to implement congressional policies and provides funding to these agencies to do so, Congress feels that it has the right and the responsibility to oversee how the agencies put those policies into action and how they spend their appropriated funds. As one analysis explained, "A fundamental objective of legislative oversight is to hold executive officials accountable for the implementation of delegated authority" (Oleszek et al. 376). Among other things, congressional oversight over federal agencies may take the form of congressional committee hearings and/or reports to Congress by inspectors general located in most federal agencies or by the General Accounting Office located in the legislative branch.

Congressional oversight of the judiciary is a very different concept. While Congress determines how many judges may sit on a specific federal court and the Senate must confirm all federal judicial nominees, Congress does not delegate authority to the federal courts. Instead, the Constitution set up a system of judicial independence in order to allow federal judges to be free of political influence in their decision-making. Thus, federal judges have life terms and Congress is prohibited from reducing their salaries. Although the judicial independence of the federal courts is widely accepted, there are a small number who disagree. For example, one conservative congressional staffer once told me, "Law schools teach the myth that there are three coequal branches of government in the U.S. In reality, the courts are subservient to the will of the majority as expressed by the legislative branch" (Miller 2009: 10). Nevertheless, most argue that judicial independence is constitutionally guaranteed, and that such independence is necessary to keep judges free from direct congressional oversight.

It is quite common for politicians in Congress or in the White House to complain about specific federal court decisions with which they disagree. Congressional committees may even hold hearings to express their opposition to particular court rulings. For example, almost immediately following the U.S. Supreme Court's decision in *Kelo v City of New London* (2005), in which the Court allowed local governments to determine whether seizing property through eminent domain would serve the public interest, a subcommittee of the U.S. House Judiciary Committee held hearings to attack the ruling (U.S. House, Committee 2005a). Sometimes congressional committees hold hearings with broader themes, such as when the same subcommittee held a hearing deploring the citing of international court decisions by various justices of the U.S. Supreme Court (U.S. House, Committee 2005b). In addition, individual members of the Senate Judiciary Committee may use judicial confirmation hearings to express their unhappiness with specific court decisions.

Congress can also overturn federal court rulings. One of the duties of the federal judiciary is to interpret federal statutes when their meaning is vague or unclear. If Congress is unhappy with a federal court's statutory interpretation decision, then it can merely enact a new statute and thus overturn the court's interpretation. However, if the judicial ruling is based on the court's reading of the U.S. Constitution, then in theory Congress's only recourse is to pass a constitutional amendment, which requires the approval of two-thirds of each house of Congress and three-quarters of the states. Congress has sometimes attempted to use federal statutes to overturn constitutionally based decisions, but the Supreme Court has usually declared these laws to be unconstitutional, as they did in 1990 when Congress passed a federal statute in an attempt to overturn the Court's ruling that flag burning is a form of constitutionally protected political speech.

A more aggressive form of congressional oversight would be to create an inspector general for the federal judiciary. Since 1978, Congress has established inspectors general in almost all federal agencies to help conduct oversight of the executive branch. The inspectors general conduct audits and investigations of agency programs and operations, and report to Congress on their findings. An inspector general for the federal judiciary, however, has never existed. In 2005, the chair of the House Judiciary Committee, Congressman Jim Sensenbrenner (R-WI), joined with the chair of the Senate Judiciary Committee, Senator Chuck Grassley (R-IA), to introduce such a bill. The legislation was approved by the House Judiciary Committee in 2006, but it never reached the floor of the House and received no consideration even in committee in the Senate (see Miller 2009, 170–179). Chairman Grassley again raised this idea in a May 2018 hearing concerning sexual harassment in the judiciary (Totenberg 2018). The proposal struck federal judges, however, as an attack on judicial independence. They claimed that the main goal of supporters of an inspector general position over the judiciary was to accumulate evidence that could be used to impeach federal judges whose decisions various politicians did not like.

A final form of congressional oversight over the federal judiciary is that Congress has the legal authority to impeach federal judges under certain extreme circumstances and remove them from the bench. Under judicial impeachment rules, the House brings articles of impeachment, and the Senate then holds a trial to determine if the judge or other federal official should be removed from office. Since 1803, the tradition has been that Congress will not remove a federal judge merely because of political disagreements with their judicial decisions. Nonetheless, various politicians continue to threaten to impeach judges with whom they disagree.

Should there be congressional oversight over the federal courts? If Congress overturns various court rulings through the normal legislative and constitutional amendment channels, then the answer should be yes. But if Congress uses oversight to attack the courts as an institution, that puts judicial independence at risk.

Bibliography

Miller, Mark C. 2009. *The View of the Courts from the Hill: Interactions between Congress and the Federal Judiciary.* Charlottesville: University of Virginia Press.

Oleszek, Walter J., Mark J. Oleszek, Elizabeth Rybicki, and Bill Heniff Jr. 2016. *Congressional Procedures and the Policy Process,* 10th ed. Thousand Oaks, CA: CQ Press.

Totenberg, Nina. 2018. "Sen. Grassley Says Report on Sexual Harassment in Judiciary Simply Kicks the Can." *NPR.* June 14. https://www.npr.org/transcripts/619701971

U.S. House, Committee on the Judiciary, Subcommittee on the Constitution. (2005a). *Supreme Court's Kelo Decision and Potential Congressional Responses: Hearing Before the Subcommittee on the Constitution of the House Judiciary Committee,* 109th Cong., 1st Session. September 22, 2005.

U.S. House, Committee on the Judiciary, Subcommittee on the Constitution. (2005b). *House Resolution on the Appropriate Role of Foreign Judgements in the Interpretation of the Constitution of the United States: Hearing Before the Subcommittee of the Constitution of the House Judiciary Committee,* 109th Cong., 1st Session. July 19, 2005.

Mark C. Miller *is a professor of political science and the director of the Law & Society program at Clark University in Worcester, Massachusetts. He is the author or editor of five books, including* Judicial Politics in the United States *(2015).*

Courts and Administrative Agencies: A Central Feature of Modern Policymaking
Joseph Postell

Our contemporary judicial system is increasingly occupied with a category of cases and controversies surrounding the exercise of policymaking power by administrative agencies. This category of law, defined as *administrative law*, has emerged because of the dramatic increase of power delegated to modern administrative agencies over the past century.

Today, most major policies are made not by Congress or state legislatures but by administrative agencies who have *rule-making* power (power to make rules that carry the force of law) as well as (in most cases) the power of *adjudication* (power to decide particular cases arising under the enforcement of their rules). Across a wide variety of areas—from environmental protection under the EPA, to communication regulations by the FCC, to workplace safety under OSHA, to health-care law made by the Department of HHS—these "alphabet soup" agencies are responsible for making and enforcing most of the federal laws that govern us today. Legislatures today typically avoid making the law directly, handing power over to the agencies instead and relying on oversight after the fact to hold the agencies accountable.

As this brief portrayal suggests, modern administrative agencies have powers that look like the legislative, executive, and judicial powers that the Constitution vests in Congress, the president, and the federal courts. Congress delegates much of its legislative powers to these agencies and entrusts them to make the specific rules that it otherwise would have to spend most of its time enacting into law. The emergence of bureaucracy as a central feature of modern governance, however, raises important constitutional and legal questions.

Given this extraordinary expansion and concentration of administrative power, it is imperative to protect citizens from the potentially arbitrary decisions that bureaucrats make. This is where administrative law enters the picture. It is increasingly seen as the job of the courts to devise and impose legal restrictions on the massive power of government agencies and administrators. At both the national and state levels, courts spend much of their time reviewing the legality of decisions of administrative agencies.

Although these decisions often involve technical, arcane legal doctrines and complicated facts, they have enormous policy

implications. For instance, when the George W. Bush administration determined in 2003 that it did not have the authority
under the Clean Air Act to regulate greenhouse gas emissions
to address climate change, the Supreme Court intervened and
rejected that claim in a 2007 case called *Massachusetts v. EPA*.
After a tragic mass shooting in Las Vegas on October 1, 2017,
the Donald Trump administration adopted a regulation rein-
terpreting guns with "bump stocks" (which was used in the Las
Vegas shooting) as "machine guns," and banned them. Litigation challenging this regulation is ongoing in the federal courts
of appeals.

These cases involve important issues such as climate change
and gun control, but they are cases involving judicial review of
administrative agencies (EPA in the former case, and ATF in
the latter). In sum, administrative law is now an important feature of the modern judiciary and is central to how government
policy is made today.

Administrative law is increasingly important in state courts
as well. The COVID-19 pandemic led to emergency lockdown
orders issued by state health departments in many states. These
state agencies typically relied on existing laws that delegated
power to the state's executive branch to impose such restrictions. In Wisconsin and Michigan, however, state supreme
courts ruled that these restrictions violated their respective
state constitutions. Even at the state level, power is increasingly granted to the executive branch, and the state courts are
tasked with reviewing the decisions made by state agencies and
officials.

The emergence of administrative law as a core function of
the judiciary has inserted courts into important areas of public policy. Now, when an agency makes a rule or a policy, it
is almost inevitable that someone will sue the agency to challenge the legality of its decision. These challenges can take a
number of forms. First, plaintiffs can challenge whether the
agency's decision was constitutional. They may challenge the
agency's policies by claiming that they infringe on the plaintiff's

constitutional rights or is based on an unconstitutional delegation of power. Additionally, plaintiffs may assert that the agency's structure violates constitutional principles or that the agency violated procedural requirements that the Congress or state legislatures have imposed on them.

Both the federal government and various state governments have passed Administrative Procedure Acts that require agencies to take specific steps before issuing their rules or adjudicating. If an agency does not disclose its proposed rule to the public, or does not allow for the public to comment on its decisions, it may violate these procedural requirements. Third, the substance of the agency's decision may be challenged as inconsistent with the law passed by the legislature, as arbitrary and capricious, or as based on inaccurate information.

Consequently, lawyers have many options for challenging the decisions made by administrative agencies. This gives both courts and litigants tremendous power over the policy decisions made by the bureaucracy. In other words, administrative law affords interest groups opportunities to use judicial review to challenge and change public policy. Unsurprisingly, this has led to the creation of a wide variety of public interest law firms, from the Natural Resources Defense Council to the Environmental Defense Fund to Common Cause on the progressive side, and the Kirkwood Institute and the Center for Individual Rights on the conservative side. They seek to use the court system to intervene in decisions made by the bureaucracy to which they object. These lobbying groups spend an increasing portion of their efforts on litigation to accomplish their goals (in addition to trying to influence legislators), because the decisions that matter to them are now made by agencies that are reviewed by courts.

In summary, administrative law is an extremely important and growing part of the workload of national and state courts. Administrative law affects major public policy outcomes in almost every area of public policy. It has involved courts in public policy decisions to a much greater degree, and has also provided interest groups with opportunities to use litigation to lobby for changes to public policies. Much of this happens outside the legislative process, so the public does not understand or follow these decisions as carefully as they would if the decisions were made by their elected representatives.

Joseph Postell *is associate professor of politics at Hillsdale College, Michigan. He is author of* Bureaucracy in America: The Administrative State's Challenge to Constitutional Government *(2017) and editor* of Rediscovering Political Economy *(2011) and* Congress: Core Documents *(2020).*

Transgender Rights and the American Judicial System
Chuck Stewart

Transgender rights have become a hot topic in U.S. politics. The public and courts have often confused the issue, however, by conflating terms with different meanings such as "gender," "sex," and "sex roles" under the umbrella word "sex." For example, Title VII of the U.S. Civil Rights Act of 1964 prohibited discrimination in employment based on race, color, religion, sex, and national origin. Unfortunately, "sex" was not defined. For more than fifty years, legal arguments that revolve around that Title VII wording have been made for and against gay, lesbians, bisexual, transgender (LGBT) rights. Some attorneys have argued that "sex" simply meant "women" and "men." This argument, though, misleadingly conflates sex with gender. Other attorneys have argued that Title VII prohibits employment decisions in which the "sex" of the person involved is taken under consideration. But what is sex? What is gender? What does it mean to be a "woman" or a "man"? And the prefix for "transgender" is "trans," meaning "beyond." What does it mean to be "beyond" gender?

"Gender identity" is a person's conviction of being "female" or "male." The public display of acting "masculine" or "feminine" and engaging in behaviors deemed acceptable for those characteristics is identified as the "social sex-role" (sexologist John Money in 1955 used the term "gender role"). Clothing, hair styles, type of employment are some of the major sources of establishing a feminine or masculine persona. A person's "sex" (better called "biological sex") is a concept based on: <u>primary</u> sexual characteristics determined by chromosomes factors (XX-female, XY-male) as expressed in internal and external genitalia (breasts, clitoris, penis), hormonal states, and <u>secondary</u> sexual characteristics (body hair, height, weight, voice). "Sexual orientation" is understood as sexual attraction for the other sex (*heterosexual*), the same sex (*homosexual*), both sexes (*bisexual*), or none of the sexes (*non-sexual*). Often, "affectional orientation" (who one is attracted to for affection) is confused with sexual orientation because sexual attraction is often strongly linked to feelings of affection. "Sexual attraction" also ranges from those strongly desiring sex to those who are *asexual* (sometimes referred to as *graysexual,* these individuals are not overly interested in engaging in sex). These characteristics fall on a spectrum and should not be viewed as exclusively binary.

For example, a <u>cis</u>gender woman is born with the internal and external genitalia, hormonal states, and secondary sexual characteristics of a woman (sex), who feels like a "female" (gender identity), acts "feminine" by wearing the clothing and hair, uses mannerisms and works a job society dictates as appropriate for women (social sex-role), has a sexual attraction for men (sexual orientation being heterosexual), and seeks affection and emotional support from men (affectional orientation). The woman is concordant on all measures for defining a "woman" by most cultural standards. However, very few people meet all these requirements and many may vary in one or more characteristic. There is a range of expressions for each of these characteristics. The binary model is not accurate and should be discarded. For example, if this same cisgender woman simply worked in heavy construction and wore traditionally "manly" clothing and no makeup, she would no longer be considered fully a woman by many people in the culture. Further, if she felt like her fundamental identity was not as a woman but rather as a man, he would be transgender whether or not he made efforts to make the transition through medical intervention. He would be classified as female-to-male (FTM) transgender and be addressed by the male pronoun "he."

Transgender people do not conform to the societal definition of gender but transcend gender norms. Some people completely reject gender norms and may identify as gender queer (or Genderqueer). Intersex (previously labeled "hermaphrodite") people have a mixed set of biological sex characteristics—for example, a baby born with both an enlarged clitoris (often mistaken for a penis) and vaginal opening. The political term for opposing binary thinking on gender and sexual orientation is the word "queer." The word queer has academic application and is widely used by younger lesbian, gay, bisexual, transgender, intersex, and queer people (LGBTIQ or LGBTQ+) but historically was used as a pejorative to denigrate non-heterosexual people.

Challenges that transgender people have made against the U.S. legal system reveal a deep confusion in both the judicial and legislative branches of government about the construction of gender. Several cases of employment discrimination based on sexual orientation and transgender status have worked their way through the courts to the U.S. Supreme Court. Transgender litigants have claimed that Title VII inclusion of "sex" as a protected class applies to them. The U.S. Supreme Court issued a landmark ruling in June 2020 interpreting Title VII to provide employment protection for LGBT individuals (*Bostock v. Clayton County* 2020). In the 5-to-4 ruling, the conservative jurist Justice Gorsuch took a literalist approach to the case and delivered the opinion of the court. He summarized:

> An employer violates Title VII when it intentionally fires an individual employee based in part on sex. It makes no difference if other factors besides the plaintiff's sex contributed to the decision or that the employer treated women

as a group the same when compared to men as a group. A statutory violation occurs if an employer intentionally relies in part on an individual employee's sex when deciding to discharge the employee. Because discrimination on the basis of homosexuality or transgender status requires an employer to intentionally treat individual employees differently because of their sex, an employer who intentionally penalizes an employee for being homosexual or transgender also violates Title VII. . . . An employer who fires an individual for being homosexual or transgender fires that person for traits or actions it would not have questioned in members of a different sex. Sex plays a necessary and undisguisable role in the decision, exactly what Title VII forbids. . . . For an employer to discriminate against employees for being homosexual or transgender, the employer must intentionally discriminate against individual men and women in part because of sex. That has always been prohibited by Title VII's plain terms (page 2).

The decision surprised many Court observers and legal experts, since Justice Gorsuch had been nominated by President Trump for his conservative views. Instead, his literalist approach to interpreting the Constitution resulted in a conclusion that discrimination against LGBT people is unconstitutional discrimination based on cultural sexual roles. Still, the ruling leaves gaps in LGBT rights. The ruling does not apply to businesses with fewer than fifteen workers, doesn't address the "bathroom issue" or dress code challenges faced by transgender workers, doesn't address the disparity in health plans provided by employers, and doesn't clarify whether or not employers and service providers can deny LGBTQ persons based on religious convictions.

The presidency of Donald Trump was difficult for lesbians, gays, bisexual, and especially for transgender people. Although Trump was the first Republican presidential nominee to openly state support for the LGBTQ community, his actions as president were quite the opposite. His administration took more than thirty-five actions seen as hostile to LGBTQ Americans, including banning transgender service members from the military; creating a Religious Discrimination Division of the HHS to defend physicians and other medical professionals who refuse service to LGBTQ patients on religious grounds; allowing emergency shelters to deny access to transgender and gender-nonconforming people; and refusing entry to LGBTQ asylum seekers fleeing violence and persecution in their home countries.

Bibliography

Acosta, Lucas. 2020. "The Real List of Trump's 'Unprecedented Steps' for the LGBTQ Community," June 11. Human Rights Campaign. https://www.hrc.org /blog/the-list-of-trumps-unprecedented-steps-for-the-lgbtq -community

Bostock v. Clayton County, Georgia, No. 17-1618, Certiorari for the Eleventh Circuit, June 15, 2020.

Chuck Stewart *is an independent researcher and writer on LGBT topics. He is the published author of several books on the topic. His doctorate is in education, and he teaches math and statistics courses at National University.*

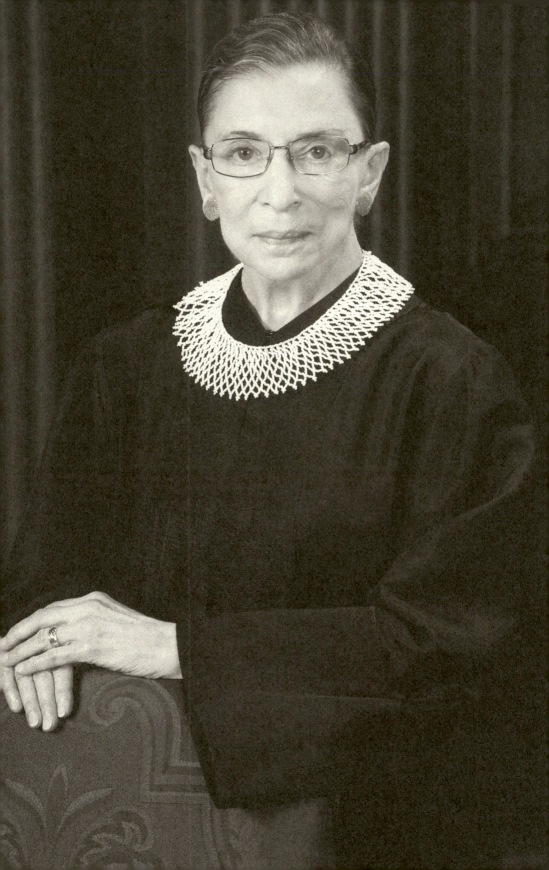

4 Profiles

Introduction

This chapter presents profiles of important organizations and activists involved in the American judicial system and the politics thereof. They have influenced courts and the judicial system in the halls of Congress by advocating for or against enactment of laws affecting or reforming the judicial system. The efforts of these individuals and groups resulted in landmark judicial decisions that affected the judicial system and set precedents influencing the operation and authority of courts at all levels. They did and continue to do so by engaging in the politics of judicial appointments at the federal courts level, and by engaging in judicial electoral politics at the state and local government level. The chapter describes twenty-nine key stakeholder organizations and presents profiles of twenty-two individual actors in the arena of judicial politics and processes. They include both government officials and leading activists from nongovernmental groups who have impacted judicial system issues across a spectrum of ideological perspectives. These sets of organizational and individual profiles are presented in alphabetical order.

Ruth Bader Ginsburg, whose litigation on behalf of women's rights transformed the legal landscape of the 1970s, was the second woman and the first Jewish justice since Abe Fortas to serve on the U.S. Supreme Court. She served on the Supreme Court from 1993 until her death in 2020. (Steve Petteway, Collection of the Supreme Court of the United States)

Organizations

Alliance for Justice (AFJ)

Founded in 1979, the Alliance for Justice (AFJ) is a progressive judicial advocacy group that monitors judicial appointments. It represents a coalition of 120 politically liberal groups active in U.S. judicial politics. AFJ works in collaboration with organizations representing women's rights, LGBTQ rights, workers' rights, civil rights, disability rights, immigrants' rights, and environmental protection. These groups advocate to ensure that the U.S. justice system advances core constitutional values, preserves fundamental rights, and offers unfettered access to the courts for all, not just the wealthy and politically powerful. AFJ advocates for a fair and independent judicial system through its justice programs, and by promoting nonprofit advocacy via their Bolder Advocacy Program (1999). AFJ was founded by attorney and activist Nan Aron in response to the efforts of conservative groups such as the Federalist Society to pack the courts with ultraconservative judges, which the AFJ and its member groups see as a direct threat to the public interest and civil rights.

AFJ, which began in a Georgetown University campus building, launched its Judicial Selection Project in the mid-1980s. AFJ was a leading organization against the federal judicial nominations of Robert Bork, Clarence Thomas, and Brett Kavanaugh. It highlights the importance of judicial nominations by championing public involvement during the nomination process. It also has launched a Building the Bench initiative to pinpoint diverse candidates for federal bench positions.

American Association for Justice (AAJ)

American Association for Justice (AAJ) was launched in 1946 in Portland, Oregon, by a group of nine attorneys involved in workers' compensation litigation. They put together a national organization to oppose new threats facing trial lawyers across the country. Operating first as the National Association of

Claimant's Compensation Attorneys, they advocated for and offered strong representation for victims of industrial accidents. The organization quickly attracted additional lawyers who specialized in admiralty law, railroads, and personal injury cases, and then expanded to almost all facets of trial advocacy. The group changed its name three times as it expanded its fields of focus, emerging first as the Association of Trial Lawyers of America. In 1977, the organization moved its headquarters from Boston to Washington, D.C. In 2006, the group adopted its new name, AAJ, to reflect its broad-based membership coalition of attorneys, law professors, paralegals, and law students.

Today, AAJ describes itself as an organization that seeks justice for victims and protects their rights—especially the right to trial by jury—and seeks to "strengthen the civil justice system through education and disclosure of information critical to public health and safety." AAJ has members worldwide, with networks in the United States and Canada.

American Bar Association (ABA)

Founded in 1878, the American Bar Association (ABA) is a professional membership organization whose stated mission is to serve its members and the public in defending liberty and delivering justice as the premier national representative organization of the legal profession. It promotes quality legal education, attorney competence, ethical conduct and professionalism, and promotes pro bono and public service by legal professionals. It promotes equity among all persons within the justice system, and aims to eliminate bias within legal professions. The ABA promotes the advancement of the rule of law, and seeks to preserve the independence of the legal profession and the judiciary.

The ABA formally adopted its standards for legal education in 1921, and in 1952 began its program of law school accreditation. It sponsored National Law Day in 1958. In 1974, it established its Legal Services Corporation. The ABA is headquartered in Chicago, Illinois. It began its judicial rating system in 1956 when it established its standing committee of fifteen members to rate nominees to the federal bench. The current chair of the Standing Committee on the Federal Judiciary is Randall Noel. In 2015, the ABA selected attorney Paulette Brown of New Jersey as the first African American to serve as the ABA president. In 2019, it selected Judy Perry Martinez, a Louisiana attorney, as ABA president.

American Civil Liberties Union (ACLU)

The ACLU is a nonpartisan, non-profit organization formed to "defend and preserve individual rights and liberties" of every person in America as guaranteed by the Constitution and the laws of the United States. ACLU was founded in 1920 in reaction to then attorney general Mitchell Palmer's "Red Scare" raids. Those raids rounded up thousands of radicals solely for their alleged political beliefs and deported hundreds of them. These victims of the raids, many of whom were American citizens, were arrested without warrants and without regard to constitutional protections against unlawful search and seizure. The raids literally constituted "guilt by association." Among the small group of founders of ACLU were Helen Keller, Roger Nash Baldwin, Jane Addams, Walter Nelles, Elizabeth Gurley Flynn, Felix Frankfurter, Norman Thomas, and Crystal Eastman. As of 2021, ACLU is headquartered in New York City and is led by CEO Anthony Romero, deputy CEO Dorothy Ehrlich, and its national legal director, David Cole. Currently, ACLU claims a national membership of over 1.5 million. Its annual budget exceeds $234 million, and it has a staff of 300 attorneys, as well as several thousand volunteer attorneys helping in offices throughout the United States.

ACLU lobbies for a broad variety of policy positions, including: (1) opposition to the death penalty that ACLU considers to be cruel and unusual punishment and unconstitutional on the basis of the Eighth Amendment; (2) support for same-sex marriage rights and equal rights for LGBT people, including an end to anti-LGBT discrimination in employment, housing, adoption, and media stereotyping; (3) support for birth control and abortion rights, and to protect against overturning *Roe v. Wade;* (4) elimination of discrimination against women in employment and compensation so that they receive equal pay for equal work; (5) support for the rights of prisoners and opposition to the use of torture; (6) opposition to government preference of religion over nonreligion, or for particular faiths over other faiths; and (7) support for the right to equal access to the ballot box (LeMay 2018, 162–163).

ACLU is comprised of two separate but closely affiliated nonprofits: the ACLU, a 501(c)(4) social welfare group; and the ACLU Foundation, a 501(c)(3) public charity. Both organizational platforms engage in civil rights litigation, advocacy, and education, but only the 501(c)(3) donations to the ACLU Foundation are tax deductible, and only the 501(c)(4) group can engage in unlimited political lobbying. The ACLU has supported countless suits by filing amicus curiae briefs. These "friends of the court" briefs are legal filings that lay out the legal arguments the group wants the court to consider even though it is not a litigant in the case. It has supported Native American suits to protect their rights to use controlled substances in religious ceremonies. It has supported the rights of Jehovah's Witnesses to canvass door-to-door, to resist the draft as conscientious objectors, and to refuse to salute the American flag. The ACLU has also been at the forefront of legal battles over the separation of church and state in cases like *Everson v. Board of Education* (1947), *McCollum v. Board of Education* (1948), and *Engel v. Vitale* (1962). It has lobbied in opposition to proposed constitutional amendments to mandate school prayer, and has consistently opposed local ordinances mandating the closure of businesses on Sunday. During the Trump administration, it attracted considerable attention for its opposition on constitutional grounds to President Donald Trump's Muslim travel ban.

Some of ACLU's more famous battles over the decades have included partnering with Clarence Darrow to defend schoolteacher John Scopes and the teaching of evolution in the Scopes Trial of 1925; the defense of Japanese American citizens incarcerated in internment camps by the U.S. government in 1942; support for ending the "separate-but-equal" doctrine in *Brown v. Board of Education*; championing privacy rights in *Roe v. Wade*; defending the free speech rights of Nazi demonstrators in *National Socialist Party of America v. Skokie* (1977); opposition to the USA Patriot Act in 2001 on privacy rights grounds; defending the rights of immigrants; supporting enactment of the Americans with Disabilities Act; protecting free speech in *Tinker v. Des Moines* (1969); fighting against the compulsory teaching of creationism in Arkansas in 1981; defending internet free speech in 1997 in *ACLU v. Reno*; defending LGBT rights in *Lawrence v. Texas* (2003) and many other cases; keeping religion out of science classrooms in *Kitzmiller v. Dover Area School District* (2005); and in 2009, protecting the constitutional rights of a thirteen-year old girl from being strip-searched in *Safford Unified School District v. Redding* (Cole 2016).

American Constitution Society (ACS)

The ACS is a nationwide network comprised of 200 chapters of lawyers and law students that promote and conduct debates and discussion of legal issues of the day. It has chapters in forty-eight states and on the campuses of most law schools. It has lawyers' chapters in forty cities. Its formal title is the American Constitutional Society for Law and Public Policy, and it is a progressive legal organization established as a counterbalance to the Federalist Society (which it is nonetheless modeled after in some ways). Its stated mission is to uphold the everlasting promises of the U.S. Constitution and the fundamental values expressed therein: individual rights and liberties, genuine equality, access to justice, democracy, and the rule of law.

Founded in 2001 and headquartered in Washington, D.C., the organization promotes and facilitates discussion and debate of progressive public policy ideas and issues, and provides forums for legal scholars, lawmakers, judges, lawyers, public policy advocates, law students, and members of the media. Recent forums are exemplified by a September 2020 ACS meeting in Arizona on "2020 Supreme Court Review," one in Nashville titled "Supreme Court Preview," and another on "What Is Criminal Justice Reform to an Exoneree?"

The society was founded by Peter Rubin, a Georgetown Law School professor who served as counsel to Al Gore in the legal battle over the 2000 presidential election. Initially called the Madison Society for Law and Policy, it received initial funding from the William and Flora Hewlett Foundation. Among its distinguished board members are David Halperin, who was its founding executive director, and Eric Holder, former attorney general of the United States. ACS hosts press and Capitol Hill briefings and public policy debates, disseminates ACS Issue Briefs, the ACSBlog, and publishes a variety of books as well as two journals: *Harvard Law and Policy Review* and *Advance: The Journal of the ACS Issue Groups.*

American Heritage Society

The Heritage Foundation was founded in 1973 and exemplifies the "think tank," as well as an advocacy organization, supporting research and education on the conservative right that directly impacts judicial system politics. It has grown to roughly one-half million claimed dues-paying members supporting its attempts to promote libertarian-based policies on freedom, property rights, and a more conservative civil society. The Heritage Foundation is a 501(c)(3) public policy advocacy organization that formulates and promotes conservative policy to limit government, promote individual liberty, traditional values, and a strong national defense. Its members assert that the organization's activities reflect the principles and ideas of the Founding Fathers, and that those principles and ideas are worth conserving and renewing. The Heritage Foundation has become an important lobbying organization for the appointment of conservative "originalist" judges to all levels of courts, especially in the federal judicial system. Conversely, it opposes "liberal" or even "centrist" judges nominated by Democratic presidents.

The foundation's staff, with years of experience in business, government, communications, and on Capitol Hill, regularly delivers conservative policy research and policy proposals to the Congress, the executive branch, the judiciary (through amicus briefs), and the media and American public. The foundation is governed by a twenty-two-member board of trustees.

American Judicature Society (AJS)

The American Judicature Society (AJS) was informally begun in 1912 by Herbert Harley and formally established one year later as an independent, nonprofit, nonpartisan organization dedicated to bettering the field of justice administration in the United States and to increasing the general public's comprehension of the justice system. Harley served as its secretary-treasurer from 1913 to 1945. Over the course of its century-long existence the AJS has focused on judicial diversity, judicial ethics, judicial selection, access to justice, criminal justice reform, and the jury system. It promoted a merit-based system for selecting judges, greater transparency during judicial proceedings, and enhanced access to the courts and to justice for all. It is credited with development of the Missouri Plan for judicial selection, and later for the creation of state judicial conduct commissions and nominating committees. For many years it also published an award-winning peer-reviewed journal, *Judicature*. In 2014, its board voted to dissolve due to funding constraints and to move the organization's operations and assets at the Dwight D. Opperman Center at Drake University to the AJS Hawaii Chapter. These include the National Center for State Courts, the Duke Law Center for Judicial Studies, the Hunter Center of the Communities Foundation of Texas, and the South Texas College of Law. The Hawaii chapter formed the new American Judicature Society. It maintains standing committees to monitor issues affecting the judiciary, develop programs related to the judiciary, and publish newsletters, articles, and reports.

Brennan Center for Justice

The Brennan Center for Justice at the New York University School of Law was founded in 1995 by former law clerks to Supreme Court justice William Brennan (1906–1997) to honor the memory and promote the ideals of Justice Brennan. These ideals include a commitment to inclusive and equitable democracy to aid the disadvantaged, respect for individual rights and liberties, and the value of "human dignity" as the core of the law. Justice Brennan was widely regarded as one of the most influential justices on the Supreme Court. He was a key member of the Warren Court, especially in regard to consequential Court decisions regarding civil rights and civil liberties. He was appointed to the Supreme Court by President Dwight D. Eisenhower in 1956. Brennan authored such landmark majority opinions as *Baker v. Carr* (1962) with its judicial principle of "one man, one vote," and *New York Times Co. v. Sullivan* (1964), which expanded press freedoms. The center has experienced exponential growth over the years, transforming from a small start-up to an organization nationally renowned for its work in the legal system. It has a current staff of 130 attorneys, scholars, and legal journalists and an annual budget of $27 million, maintaining offices in New York and Washington, D.C. Since 2006, it has expanded from litigation to a focus on research, public policy, and communication. It combines the elements of a think tank and legal advocacy group, and it has helped form a new agenda for legal reform in the states and nationally. It regularly publishes reports on the status of state and local courts and state laws affecting rights, such as the recent wave of state laws restricting voting rights.

Bureau of Justice Statistics (BJS)

The U.S. Bureau of Justice Statistics (BJS) is an agency of the Department of Justice and is a principal agency within the Federal Statistical System, the large network of government agencies primarily responsible for gathering data and statistics on various socioeconomic issues. Formed in 1979 and head-quartered in Washington, D.C., BJS publishes authoritative data gathered from the more than 50,000 agencies comprising the U.S. justice system. Its mission is to "collect, analyze, pub-lish, and disseminate statistical information on crime, crimi-nal offenders, victims of crime, and the operation of justice systems at all levels of government" (Bureau of Justice Statis-tics 2020). It publishes data critical to federal, state, and local policymakers in their efforts to combat crime and ensure that justice is efficient and evenhanded. It is an agency within the Office of Justice Programs of the Department of Justice. Prior to 2012, the director of the BJS required Senate approval, but since 2012, it now only requires the president's appointment.

Cato Institute Center for Constitutional Studies (CICCS)

The Center for Constitutional Studies is one of several research centers established at the Cato Institute. The work of the Cen-ter for Constitutional Studies and its scholars reflects the Cato Institute's emphasis on securing and maintaining individual freedom by constitutionally limiting the government. The cen-ter asserts that the judiciary should "neither make nor ignore the law, but rather to interpret and apply it through the natural rights tradition inherited" from the Founding Fathers (Cato Institute 2020). Scholars affiliated with the center conduct rigorous legal research ranging over such subjects as constitu-tional theory and history, the Supreme Court, property rights, and environmental law. The center publishes the annual *Cato*

Supreme Court Review and hosts an annual Constitution Day Conference featuring leading legal scholars analyzing the most important decisions of the Supreme Court's most recent term. Resident scholars at the center also file amicus curiae briefs with the Supreme Court aimed at presenting libertarian legal perspectives on cases being considered by the Court.

Center for American Progress (CAP)

Founded in 2003, the Center for American Progress (CAP) is a public policy think tank headquartered in Washington, D.C. As of mid-2021, its president is Patrick Gaspard, and its board of directors is chaired by former U.S. senator minority leader Tom Daschle. The center describes itself as an "independent nonpartisan policy institute that is dedicated to improving the lives of all Americans through bold, progressive ideas, strong leadership," and policy advocacy (Center for American Progress 2020). The organization adheres to liberal viewpoints on a host of economic and social issues. Its founder and first president and CEO was John Podesta, White House chief of staff to President Bill Clinton. In 2003, CAP established a youth-engagement organization, the Generation Progress. It works with its sister advocacy organization, the Center for American Progress Action Fund, to counterbalance the libertarian Heritage Foundation. From 2005 to 2019, CAP hosted a progressive news website, *ThinkProgress*. CAP is a 501(c)(3) nonprofit. *CAP Action* is a 501(c) (4), allowing it to devote funding to lobbying, and it plays an important role in Democratic Party politics. CAP is funded in the $50 million range from a mix of individual donors and foundations, as well as various corporate donors.

Center for Individual Rights (CIR)

Founded in 1989, CIR is a conservative public interest law organization that emerged from the Washington Legal Foundation. Its founders, Michael McDonald and Michael Greve, both launched the Washington Legal Foundation in response to the success of liberal public law organizations like the ACLU and Public Citizen. They created a conservative firm to defend individual liberties concerning civil and economic rights. Rather than concentrating on amicus briefs, CIR's attorneys have worked on precedent-setting cases. For example, in 2011, they won a U.S. Court of Appeals case for the Second Circuit in *US v. New York City Department of Education*. In 2014, they won similar cases in Michigan, upholding the Michigan amendment barring the use of racial preferences in state programs. In 2017, they won in *Doe v. Alger*, a U.S. District Court ruling against James Madison University on due process grounds; and won a settlement with the attorney general of California versus using a law prohibiting the flying of a confederate flag on public property. In 2018, the Supreme Court issued a landmark ruling in *Janus v. AFSCME*, ruling that compelling nonmembers to pay union dues violated their First Amendment rights (Center for Individual Rights.org 2020).

Center for Justice and Democracy (CJD)

The Center for Justice and Democracy (CJD) was established in 1998 by consumer advocates. It was originally named the Citizens for Corporate Accountability and Individual Rights. Its initial funding came from a grant from the Stern Family Fund. It has since released hundreds of studies, white papers, and fact sheets on civil justice issues. CJD members have testified before Congress, state legislatures, and organized numerous press events advocating for the rights of consumers and patients. In 2011, it began a partnership with the New York Law School, and changed its name to the Center for Justice and Democracy. It established a clinical course at the law school, Civil Justice and National Advocacy, allowing students to work on various projects, including researching and analyzing civil justice topics, preparing advocacy papers for CJD and the consumer rights community, and preparing policy papers for congressional presentation. It advocates for the civil justice system through its research, legal analysis, and grassroots mobilization. In 2007, it led a large-scale organizing effort around Supreme Court cases for victims of securities fraud (the Enron fraud victims). It launched a "boutique" project for states, creating a website called "Caps Harm" providing information about harm done by caps and tort reform. In 2011, the CJD added staff to organize medical malpractice victims and groups. The office built coalitions with progressive and public interest groups on a variety of interests to focus on civil justice issues (Center for Justice and Democracy.org 2020).

Center for the Study of Law and Religion (CSLR)

Founded in 1982, the Center for the Study of Law and Religion (CSLR) is an organization at Emory University that is dedicated to studying the religious dimensions of law and religion and how the two interact in institutions, norms, customs, and practices of the federal and state judicial systems. It exemplifies the "think-tank" organization that is founded on the assumption that religion gives law its spirit, and inspires adherence to ritual and justice; that law gives religion its structure and encourages the devotion of religious institutions to order and societal organization. The center encourages thousands of scholars and students each year through its courses, degree programs, fellowships, sponsored research projects, and public programming. It publishes a leading periodical, *Journal of Law and Religion*, as well as two book series: *Law and Christianity* and *Law and Judaism*.

The center offers six degree programs, pursues multiyear research projects, and has produced more than 300 books, as well as hosting national and international conferences and distinguished lecture series. Law professor John Witte Jr. is director of the center, which in 2000 received a $3.2 million grant from the Pew Charitable Trust and was officially designated a Pew "Center of Excellence." In recent years, it has been supported with some $20 million in grant funding, as well as the generous Emory University endowment of its general operations.

Economic Policy Institute (EPI)

The Economic Policy Institute (EPI) is a nonprofit, nonpartisan think tank that was established in 1985 with the mission to include the needs of low- and middle-income workers in economic policy discussions. It conducts research and analysis on the economic status of working-class Americans and proposes public policies that affect those workers. It also maintains the *State of Working America Data Library*, which provides data analysis of government statistics related to income inequality, wage trends, and other socioeconomic data. Policymakers, the media, national progressive advocacy organizations, and state research organizations often utilize EPI data and analysis, as do scholars and other researchers.

EPI research associate and Yale university professor Jacob Hacker developed the concept of the public insurance option to compete with private health insurers to make health insurance more affordable and assure robust competition across the industry. EPI also helped form the Economic Analysis and Research Network. It works on a wide range of economic policy issues, such as the federal budget, deficits and taxes, immigration, jobs, wages and living standards, the economy, labor policy, macroeconomic performance, public investment, regulation, and trade and globalization. EPI is a 501(c)(3) corporation that receives foundation grants, funding from labor unions, individuals, corporations, and other organizations.

Federalist Society for Law and Public Policy Studies

The Federalist Society for Law and Public Policy Studies (usually known as the Federalist Society-FS) was founded in 1982 as an organization of conservatives and libertarians aiming at reforming the legal order. It was initially funded with a grant of the Institute for Educational Affairs, and then by a grant of $5.5 million from the Olin Foundation. Other donors to its annual budget of more than $20 million in 2017 included the Scaife Foundation, the Koch Family Foundation, Google, Chevron, Robert Mellon Scaife Foundation, and the Mercer family. It is headquartered in Washington, D.C.

The Federalist Society advocates for what it describes as a textualist and originalist interpretation of the U.S. Constitution, and it asserts that its core values are preserving individual freedom and limiting government authority and power in accordance with the provisions of the Constitution. During Republican administrations, and especially since the Trump administration, FS has played a substantial role in the nomination and confirmation of conservative judges to all levels of the federal bench. It influenced most of President Trump's appointments to the federal bench throughout his term in office. For example, of the fifty-one judges Trump appointed to U.S. appellate courts, forty-three belonged to the Federalist Society.

The Federalist Society is a membership organization that has three divisions: Student, Lawyer, and Faculty. Its Student Division has more than 10,000 law students at all 204 of the ABA-accredited law schools, as well as ten chapters based at nonaccredited law schools. It provides speakers and assists student chapters in organizing lectures, debates, and educational activities. Its Lawyer Division has more than 65,000 members and has active chapters in ninety cities. It hosts an annual National Lawyers Convention. It has a speakers' bureau for organizing lectures and debates, and fifteen legal practice groups. It established its Faculty Division in 1999, and fosters the growth and development of rigorous traditional legal scholarship. As of 2021, six Supreme Court justices (all conservative) are or were members of the Society: Brett Kavanaugh, Neil Gorsuch, Clarence Thomas, John Roberts, Samuel Alito, and Amy Coney Barrett. The society also publishes the *Harvard Journal of Law and Public Policy*.

Federal Judicial Center (FJC)

The Federal Judicial Center (FJC) is a research and education agency within the judicial branch of the U.S. government. It was established in 1967 to support the swift and accurate carriage of justice while safeguarding judicial independence. It has no policymaking or enforcement authority. Its mission is to provide accurate, objective information, and education that encourages thorough and candid analysis of policies, best practices and procedures for the federal judiciary. The chief justice of the U.S. Supreme Court serves as chair of the FJC Board, which includes the director of the Administrative Office of the U.S. Courts, and seven judges elected to serve on its board by the Judicial Conference. The board appoints the center's director (currently John Cooke) and deputy director (currently Clara Altman), and the director appoints the center's staff. The center's Research Division "examines and evaluates current and alternative federal court practices and policies" (Federal Judicial Center.org 2020). Its research assists the Judicial Conference and contributes to its educational mission. Its Education Division conducts education and training for judges and court staff. Its Judicial History Office contributes to the study and preservation of the judicial past. Its International Judicial Relations Office provides information to judicial and legal officials from foreign countries and other court systems. The Technology Office and the Editorial and Information Services Office—two units of the Director's Office—support the center's missions through technology. It is funded by annual appropriations from Congress, and it is authorized to accept gifts to support its programs (Federal Judicial Center.gov 2020).

Institute for Justice (IJ)

The Institute for Justice (IJ) is a libertarian organization that litigates cases to limit the size and scope of governmental power. IJ asserts that it does so to keep power in the hands of the people so that they can achieve their own version of the American dream and participate as conscientious members of society. Founded in 1991, it is a 501(c)(3) organization that combines litigation, media relations, strategic research, and grassroots advocacy to advance its libertarian goals. IJ has litigated 290 cases, including eight before the U.S. Supreme Court, losing only one case (*Kelo v. New London*, 545 U.S. 469, 2014). Some notable wins for the institute, decided in various courts since 1997, include the following: *Kelo Eminent Domain* (1997); *Zelman v. Simmons-Harris* (2002); *Granholm v. Heald* (2005); *Arizona Campaign Finance* (2011); *Arizona Individual Tax Credit Scholarships* (2011); *Tennessee Wine and Spirits Retailers Association v. Thomas* (2019); *Timbs v. Indiana* (2019); *Brownback v. King* (2020); and *Espinoza v. Montana Department of Revenue* (2020).

IJ is headquartered in Arlington, Virginia, but has five satellite offices located in Florida, Minnesota, Texas, Arizona, and Washington state. It has a Clinic on Entrepreneurship located at the University of Chicago Law School.

Law and Economic Center (LEC)

Founded in 1974, the Law and Economics Center (LEC) at the Antonin Scalia Law School at George Mason University serves as a hub for economic and legal research, educating current and future policymakers by ensuring that they know how to analyze and address current issues around the globe. The Law and Economics Center provides a classroom forum where federal and state judges, state attorneys general, law professors, and other legal professionals can be trained in basic economics, accounting, statistics, regulatory analysis, and related disciplines. It reaches an audience of esteemed policymakers, practitioners, and scholars. To date, more than 5,000 federal judges and state court judges, from all fifty states and the District of Columbia, including three current U.S. Supreme Court justices, have participated in one or more of LEC's education programs. LEC has hosted 1,000 state attorneys general and senior AG staff lawyers, and thousands of other legal professionals. It also sponsors seminars and conferences that focus on economics, finance, accounting, statistics, and the scientific method. Among its programs are the following: the Henry G. Manne Program for Law and Economic Studies; the Mason Attorneys General Education Program; the Congressional Civil Justice Academy; the Program of Economics and Privacy; and the Economics for Lawyers Online Program. Its online courses are taught by the Scalia Law Faculty for credit at over fifty ABA-accredited law schools.

Legal Information Institute (LII)

The Legal Information Institute (LII) is an independently funded project of the Cornell Law School. Founded in 1992 by Peter Martin and Tom Bruce, it employs technology to gather, process, and publish legal information that is accurate and objective. It founders believed that everyone should be able to access, read, and understand the laws under which they are governed. Today it electronically publishes U.S. Supreme Court opinions (all since 1992, and some historically important decisions ruled on pre-1992), the Uniform Commercial Code, the U.S. Code of Federal Regulations, and some treaties and United Nations materials. It serves more than 40 million unique visitors annually. LII publishes the *Wex Legal Dictionary/ Encyclopedia*, a collaborative legal reference guide written by experts in the field. Its other website is the *Oyez Project*, which is focused on Supreme Court decisions (Hall and Patrick 2006; Lawrence and Miller 2000; Trinkle and Merriman 2001).

National Constitution Center

In 1988, President Ronald Reagan signed the Constitution Heritage Act. This legislation established a private, nonpartisan, nonprofit organization called the National Constitutional Center to serve as the nation's leading platform for constitutional education and debate. Construction of the center began in 2000 in Philadelphia, and it opened its doors on July 4, 2003. Since 2006, the center has administered the Liberty Medal, on an annual basis, to individuals actively working toward securing liberty around the globe. Recent recipients include President George W. and Laura Bush for their support of veterans, Representative John Lewis for his civil rights work, and Malala Yousafzai for her work on behalf of young women. In 2006, the center also launched its Constitution High School, a history- and civics-themed magnet school in Philadelphia. In 2008, the center hosted a Democratic presidential primary debate and a town-hall meeting with Senator John McCain. It was the site for a pivotal speech on race by then-Senator Barack Obama. In 2010, the center launched two online platforms: a blog called *Constitution Daily* and *Constitution Hall Pass*, a free video lesson and live chat series exploring America's civic holidays and history that reached millions of students every year. In 2011, it was accredited by the American Association of Museums. In 2013, to honor the one-hundred-year agreement between the Commonwealth of Pennsylvania and the New York Public Library, the center began displaying one of twelve surviving copies of the Bill of Rights and its "We the People" institution exhibiting the historic document to the general public. In 2015, the center, in partnership with the American Constitution Society and the Federalist Society, under a grant from the John Templeton Foundation, launched the "Interactive Constitution," a free, online tool exploring the meaning of each of the amendments to the Constitution, and bringing together scholars from across the legal and political spectrum to explore the meaning of each provision of the Constitution, with informed, up-to-date discussions and debates about the Constitution. The organization also renovated the Sidney Kimmel Theater, home to *Freedom Rising*, Philadelphia's longest running theatrical show.

Olin Foundation

The Olin Foundation was established in 1953 by industrialist John M. Olin (1899–1982), founder of a chemical and munitions manufacturing company. It closed down in 2005 after it had disbursed more than $370 million in funding. It funded a number of conservative think tanks and media outlets, as well as law programs at some of the nation's most prestigious university law schools. When John Olin founded it, he specified that it spend all of its assets within a generation of his death. During its span of fifty-two years, the Olin Foundation had a significant impact on the American judiciary. Law schools at the University of Chicago, Harvard, Stanford, Virginia, and Yale all have law and economic programs named in Olin's honor. The foundation also provided funding to a number of conservative, law-related organizations including the Federalist Society, the Center for Individual Rights, the Heritage Foundation, the Hoover Institution, the Manhattan Institute, the National Association of Scholars, the New Criterion, the Philanthropy Roundtable, and the Collegiate Network (a consortium of conservative college newspapers). It was charged with promoting projects intended to strengthen the economic, political, and cultural institutions on which the American heritage of constitutional government and private enterprise is based. Its executive director in its early years was conservative activist Michael Joyce, and James Pierson served as the foundation's executive director for twenty of its fifty-two years. William Simon, U.S. secretary of the treasury under President Richard Nixon, was its president from 1977 until his death in 2000. It dispensed hundreds of millions of dollars to scholars, think tanks, publications, and other organizations that shaped and aided the growth of the modern conservative movement, and its grants promoted the intellectual architects of the right-wing movement for decades (Miller 2005; Mayer 2016).

Pew Research Center

The Pew Research Center was founded in 2001 as a nonpartisan research organization supported by the Pew Charitable Trust and is a leading think tank and trusted source for nonpartisan research on the American judiciary, particularly concerning racial and ethnic disparities in the courts and with respect to incarceration of minorities. Its research is noted for its timeliness, relevance, and scientific rigor. It is a classic example of the think tank, taking no advocacy positions for or against specific public policy proposals. Located in Washington, D.C., its research data are regularly reported on by the mass media, which thereby influences public opinion, notably regarding judicial reform and reforms in the criminal justice system. In recent reports (July and September 2020), for example, the Pew Research Center reported data on the growth in public support for giving civilians the right to sue police over officer misconduct, and on the widening partisan divide over freedom to peacefully protest (Pew Research Center 2020).

Southern Poverty Law Center (SPLC)

The Southern Poverty Law Center (SPLC) was founded in 1971 by two civil rights lawyers, Morris Dees and Joseph Levin Jr., to advance landmark civil rights litigation on behalf of the powerless, the exploited, and the forgotten. Its lawsuits over the years attacked institutional racism and the remnants of Jim Crow segregation. The lawsuits crippled some white supremacist groups and protected the civil rights of children, women, the disabled, immigrants and migrant workers, the LGBTQ community, prisoners, and others who faced discrimination, legal abuse, or exploitation. Since the 1980s, the SPLC has maintained an Intelligence Project that tracks and exposes the activities of hate groups and domestic terrorists. In the 1990s, it launched its Teaching Tolerance program, which produces and distributes free materials aimed at reducing prejudice and promoting equality in schools, including documentary films, books, lesson plans, and educational materials. It built and maintains the Civil Rights Memorial and its interpretive center, the Civil Rights Memorial Center, in Montgomery, Alabama. SPLC is based in Montgomery, with offices in Atlanta, Miami, New Orleans, and Jackson, Mississippi.

At its inception, SPLC took pro bono cases others were unwilling to pursue, and their litigation had far-reaching effects. Early lawsuits that SPLC won resulted in the desegregation of recreational facilities, the reapportionment of the Alabama legislature, the integration of the Alabama state troopers, and reforms in the state prison system. In 1971, civil rights activist Julian Bond was named the SPLC's first president. SPLC began monitoring white supremacist groups in the 1980s and publishes an online Hate Crimes and Hate Groups map site (Southern Poverty Law Center.org 2020).

The Sentencing Project

The Sentencing Project is a Washington, D.C.-based "research and advocacy center working to reduce the use of incarceration in the United States and to address racial disparities in the criminal justice system" (The Sentencing Project.org. 2021). Founded in 1986, it produces groundbreaking research to promote reforms in sentencing policy and to advocate for alternatives to incarceration. For example, the group focuses considerable resources on the issue of disenfranchisement of felons after they have served their time—over 6 million Americans who can't vote because of past felony convictions—as well as helping thousands of women and children who have lost food stamps and cash assistance as a result of convictions for drug offenses.

The Sentencing Project was an offshoot of a pilot program started by lawyer Malcolm Young in the 1980s. In 1981, Young became director of the National Legal Aid and Defender Association, where he advocated for fair sentencing for criminal defendants. In 1986, the association was incorporated as the Sentencing Project, an independent organization committed to research and public education work centering on current criminal justice policy. It is part of a national coalition supporting the bipartisan Sentencing Reform and Corrections Act, and has lobbied for the bill before the Senate Judiciary

Committee. It helped secure passage of the Fair Sentencing Act (2016), which reduced the disparities in sentencing for convictions of possessing or trafficking in crack cocaine compared to powder cocaine. It has been a prominent participant in debates about racial and ethnic disparities in arrests, sentencing, and incarceration within America's legal system, and has monitored and reported on the denial of voting rights to persons with prior felony convictions. Since 2012, it has provided a state-by-state breakout on disenfranchisement titled "Six Million Lost Voters." It showed that Florida led the nation with 1.5 million persons disenfranchised for felony convictions (Chesney-Lind and Mauer 2003; Mauer and Jones 2013).

U.S. Department of Justice (DOJ)

The DOJ was established in 1870 by President Ulysses S. Grant. It is home to several divisions and bureaus that regularly involve the DOJ in federal judiciary matters. The department assumed control of federal prisons in 1884 (from the Department of the Interior) and established its Civil Rights Division in 1957. In 1909, DOJ established a Public Lands Division that subsequently became its Environment and Natural Resources Division. This division's focus on environmental policies has spilled over into First Amendment issues on a number of occasions, such as disputes over policies regarding claimed sacred sites of Native American Indian religious groups and policies concerning oil pipelines and timber harvesting on lands claimed by Indian tribes. DOJ also established a National Security Division in 2007.

DOJ houses several law enforcement agencies, including the U.S. Marshals Service (USMS); the Federal Bureau of Investigation (FBI); the Federal Bureau of Prisons; (BOP); the Bureau of Alcohol, Tobacco, Firearms and Explosives (ATF); the Drug Enforcement Agency (DEA); the Office of Inspector General; the Executive Office of Immigration Review; the Office of Immigration Litigation; and the Office of Tribal Justice, all of which on occasion embroil it in federal judicial cases. The DOJ is led by the attorney general (AG) of the United States, who is the leading law enforcement officer of the country. The DOJ's Office of Solicitor General represents the federal government in arguing all cases before the U.S. Supreme Court in which the federal government is involved as a litigant or has an interest in the decision of the Court.

U.S. Senate Judiciary Committee

Established in 1816, the Senate Judiciary Committee is among the oldest standing committees of the Senate. It is widely considered one of the most important and influential committees in Congress. Its broad jurisdiction gives it a primary role as a forum for the public discussion of a wide range of social and constitutional issues. It is responsible for oversight of key activities of the executive branch, especially the Department of Justice, and is also responsible for the initial stages of the confirmation process of all judicial nominations for the entire federal judiciary.

After the Judiciary Act of 1789 established the three-tiered hierarchy of the federal judicial system and the Office of the Attorney General, temporary committees were used in the House and the Senate as the small size of the Congress made permanent committees unnecessary (Hagedorn and LeMay 2019). In 1816, the Senate established its original standing committees, of which the Committee on the Judiciary was one. The House Judiciary Committee was established as a standing committee in 1819. Leadership of and membership on the committee ebbs and flows between the nation's two main political parties depending on whether Democrats or Republicans control the wider U.S. Senate.

In addition to its consideration of judicial appointments, the committee considers the presidential nominations for all appointive positions at the Department of Justice and certain positions in the Department of Homeland Security. It is in charge of holding hearings and investigating all federal judicial nominations.

U.S. Supreme Court (SCOTUS)

As indicated by a plethora of landmark decisions discussed herein, SCOTUS is *the* federal organizational entity that has had the most profound and continuous impact on the judicial systems of the United States at all three levels of government. With respect to the federal judicial system, SCOTUS oversees the federal court system of ninety-four district courts in twelve regional circuits, and thirteen courts of appeals. The federal district courts are the workhorses of the federal judicial system in that almost every civil or criminal case heard in the federal courts starts at the district court level. These courts review petitions, hear motions, hold trials, and issue injunctions (U.S. Courts.gov 2020a).

SCOTUS was created in accordance with the Judiciary Act of September 24, 1789 (1 Stat. 73), which states that its jurisdiction extends to "all cases in law and equity arising under the Constitution, the laws passed by Congress, and treaties made under congressional authority, and all cases affecting ambassadors, other cabinet ministers, all maritime cases, and cases between citizens of two or more states, and between a state or citizen thereof and foreign states."

The Supreme Court today consists of the chief justice and eight associate justices. Appointments of the chief justice and of associate justices are made by the president of the United States with the advice and consent of the U.S. Senate. As of 2021, SCOTUS consists of Chief Justice John Roberts and Associate Justices Clarence Thomas, Stephen Breyer, Samuel Alito Jr., Sonia Sotomayor, Elena Kagan, Neil Gorsuch, Brett Kavanaugh, and Amy Coney Barrett.

SCOTUS essentially gave itself the power of judicial review of the constitutionality of acts of Congress, the president, executive branch departments and agencies, and of state government laws and actions in the decision of *Marbury v. Madison* (5 U.S.C. 137, 1803) (see Document 5.4). The Court, in the majority opinion written by Chief Justice John Marshall, affirmed for the first time the principle that courts may declare an act of Congress void if it is found by the Court to be inconsistent with or in violation of the U.S. Constitution. Through its judicial doctrine of incorporation, the Supreme Court has gradually applied many Bill of Rights protections to the states, thereby also ruling on the constitutionality of state and local laws (History.com 2020a).

Vera Institute of Justice (VIJ)

In 1961, the Vera Institute was founded by philanthropist Louis Schweitzer (the organization was named after his mother) and magazine editor Herb Sturz. They were concerned about the injustice of the bail system as it was then conducted in New York City because it essentially locked up people simply for being poor. They conducted an experiment—the Manhattan Bail Project—that demonstrated that New Yorkers with strong ties to their communities could be released from custody without bail or by posting a small, token bail amount and they would still show up for trial. The Manhattan Bail Project spurred dozens of similar projects in other cities and counties across the nation. It also began a legislative movement to reform the federal bail system.

The Vera Institute of Justice is a 501(c)(3) nonprofit, nonpartisan organization that today uses new tools, such as mining big data, to tackle such pressing issues as mass incarceration; racial disparities in arrests, convictions, and sentencing; the general public's mistrust of law enforcement officials; and the often marginalized victims of crimes and violence. The Vera Institute works in partnership with local, state, and national government officials to study problems, pilot solutions, engage with diverse communities, and harness the compelling power of evidence to drive effective policy and practice. It has ongoing projects in more than forty states and is an example of how a think-tank organization can be an advocate for and an instrument of change.

People
Samuel Chase (1741–1811)

Samuel Chase was a signer of the Declaration of Independence and served as associate justice of the Supreme Court from 1796 until his death by a heart attack in 1811. He also holds the distinction of being the only Supreme Court justice ever to be impeached. A Federalist, Chase was impeached for letting his partisan political leanings affect his court decisions. Chase was acquitted in the Senate on all counts, however, and since then, all impeachments of federal judges at all levels (district, appellate) have been on grounds of legal or ethical misconduct, not ideology or partisan-relevant judicial philosophy.

Chase was born in Maryland, the only child of an Episcopal clergyman. He was educated at home until he moved, at age eighteen, to Annapolis, Maryland, where he studied law under attorney John Hall. He was admitted to the bar and practiced law there. In 1764, he was elected to the colony's General Assembly, where he was noted for his fierce opposition to the Stamp Act of 1765. He served in the assembly for twenty years, but was also a delegate from Maryland to the Continental Congress, where he signed the Declaration of Independence in 1776. He cofounded the Anne Arundel County's chapter of the famous revolutionary group, the Sons of Liberty. He moved to Baltimore in 1786 and was appointed chief justice of the District Criminal Court in Baltimore two years later. In 1791, he rose to chief justice of the Maryland General Court. In 1796, President George Washington appointed Samuel Chase associate justice of the U.S. Supreme Court.

His most notable majority opinion decision was in *Calder v. Bull* (3 U.S. 386, 1798). The decision defined four important points of constitutional law, and in his opinion, Chase held that natural law guaranteed rights and liberties not expressly written in the due process clause. When Thomas Jefferson was elected president in 1800, he opposed what he viewed as an illegitimate seizure of power by the judiciary through its use of the claim of exclusive judicial review. Jefferson tried to remove some Federalist judges from the bench, and with his allies in Congress, he led the repeal of the Judiciary Act of 1801, abolishing the lower courts and thereby terminating Federalist judges despite their lifetime appointments. Chase vigorously denounced this, leading to his impeachment by the House of Representatives, which was then dominated by the Jeffersonian Democrat-Republican Party. The impeachment charges against Chase were seen as politically motivated, and he was acquitted in the U.S. Senate. His impeachment and acquittal was a victory for the independence of the judiciary, and set the precedent that a judge should not be removed for stating political views from the bench. His case also demonstrated that judges should remain nonpartisan by demonstrating the dangers of speaking about his political philosophy directly from the bench. Chase remained on the Supreme Court until his death from a heart attack in 1811 (Oyez.org 2020, "Samuel Chase").

William O. Douglas (1898–1980)

President Franklin D. Roosevelt appointed William Douglas as associate justice of the U.S. Supreme Court in 1939. He served on the Court for the next thirty-six years, setting the record for the longest continuous service on the Supreme Court. He was just forty years old when appointed, the youngest justice to be confirmed to the Court. The Senate confirmation vote was 62 to 4.

William Douglas rose from relative poverty. He worked his way through schools, including Whitman College in Yakima, Washington, where he distinguished himself with excellent grades, as an outstanding debater on the debate team, as student congress president, and as president of his fraternity. He also wrote for the campus literary magazine (and went on to be a lifelong, prolific writer, authoring thirty books) and tutored students in economics. He graduated with a BA degree in economics.

Douglas studied law at Columbia Law School, again working his way through law school by tutoring high school seniors intending to attend an Ivy League school. He graduated in 1925 with his law degree and secured work at a prestigious Wall Street law firm, but also taught at Columbia Law and later at Yale Law School. He left Yale Law to work in the administration of Franklin D. Roosevelt. He championed Roosevelt's New Deal policies and served as chairman of the Securities and Exchange Commission from 1937 to 1939. He then was confirmed to a seat on the Supreme Court, where he became known for his fearsome work ethic. He dissented in about 40 percent of the cases he heard during his career on the Supreme Court. He argued for a literalist interpretation of the First Amendment, arguing that Congress could pass no law restricting its fundamental freedoms. He voted with the majority in 1944, upholding the constitutionality of the Japanese internment program in *Korematsu v. United States.* He wrote the majority opinion in *Griswold v. Connecticut* (1965) asserting the right to privacy that laid the legal groundwork for *Roe v. Wade* (1973). He faced impeachment for his granting of a temporary stay of execution of the Rosenbergs in 1953 (Julius and Ethel Rosenberg were an American married couple convicted of spying for the Soviet Union; they were executed in 1953 despite Douglas's temporary stay of the sentence). Douglas was notably strongly opposed to the Vietnam War. He issued a judicial order in 1974 to stop the U.S. government's bombing of Cambodia, and he compiled a strong anti-segregation record.

A lifelong environmentalist, he wrote eight travel books among his thirty published books. In 1948, Douglas was briefly considered as the vice-presidential running mate for President Harry Truman. He wrote an autobiography, *Of Men and Mountains* (1950), and two memoirs: *Go East Young*

Man: The Early Years, 1939–1975 (1974), and *The Court Years: 1939–1975* (1980). Douglas suffered a stroke in 1974, leaving him partially paralyzed. He retired from the Court in 1975 and died in 1980 (Oyez.org 2020, "William O. Douglas"; Murphy 2003).

William M. Evarts (1818–1901)

William Evarts was a distinguished U.S. senator who served the state of New York from 1885 to 1891. He was also a states-man, serving as the twenty-seventh secretary of state from 1877 to 1881 in the cabinet of President Rutherford B. Hayes; and as the twenty-ninth U.S. attorney general (1868–1869) in the cabinet of President Andrew Johnson. He was most famous, however, as a litigator, and argued two of the most important issues in political jurisprudence during his time: the 1868 impeachment of President Johnson, and the contest before the electoral commission to settle the presidential election of 1876. He was also the author (chief sponsor) of the Judiciary Act of 1891, which established the United States Courts of Appeals.

Evarts attended Yale College, where he was a member of the school's famous Skull and Bones secret society, and was a cofounder of the *Yale Literary Magazine* in 1836. He graduated in 1837, then moved to Vermont, where he studied law in the office of Horace Everett and taught school to save money to attend Harvard Law School. He was admitted to the New York bar in 1841 after graduating from Harvard. He practiced law in New York, where he became a member of the Whig Party. When the Whigs went into decline, he joined the emerging Republican Party. Evarts was a delegate to the 1860 Republican National Convention, and served on New York's Union Defense Committee during the Civil War.

Evarts served as chief counsel to President Andrew Johnson during his 1868 impeachment trial pushed by the Reconstructionist U.S. senators who opposed President Johnson's plans for reinstating the Confederate States into the Union. Having won

Johnson's acquittal in the U.S. Senate, Evarts went on to serve as U.S. attorney general under Johnson from 1868 to 1869. In 1872, he was counsel for the United States before the tribunal of arbitration over the ownership claims of the *Alabama* (a Confederate ship during the Civil War) held in Geneva, Switzerland. He was a founding member of the New York City Bar Association and its first president, serving in that capacity from 1870 to 1879. He was counsel to President-elect Rutherford B. Hayes in negotiations that resolved the disputed presidential election of 1876. The compromise, in which Hayes agreed that as president he would remove Union troops from the South, essentially brought the Reconstruction era to a close. Evarts went on to serve as Hayes's secretary of state. He ran for the U.S. Senate seat from New York, serving just one term (1885–1891), during which time he chaired the Senate Committee on the Library, and sponsored the Evarts Act. He led the fundraising campaign for the pedestal for the Statue of Liberty. Evarts retired in 1891 due to ill health. He died in New York City in 1901 (History .state.gov 2021).

Clarence Earl Gideon (1910–1972)

Clarence Earl Gideon was a poor and often homeless man who sometimes survived through thievery. He also had a profound impact on U.S. criminal law procedure due to a case— *Gideon v. Wainwright* (372 U.S. 335, 1963)—in which he became involved. A man with little formal education, Gideon spent his adult life in and out of prisons for various nonviolent crimes (robbery, burglary, larceny, and theft). In 1961, Gideon was charged with breaking and entering with the intent to commit a misdemeanor, which under Florida law is a felony. He was tried without an attorney. Gideon had asked the court to appoint an attorney, but his request was denied because Florida law only permitted appointment of counsel for poor defendants charged with capital offenses. He represented himself but lost and was sentenced to five years imprisonment.

He challenged his conviction on the grounds that the judge's refusal to appoint counsel violated his constitutional rights to a fair trial. The Florida Supreme Court denied his petition, and he was sent to prison to begin his sentence.

While in prison, however, Gideon studied the American legal system and concluded the Florida trial judge had denied him his constitutional right to counsel under the Sixth Amendment and applicable to Florida through the due process clause of the Fourteenth Amendment. In January 1962, Gideon appealed his conviction to the U.S. Supreme Court in a handwritten, five-page petition. The Court agreed to hear his argument, which held that the right to counsel guaranteed under the Sixth Amendment applied to defendants in state court via the due process clause of the Fourteenth Amendment. On March 18, 1963, in a unanimous decision in which Justice Hugo Black wrote the majority opinion, the U.S. Supreme Court held that the Sixth Amendment's guarantee of the right to counsel is a fundamental right essential for a fair trial and applies to the states, overturning a prior Supreme Court decision in *Betts v. Brady* (316 U.S. 455, 1942). The decision in *Gideon* resulted in overturning the convictions of about 2,000 people in Florida.

Gideon himself was not freed. The U.S. Supreme Court decision, however, had remanded his case back to a Florida trial court. Gideon received another trial, this time with a court-appointed counsel representing him, and was acquitted. The attorney who represented him in the retrial was Abe Fortas, who later served on the U.S. Supreme Court from 1965 to 1969. Gideon died of cancer in Florida in 1972 at age sixty-one. His story was later told in the film *Gideon's Trumpet* (1980), starring Henry Fonda (U.S. Courts.gov 2020b).

Ruth Bader Ginsburg (1933–2020)

Ruth Bader Ginsburg (known widely and affectionately simply by her RBG initials) was appointed an associate justice to the U.S. Supreme Court in August 1993 by President William

Clinton. She filled the seat vacated by Justice Byron White's retirement. Ginsburg became a central pillar of the Supreme Court's liberal ideological bloc, regularly joined by Justices Stephen Breyer, Sonia Sotomayor, and Elena Kagan. After her appointment, Justice Ginsburg cast votes on dozens of important Supreme Court decisions on cases related to civil rights and liberties. Justice Ginsburg wrote the majority opinion in some, joined with the majority decision on some others, or voted with the liberal justices in dissenting opinions on many other cases in which they were outvoted by the Court's conservative justices (Carmon 2015; Kanefield 2016; Wainwright 2019). Throughout Justice Ginsburg's long and respected career, she was notably vocal about gender discrimination.

Justice Ginsburg earned her BS from Cornell University, attended Harvard Law, and received her LLB from Columbia Law School, where she graduated first in her class. She clerked for Edmund Palmieri, a judge of the U.S. District Court for the Southern District of New York, 1959–1961. From 1961 to 1963, Ginsburg was a research associate of the Columbia Law School Project on International Procedure. During that time Ginsburg lived in Sweden, where she published a book on Swedish civil procedure. In 1963, she became a professor at Rutgers University Law School. In 1972, she began teaching at Columbia Law, the first female to earn tenure there. She directed the Women's Rights Project for the ACLU, successfully arguing six landmark cases before the Supreme Court. In 1977–78, Ginsburg was a fellow at the Center for Advanced Study in the Behavioral Sciences at Stanford University. Two years later, President Jimmy Carter appointed her to the U.S. Court of Appeals for the District of Columbia, a court that has often been a stepping-stone to appointment to the U.S. Supreme Court. She served on the court of appeals until President Clinton appointed her to the U.S. Supreme Court in 1993.

Ginsburg was born Ruth Bader in Brooklyn, New York. She married Martin Ginsburg in 1954. They had a son and daughter. Martin battled cancer off and on from 1956 until he passed away in 2010. Although she disagreed with fellow Supreme Court Justice Antonin Scalia on most of the cases they heard, Ginsburg and Scalia were close friends in their personal lives, sharing a love for the opera. They voted together, however, on four religious freedom cases: *Church of the Lukumi Babalu v. City of Hialeah* (1993), *Elk Grove v. Newdow* (2004), *Gonzales v. U.D.V.* (2006), and *Hosanna-Tabor v. E.E.O.C.* (2012).

Ginsburg wrote the majority opinions in *Chandler v. Miller* (1997), an 8-1 Fourth Amendment ruling; and in *Vermont v. Brillon*, a 7-2 ruling regarding the Sixth Amendment's right to a speedy trial. Justice Ginsburg dissented in two Second Amendment cases that were decided 5-4. She participated in several 9-0 rulings on civil rights matters; for example: on the Fourth Amendment challenge of a stop and frisk case (*Florida v. J.L.*, 2000); in *Berghuis v. Smith* (2010) and *Thaler v. Haynes* (2010). Justice Ginsburg voted with the majority in four landmark capital punishment cases: *Harris v. Alabama* (1995, 8-1), *Atkins v. Virginia* (2000, 6-3), *Roper v. Simmons* (2005, 5-4), and *Hurst v. Florida* (8-1) (LeMay 2018, 182–184). Ginsberg became a pop culture icon of sorts later in her career. Her life was the subject of an Academy Award-nominated 2018 documentary called *RBG*, as well as a dramatic rendering of her early career and first appearance before the Supreme Court in the feature film *On the Basis of Sex*. She also wrote an autobiography, *My Own Words,* that was published in 2018.

Ginsburg was a champion of expanding LGBTQ rights. She voted with the majority in *Romer v. Evans* (1996), which struck down a Colorado law barring local governments from recognizing gay men and lesbians as protected classes. She also voted with the majority in *Lawrence v. Texas* (2003), which decriminalized same-sex sexual activity; *United States v. Windsor* (2013), which struck down the Defense of Marriage Act; *Obergefell v. Hodges* (2015), which made same-sex marriage legal across the United States; and *Bostock v. Clayton County,*

Georgia (2020), in which the Court ruled that Title VII of the Civil Rights Act of 1964 prohibited workplace discrimination based on sexual orientation and gender identity.

Justice Ginsburg had initially planned to retire in 2016, assuming Secretary Hillary Clinton had won the presidency. She had wanted the nation's first woman president to appoint her successor. When President Trump beat Clinton in the electoral college that year, Ginsburg stayed on the Court, hoping to last beyond Donald Trump's first term. However, Ruth Bader Ginsburg died of pancreatic cancer on September 18, 2020. Her vacant seat on the Court was filled during Trump's last months in office by conservative jurist Amy Coney Barrett (Ginsburg 2018).

Charles Evans Hughes (1862–1948)

Charles Evans Hughes was one of the most influential Supreme Court justices in the history of American jurisprudence. He served as an associate justice from 1910 to 1916 and as the Court's eleventh chief justice from 1930 to 1941. He was also a prominent Republican Party politician and the thirty-sixth governor of New York (1906–1910). He was U.S. secretary of state under Presidents Warren G. Harding and Calvin Coolidge (1920–1925).

Hughes was born in New York, attended Madison College (now Colgate University), and graduated from Brown University. He earned his law degree from Columbia Law School by age twenty-two, and practiced law in New York for twenty years, during which time he also taught at Cornell Law School. He had a national reputation for investigating illegal rate-making and fraud in the insurance industry. The support of Theodore Roosevelt helped him win the New York governorship in 1906. President Howard Taft appointed him associate justice to the Supreme Court in 1910. He resigned from the Court to seek the Republican presidential nomination in 1916, only to go on to lose to Democrat Woodrow Wilson in the presidential election.

Hughes authored twice as many constitutional majority opinions as any other member of the Supreme Court. While associate justice, he wrote or was involved in several landmark cases. *Baltimore and Ohio Railroad v. Interstate Commerce Commission* (1911) held that the federal government could regulate interstate commerce. In *McCabe v. Atchison, Topeka, and Santa Fe Railroad Company* (1914), the Court ruled for equal treatment of African Americans employed by the railroad. In *Guinn v. United States* (1915), the Court outlawed the use of the grandfather clause by state governments in local and state elections.

As chief justice, he wrote the opinion on *Near v. Minnesota* (1931) held that the free press clause of the Bill of Rights incorporated state law. In *O'Gorman and Young Inc. v. Hartford Fire Insurance Company* (1931), the Court held that states could regulate the sale of fire insurance. Other cases in the 1930s were important cases that involved the Court's clashing with FDR's New Deal programs: *Railroad Retirement Board v. Alton Railroad Company* (1935), *United States v. Butler* (1936), *Morehead v. New York ex rel Tipaldo* (1936), *United States v. Curtiss-Wright Export Corporation* (1936); *West Coast Hotel Company v. Parrish* (1937), and *National Labor Relations Board v. Jones and Laughlin Steel Corporation* (1937). President Roosevelt's dissatisfaction and conflict with the Supreme Court over its hostility to his New Deal programs and agencies led him to push his "court-packing plan" in 1937. This scheme to add justices who would be more supportive of his administration's Depression-fighting policies failed in the U.S. Senate. But after the court-packing episode, Chief Justice Hughes and the Court issued rulings welcomed by Roosevelt and his fellow liberals in several landmark cases: *Missouri ex rel. Gaines v. Canada* (1938); *Chambers v. Florida* (1940), and *Minersville School District v. Gobitis* (1940). Justice Hughes retired from the Court in 1941 and retired to New York City. He died in 1948 at the age of eighty-six (Gould 2016).

Edward "Ted" Kennedy (1932–2009)

Known as the "Lion of the Senate," Edward Moore "Ted" Kennedy was an icon of the progressive wing of congressional Democrats in the second half of the twentieth century. Ted Kennedy was the youngest brother of John F. Kennedy, America's thirty-fifth president, and Robert F. Kennedy, who served as both U.S. attorney general and a New York senator. Ted Kennedy was elected to the U.S. Senate in 1962, at age thirty, and served until his death in 2009. He was the grandson of John "Honey Fitz" Fitzgerald, mayor of Boston. His father was millionaire businessman Joseph Kennedy, who held many important positions both in and out of government. Ted Kennedy attended Harvard University, the International Law School at the Hague, and then Virginia Law School. He received his JD in 1959. In 1960, he campaigned on behalf of his older brother John in the latter's successful bid for the presidency.

In 1962, Ted Kennedy was elected to fill his brother's former Senate seat in Massachusetts. After the assassinations of John in 1963 and Robert in 1968, Ted became the patriarch of the Kennedy clan. He became majority whip in the Senate in 1969, but later that same year he was behind the wheel in an automobile accident that killed his twenty-eight-year-old female passenger. Rumors and speculation about the circumstances of that accident dogged Kennedy for the rest of his life, even as his stature in the Senate continued to grow.

In 1980, Kennedy challenged incumbent President Jimmy Carter for the Democratic presidential nomination but ultimately went down to defeat. He returned to the Senate, where he continued to champion a variety of liberal causes related to immigration reform, criminal code reform, fair housing, public education, health care, AIDs research, and various programs for aid to the poor. His most significant impact on the judicial system came from his service on the Senate Judiciary Committee, from which he advocated liberal positions on abortion, capital punishment, and busing. His vote was crucial on judicial nominations by Democratic presidents. He served as chairman of the Judiciary Committee from 1979 to 1981, and was its ranking member as well. Ted Kennedy maintained notable bipartisan friendships with several conservative Republican senators, including Nancy Kassebaum, John McCain, and Orrin Hatch. He also was a critical vote and progressive voice in support of President George W. Bush's No Child Left behind Act (2001). Kennedy suffered a seizure in 2008, and was diagnosed with a brain tumor, which was surgically removed. He suffered another seizure the following year and passed away in August 2009 at the Kennedy compound at Hyannis Port, Massachusetts (Hagedorn and LeMay 2019; Littlefield 2016).

Patrick Leahy (1940–)

When Patrick Leahy was elected to the U.S. Senate in 1974, he was the youngest senator to be elected from the state, and in 2021 he remained the only Democrat elected to the Senate from Vermont.

Leahy attended St. Michael's College in Colchester, graduating with a BA degree in 1961. He earned his JD from Georgetown University Law Center in 1964. For eight years (1966–1974) he was state's attorney in Chittenden County. Leahy has been the president pro tempore emeritus of the U.S. Senate since 2015 and was the president pro tempore from 2012 to 2015. He was chairman of the U.S. Senate Judiciary Committee from 2007 to 2015 and was the senior member of that committee in 2021. He is also the chair of the Senate Appropriations Committee, on which he is a member of the subcommittee on Homeland Security. Long active on human rights and civil rights issues, he is a leader in the international campaign against the production, export, and use of antipersonnel land mines, and wrote the first law by any government to ban the export of those weapons. Senator Leahy also wrote and enacted the civilian war victims relief programs in Afghanistan and Iraq. He headed the Senate's negotiations on the USA

Patriot Act in 2001, adding checks and balances provisions to the bill to protect civil liberties, and to triple the staffing along the U.S.–Canada border. He led the Judiciary Committee's investigation into the mass firings of U.S. attorneys that led to the resignation of Attorney General Alberto Gonzales in 2008. Leahy is the chief sponsor of the Innocence Protection Act addressing flaws in the administration of capital punishment. In 2004, his death penalty reform bill was enacted, requiring post-conviction DNA testing and better access to competent legal counsel. He has been a leader of open government and the Freedom of Information Act in 1996, and is one of only two politicians to be awarded the John Peter Zenger Press Freedom Award (Leahy.Senate.gov. 2020).

John Marshall (1755–1835)

John Marshall was the fourth chief justice of the United States (1801–1835). He ranks as the longest-serving chief justice and fourth-longest-serving justice in Supreme Court history. He was nominated to the Court by President John Adams, and was succeeded as chief justice by Roger Taney. Prior to his appointment as chief justice, John Marshall served as the fourth U.S. secretary of state in President John Adams's cabinet. He was a member of the U.S. House of Representatives from Virginia (1799–1800). An active Federalist, Marshall was educated at the College of William and Mary, and served as a lieutenant in the Continental Army during the Revolutionary War.

In 1797, as a special envoy of President Adams, Marshall negotiated with France to end French navy attacks on U.S. commercial shipping in what became known as the XYZ Affair. He was appointed secretary of state in 1800, and one year later President Adams appointed him to the Supreme Court. In 1803, he authored the majority opinion in *Marbury v. Madison,* a landmark legal decision that upheld the principle of judicial review. He led the Court to several decisions that confirmed the supremacy of the federal government and the

U.S. Constitution over the states, including *Fletcher v. Peck* (1810) and *Dartmouth College v. Woodward* (1819). Both of these Supreme Court decisions invalidated state laws that violated the contract clause of the U.S. Constitution. In *McCulloch v. Maryland* (1819), the Court upheld the constitutionality of the Second Bank of the United States and held that states could not tax federal institutions. In *Martin v. Hunter's Lessee* (1816), and *Cohens v. Virginia* (1821), the Court established that it could hear appeals from state courts in both civil and criminal matters. Marshall wrote the majority opinion in *Gibbons v. Ogden* (1821), which ruled that the commerce clause bars states from restricting navigation. In *Worcester v. Georgia* (1835), Marshall's majority opinion held that Georgia's criminal statute that prohibited non-Native Americans from being on tribal lands without a state license was unconstitutional. After Marshall's death in 1835, President Andrew Jackson appointed Roger Taney to replace him as chief justice (Brookhiser 2018; Johnson 1998; Newmyer 2005; Simon 2003).

Thurgood Marshall (1908–1993)

Thurgood Marshall was one of the most significant contributors to civil rights law in U.S. history—as a lawyer for the National Association for the Advancement of Colored People (NAACP), as U.S. solicitor general, and finally as the first African American associate justice of the U.S. Supreme Court. The grandson of a slave, Marshall graduated from Lincoln University (a predominantly black institution) in 1930. He went on to Howard University Law School (another predominantly black school), and earned his law degree in 1933. Marshall was greatly influenced at Howard by its dean, Charles Hamilton Houston (Rawn 2010). After graduating from Howard Law, Marshall became a special counsel for the Baltimore branch of the NAACP (Mack 2012). His first successful case was in 1935–36, when he won a Maryland Court of Appeals case against the University of Maryland for refusing to admit an African American applicant named Donald Murray (*Murray v. Pearson*, 169 Md 478, 1936). Marshall went on to win twenty-nine Supreme Court cases, including *Smith v. Allwright* (1944), which struck down all-white primaries; *Shelley v. Kraemer* (1948), which struck down racially restrictive covenants; *Sweatt v. Painter* (1950), and *McLaurin v. Oklahoma State Regents* (1950), both of which overturned racially segregated graduate schools. In 1954, Marshall successfully argued the landmark case of *Brown v. Board of Education of Topeka, Kansas*. The Court's decision in this case overturned *Plessy v. Ferguson's* (1896) separate-but-equal doctrine, and held all segregated public schools to be unconstitutional. In the view of many historians, *Brown* launched the modern Black civil rights movement (Davis and Clark 1992; Mack 2012; Rawn 2010; Tushnet 1994; Vile 2003).

In 1961, President John F. Kennedy appointed Marshall to the Second Court of Appeals. As court of appeals judge, Marshall made 112 rulings, all of which were upheld by the U.S. Supreme Court. In 1965, President Lyndon Johnson appointed Marshall as U.S. solicitor general (1965–1967), during which time he won fourteen of the nineteen cases that he argued for the government. Over his career, Marshall won more cases before the Supreme Court than any other American (Vile 2003). In 1967, President Johnson nominated him to the U.S. Supreme Court, and after his Senate confirmation, Marshall became the first African American to so serve.

While on the Supreme Court, Marshall was its most consistent proponent of civil rights and one of its most influential liberal justices. He wrote the majority opinion in a number of important cases that expanded civil rights and personal freedoms for Americans.

In the 1980s, however, when the Court became more conservative under Chief Justice William Rehnquist, Justice Marshall increasingly joined the dissent side. Indeed, Marshall has been described as a warrior at the bar—a reference to his years as a crusading civil rights lawyer—and a rebel on the bench (Davis and Clark 1992; Tushnet 2008). Thurgood Marshall retired from the Supreme Court in 1991 due to declining health and passed away in 1993 (Marshall and Tushnet 2001).

Ralph Nader (1934–)

Ralph Nader exemplifies the attorney/activist and politician who helped spark reform movements for auto safety, consumer advocacy, and environmentalism. He ran for U.S. president as an independent or on the Green Party ticket in every election from 1992 to 2008. In the 2000 election, many critics claim his Green Party run cost Al Gore Florida's electoral college vote and tipped the presidency to George W. Bush. He founded or cofounded several think-tank or public advocacy organizations, most prominently the Public Interest Research Group (often more commonly and derisively called "Nader's Raiders"), the Center for Responsive Law, and Public Citizens, Inc.

Born in 1934 in Connecticut, Nader graduated from the Gilbert School at Princeton University before earning a law degree at Harvard Law School in 1958. At Harvard, he edited the *Harvard Law Record.* After serving in the U.S. Army, he began to practice law in Hartford and to teach history and government at the University of Hartford. In 1965, he worked part-time for the Department of Labor, and his research there led to his writing *Unsafe at Any Speed* (1965), which documented the American auto industry's indifference to invest in car safety features. The publication of the book drew a concerted attack on him by GM, but also led to reforms of the auto industry and promoted the philosophy of government regulation of industry whose economic interests often ignore the harmful effects of their technology. Nader sued GM and won a judgment of $425,000, which he used to found the Center for Auto Safety and several other public interest groups. In 1968, Congress passed and President Lyndon Johnson signed the National Traffic and Motor Vehicle Safety Act, which established the National Highway Traffic Safety Administration. Nader also led a campaign on food safety that contributed to passage of the Wholesome Meat Act (1967).

Nader went on to write three dozen books, including *The Menace of Atomic Energy* (1977), *Who's Poisoning America* (1981), *Good Works* (1981), and *No Contest* (1996) (Nader .org. 2020).

Barack Obama (1961–)

The forty-fourth president of the United States, Barack Hussein Obama was also the country's first African American commander in chief. Born in Hawaii in 1961, he was educated at Occidental College, Columbia University (BA), and at Harvard Law School (JD), where he was the first African American editor of the prestigious *Harvard Law Review*. After graduation from Columbia University, he moved to Chicago, where he worked with a group of churches to help rebuild communities devastated by the closure of local steel plants. He then attended Harvard Law, but after graduating from that school he turned down opportunities to join a lucrative Wall Street law firm. Instead, Obama returned to Chicago to lead a voter registration drive, teach constitutional law at the University of Chicago, and remain active as a community organizer. He also served in the Illinois State Senate (2005–2008), where he sponsored a bill that was the first major ethics reform law in twenty-five years.

He authored several best-selling books, notably *Dreams of My Father* (1995), *The Audacity of Hope* (2008), *Change We Can Believe In* (2008), and *Of Thee I Sing* (2010). Also published in 2008 was a book by Lisa Rogak, entitled *Barack Obama in His Own Words*.

In terms of his impact on the federal judiciary, as president, Obama appointed two associate justices of the Supreme Court, Sonja Sotomayor in 2009 and Elena Kagan in 2010. As noted earlier, President Obama appointed more minority judges to the federal bench than did any other U.S. president. He was awarded the Nobel Peace Prize in 2008 and the Profile in Courage Award in 2017 (White House. Gov. 2020).

Sandra Day O'Connor (1930–)

Sandra Day O'Connor was the first woman appointed to the U.S. Supreme Court. Throughout her distinguished judicial career, she was considered to be a moderate conservative, and during her quarter-century on the Supreme Court (1981–2006), she provided the swing vote between the Court's conservative and liberal blocs. She wrote the majority opinion in two cases: *Lyng v. Indiana County* (1988), and *Westside v. Mergens* (1990), and she provided the swing vote on six cases: *Lee v. Weisman* (1992), *Rosenberger v. University of Virginia* (1995), *Mitchell v. Helms* (2000), *Zelman v. Simmons-Harris* (2002), *McCreary County v. ACLU* (2005), and *Van Orden v. Perry* (2005). Justice O'Connor also was the swing vote upholding the abortion-rights ruling in the famous case of *Roe v. Wade* (1973).

O'Connor was born in El Paso, Texas, in 1930. She received her BA and LLB from Stanford University. She was elected to two terms in the Arizona State Senate. She served as deputy county attorney of San Mateo County, California, from 1952 to 1953, and then as a civilian attorney for Quartermaster Market Center, Frankfurt, Germany, from 1954 to 1957. From 1958 to 1960, Justice O'Connor was in private practice in Maryvale, Arizona. She then served as the assistant attorney general of Arizona (1965–1969), and was appointed to the Arizona State Senate in 1959, then elected and reelected to two terms. In 1975, she was elected Judge of the Maricopa County Superior Court. She served in that capacity until 1979, when she was appointed to the Arizona Court of Appeals. President Ronald Reagan nominated her as associate justice of the Supreme Court in 1981, and she easily won confirmation from the Senate. She served on the Court for twenty-four years, retiring in January 2006. After her retirement from the Supreme Court,

Justice O'Connor continued her judicial service by hearing cases in the United States Court of Appeals. In 2009, President Barack Obama awarded her the nation's highest civilian honor, the Presidential Medal of Freedom (Oconnor Institute .org. 2021).

William Rehnquist (1924–2005)

With a total of thirty-three years on the Court, William Rehnquist was one of the longest-serving U.S. Supreme Court justices. He was an associate justice from 1972 to 1986, and was chief justice from 1986 to 2005. As chief justice, Rehnquist led the Court toward what has been described as "judicial activism of the right," tilting the Court increasingly toward conservative rulings (Schwartz 2003).

Rehnquist was born in Milwaukee, Wisconsin, in 1924. He married Natalie Cornell in 1953. Rehnquist graduated from Harvard University (a BA and MA in political science), and earned his JD from Stanford Law School, graduating in the same law class as Sandra Day O'Connor. Rehnquist served in the U.S. Army Air Force during World War II (LeMay 2018: 190–191).

While serving as associate justice, William Rehnquist often wrote dissenting opinions that reflected his conservative legal philosophy.

During Rehnquist's years as chief justice, the Supreme Court trended toward more split-decision rulings (e.g., more 5-4 or 6-3 decisions, as opposed to the 7-2, 8-1, or even unanimous rulings more common during the Warren Court) (Hudson 2006; LeMay 2009; Schwartz 2003; Tushnet 2005).

As chief justice, Rehnquist wrote several notable majority opinions: a Second Amendment case, *United States v. Verdugo-Urquidez* (6-3, 1990), and a Fourth Amendment case, *Ohio v. Robinette* (8-1, 1996). He wrote the majority opinion in the Fifth Amendment case, a unanimous ruling in *United States v. Felix* (1992). Rehnquist impacted the Court by managing its docket. Notable cases in which he dissented while chief justice include the abortion case of *Planned Parenthood v. Casey* (5-4, 1992) and the Fourth Amendment case *Chandler v. Miller* (8-1, 1997), in which he wrote the sole dissenting opinion. Rehnquist was among the dissenting votes in several Fifth Amendment cases including *Lawrence v. Texas* (6-3, 2003), *Rasul v. Bush* (6-3, 2004), and *Kelo v. City of New London* (5-4, 2005); and in the capital punishment case of *Atkins v. Virginia* (6-3, 2002). His record on civil rights and liberties cases can be described as consistently conservative rather than expansive of such rights.

Justice Rehnquist wrote the majority opinion in four First Amendment freedom of religion cases, all decided by 5-4 votes: *Stone v. Graham* (1980), *Bowen v. Kendrick* (1988), *Zobrest v. Catalina Foothills School District* (1993), and *Zelman v. Simmons-Harris* (2002) (LeMay 2020).

As chief justice, and as per the constitutional provision, Justice Rehnquist presided over the U.S. Senate impeachment trial of President William Jefferson Clinton. He also managed the Supreme Court in its highly controversial 5-4 decision in *Bush v. Gore* (2000) (Hudson 2006; Obermayer 2009). The *Bush v. Gore* ruling has been criticized as blatantly partisan, and the decision injected the Court into electoral politics in a way that historically has been more often eschewed by the Court. The *Bush v. Gore* decision undoubtedly contributed to his reputation as being a "judicial activist of the right" (Schwartz 2003). Rehnquist was still chief justice when he died of thyroid cancer in September 2005 (LeMay 2020, 203–205).

John Roberts (1959–)

John Roberts was appointed chief justice of the United States by President George W. Bush in 2005. As chief justice, Roberts has presided over the federal courts and over numerous decisions that were decided by close 5-4 votes. He wrote the majority opinions in *Gonzales v. U.D.V.* (8-0, 2006), a religious freedom decision allowing the U.D.V. religious group use of a banned drug in its religious practices; and in *Hosanna-Tabor v. E.E.O.C.* (9-0, 2012), which ruled that federal discrimination laws do not apply to religious organizations' selection of religious leaders. He provided the decisive vote reaffirming the legality of the Affordable Care Act by siding with the liberal wing of the Supreme Court in *California et al. v. Texas et al.* (2021). Roberts voted his conservative views in the minority on the issue of same-sex marriage that made same-sex marriage legal in all fifty states in *Obergefell v. Hodges* (2015).

Justice Roberts was born in Buffalo, New York, in 1959, but he spent much of his childhood in Indiana. He attended Harvard College (BA, 1976) and Harvard Law (JD, 1979) and served as a law clerk for Associate Justice William Rehnquist in 1980. He was special assistant to the attorney general in the Department of Justice from 1981 to 1982, and then served as associate counsel to President Ronald Reagan, in the White House Counsel's Office, from 1982 to 1986. After serving for several years as a deputy solicitor general with the Department of Justice, he practiced law in Washington, D.C., from 1993 to 2003. He was appointed to the U.S. Court of Appeals in 2003 by President George W. Bush. Two years later he was appointed to the U.S. Supreme Court by President Bush to replace the late William Rehnquist as chief justice. He was confirmed by the U.S. Senate in September 2005 by a 78-22 vote (LeMay 2021, 205–207).

Antonin Scalia (1936–2016)

Associate Justice Antonin Scalia (1986–2016) was unquestionably the leading voice of the conservative bloc on the high court during his tenure. Scalia was known as a forceful articulator of the judicial philosophy of "original interpretation," or "strict construction," and he argued fiercely against what he labeled judicial activism. Critics of Scalia asserted, though, that he was himself an activist on several decisions in which his conservative philosophy appeared to outweigh judicial precedent, court tradition, or originalist interpretations of the Constitution, including *Gore v. Bush* (2000) and *Citizens United v. F.E.C.* (2010).

Scalia was born in New Jersey in 1936. A lifelong devout Roman Catholic, he earned his AB from Georgetown University, and the University of Fribourg, Switzerland, and his LLB from Harvard Law School. After graduating from Harvard Law, Scalia went into private practice in Cleveland for several years, before becoming a professor of law at the University of Virginia (1967–1971). He went on to teach law as a professor of law at the University of Chicago (1977–1982), and as a visiting professor of law at Georgetown University and at Stanford University. Justice Scalia was chair of the American Bar Association's Section on Administrative Law (1981–1982), and the Conference Section Chair (1982–1983). In the federal government, Justice Scalia was general counsel of the Office of Telecommunications Policy (1971–1972), and assistant attorney general for the Office of Legal Counsel (1974–1977).

In 1982, President Ronald Reagan nominated Scalia to the U.S. Court of Appeals for the District of Columbia Circuit in 1982 (the appeals court from which the most justices have moved up to the Supreme Court). President Reagan nominated him to fill an associate justice opening on the Supreme Court in 1986. He was confirmed by the Senate by a 98-0 vote on September 17 of that year.

Justice Scalia died suddenly of a heart attack on February 13, 2016. The Republican Senate majority took the unprecedented stand of refusing to even hold hearings for President Obama's nominee to replace Scalia. Instead, the Republican Senate leadership held the seat open until after the presidential election of 2016. Scalia's seat was then filled by Neil Gorsuch, who was nominated by Republican president Donald Trump. Gorsuch was narrowly confirmed in a mostly partisan vote (54-45), and since joining the Court he has come to be seen by legal experts as a strict constructionist firmly in the tradition of Justice Scalia (LeMay 2021, 207–208).

William Howard Taft (1857–1930)

William Howard Taft is the only person to have served as both president of the United States (1909–1913) and chief justice of the U.S. Supreme Court (1921–1930). He was born in 1857, in Cincinnati, Ohio, son of a prominent Republican politician and statesman. Taft graduated from Yale University and went on to study law at the University of Cincinnati, passing the Ohio bar in 1886. In 1887, he was appointed to the Ohio Superior Court, and elected to a five-year term in 1888. In 1890, he was appointed judge of the U.S. Circuit Court of Appeals. In 1900, he served as President McKinley's envoy to set up a civilian government in the Philippines after the Spanish American War (1898), and he drafted its constitution and its Bill of Rights. He stayed on in the Philippines in 1901 despite being offered a Supreme Court appointment by President Theodore Roosevelt. In 1904, President Roosevelt appointed him secretary of war (1904–1908), which included overseeing the beginning construction of the Panama Canal. He was elected president in 1908 and served one term before losing the 1912 election to Woodrow Wilson. During his administration, he initiated eighty antitrust suits to rein in the power of big business and submitted to Congress constitutional amendments for implementing a federal income tax and the direct election of U.S. senators.

After his term as U.S. president, Taft taught law at Yale University Law School. In 1921, President Warren Harding appointed him chief justice of the Supreme Court. He improved the organization of the Court, and helped secure enactment of the Judge's Act of 1925, which reduced the workload of the U.S. Supreme Court by further defining the jurisdiction of the U.S. circuit courts. While chief justice, Taft wrote 250 decisions, most reflecting his conservative ideology. His most prominent opinion was in *Myers v. United States* (1926), which invalidated the Tenure of Office Act (1867–1887). The act limited presidential authority to remove federal judges, and in *Myers* the Court declared it likely invalid. President Taft remained on the Court until retiring shortly before his death in 1930 (White House.org. 2020/William Howard Taft).

Roger Taney (1777–1864)

Roger B. Taney was the fifth Chief Justice of the U.S. Supreme Court (1835–1864) and the first Roman Catholic justice to serve on the Supreme Court. He served as chief justice for twenty-eight years, the second longest (to John Marshall) in tenure. Taney is best known, however, for his infamous majority opinion in *Dred Scott v. Sandford* (1857), where he held that Congress had no power to exclude slavery from the territories, and that Negroes (even Free Blacks) could not become citizens.

A native of Maryland, Taney studied law with Judge Jeremiah Chase, of the Maryland General Court, and was admitted to the Maryland bar in 1799. He served one year in the Maryland House of Delegates, then practiced law in Frederick, Maryland. He was a member of the Federalist Party until 1812. He returned to the Maryland House of Delegates in 1816 when he was elected to the state senate, serving until 1821. In 1827, Taney was appointed attorney general of Maryland, by which time he had joined the Democratic Party as a strong supporter of Andrew Jackson. President Jackson appointed Roger Taney as his attorney general in 1831. He fought against the Second Bank of the United States, which he believed had abused its powers. In 1833, President Jackson appointed him secretary of the treasury, but the Senate refused to confirm him because he was considered too partisan, the first time that the Senate had turned down a nominee to a cabinet-level post. He returned to Baltimore to practice law. In 1834, the Senate refused once again to confirm him to a government position—this time rejecting Jackson's nomination of Taney to fill a seat as associate justice on the Supreme Court. In 1835, however, Chief Justice John Marshall died and Jackson nominated Taney once again. This time, despite strong opposition from the Whigs, he was confirmed. Taney was sworn in as chief justice in March 1836.

Justice Taney wrote numerous majority opinions during his tenure as chief justice, but he will always be best known to historians for his majority opinion in *Dred Scott v. Sandford* (1857), which exacerbated North–South tensions over slavery, undermined the prestige of the Court, and further drove the United States toward civil war. Whenever state authorities interfered with the execution of federal power, however, Justice Taney upheld federal supremacy. His opinion in *Ableman v. Booth* (1858) ruled against the state of Wisconsin for obstructing the processes of the federal courts. Taney's majority opinion in the case remains a powerful statement of constitutional federalism. He also ruled that the U.S. executive branch's authority over foreign relations was paramount and exclusive. Taney conflicted with President Lincoln over suspension of the writ of habeas corpus, even in a time of war. Taney was deeply Roman Catholic and considered slavery evil (he freed the slaves that he had owned when he became chief justice), but held that issues related to slavery needed to be resolved by the states rather than the federal government. He died at age eighty-seven, in 1864 (Oyez.org. 2020, Roger Taney).

Donald Trump (1946–)

The forty-fifth president of the United States, Republican businessman and media personality Donald J. Trump served a single term (from January 2017 to January 2021) before losing his bid for reelection to Democratic nominee Joe Biden. During his four years in the White House, however, Trump had a notable and lasting impact on the federal judicial system as a result of his appointments to the federal bench. He also became notorious for his unrelenting attacks on individuals and organizations that criticized him or opposed his wishes, including the FBI, the Department of Justice, and any federal court or judge who ruled against his preferred outcome or his executive orders. He added three hard-right conservative justices to the Supreme Court (Neil Gorsuch, Brett Kavanaugh, and Amy Coney Barrett), and well over 200 judges to the federal bench, including 54 appellate court judges (only one less than his predecessor made in two terms). In making these nominations Trump typically drew on the advice of the Federalist Society and the Heritage Foundation, prioritizing conservative judicial philosophy of nominees over their professional qualifications.

President Trump was born in New York City in 1946, the son of a multimillionaire real estate tycoon. He graduated from the New York Military Academy, attended Fordham University, and then the Wharton School of the University of Pennsylvania. He built on the family real estate empire, claiming billionaire status. He also became a television celebrity when his reality show *The Apprentice* became a hit. Trump ran a decidedly unorthodox campaign for the presidency and surprised most analysts by winning the Electoral College vote despite having lost the popular vote to Democratic nominee Hillary Clinton by more than 3 million votes. He selected Indiana Republican governor Mike Pence as his running mate, further appealing to the conservative wing of the Republican Party and to the religious right (LeMay 2019, 210–212).

Earl Warren (1891–1974)

William Rehnquist is often characterized as a "judicial activist of the right." In stark contrast, Chief Justice Earl Warren is widely viewed as the Supreme Court's primary judicial activist of the left (Belknap 2005; Newton 2006; Tushnet 1996). Warren was chief justice of the U.S. Supreme Court from 1953 to 1969, when the Court handed down many decisions that expanded civil rights and civil liberties for Americans. Warren guided the Court when it developed and most often used the judicial doctrine of incorporation to extend the protections of the Bill of Rights to state and local governments (Powe 2000; Urofsky 2001).

Earl Warren was born in Los Angeles in 1891. He attended the University of California, Berkeley, earning his BA in political science in 1913 and his LLB in 1914. During World War I, Warren served in the U.S. Army as a first lieutenant (1917–1918). He was chair of the Republican Party of California from 1932 to 1939, and was district attorney of Alameda County from 1925 to 1939. Earl Warren was elected attorney general of California in 1938. He supported the forced relocation and internment of Japanese American citizens in 1942, but he later came to regret that decision. In his memoirs, Warren wrote: "Whenever I thought of the innocent little children who were torn from home, school, friends, and congenial surroundings, I was conscience stricken. . . . It was wrong to react so impulsively, without positive evidence of disloyalty" (LeMay 2009: 83–85; Warren 1977). During World War II, however, the internment program was popular with the wider American public, and Warren's stance helped him win election as governor of California. He served as governor from 1943 to 1953, when he was appointed as chief justice of the Supreme Court by President Dwight Eisenhower. When Eisenhower nominated Warren, he thought he was appointing a solid conservative. Warren, though, took more liberal positions on cases before the Court than anyone anticipated. Eisenhower later called his appointment of Warren one of his biggest mistakes as president.

As chief justice, Warren wrote the majority opinion in a number of landmark civil rights–relevant cases: *Brown v. Board of Education* (1954, a unanimous ruling that held racial segregated schools were unconstitutional); *Klopfer v. North Carolina* (1967, a unanimous Sixth Amendment ruling that held that state courts also had to provide a speedy trial); *Reynolds v. Sims* (1964, an 8-1 ruling that state electoral districts had to be as equal in population as possible—One Man, One Vote principle); *Miranda v. Arizona* (1966, a 6-3 Fifth Amendment decision holding that upon arrest, a person must be read their constitutional rights); and *Loving v. Virginia* (1967, a unanimous Tenth and Fourteenth Amendment ruling that overturned a Virginia state law that made interracial marriage illegal). In managing the Court, Warren worked hard at achieving unanimous or highly consensus decisions (i.e., 7+ rulings).

Under Chief Justice Earl Warren, the Court issued "incorporation" rulings that applied constitutional freedoms to the states by such notable cases as: *Mapp v. Ohio* (1961), which held the exclusionary rule barring prosecutors from using illegally obtained evidence could not be used in state courts; *New York Times v. Sullivan* (1964), which held that freedom of speech rights of the First Amendment restricted public officials' ability to sue for defamation; *Griswold v. Connecticut* (1965), which held married couples had the right to buy and use contraceptives without restrictions by state or local government; and *Brandenburg v. Ohio* (1969), which held government could not punish inflammatory speech unless it was directed to incite a lawless act. The Court also upheld the constitutionality of the 1964 Civil Rights Act under Chief Justice Earl Warren in *Heart of Atlanta Motel, Inc. v. United States* (1964).

After President Kennedy's assassination, Earl Warren led the Warren Commission's investigation into the assassination. Earl Warren retired from the Court in 1969. He timed his retirement to enable President Lyndon B. Johnson, a Democrat, to replace him on the Court. Warren died in California in 1974 (LeMay 2021, 210–211; Warren 1977).

Bibliography

Alliance for Justice.org. 2020. "Our Work." https://www.afj .org/our-work/. Accessed September 10, 2020.

American Association for Justice. 2020. "About Us." https:// www.justice.org/about-us. Accessed September 10, 2020.

American Bar Association.org. 2020. "About the ABA." https://www.americanbar.org/about_the_aba/. Accessed September 10, 2020.

American Constitution Society.org. 2020. "About ACS." https://www.acslaw.org/about-us. Accessed September 10, 2020.

American Judicature Society.org. 2020. "About Us." http://americanjudicaturesociety.org/about-us. Accessed September 10, 2020.

American Progress.org. 2020. "Mission." https://www.americanprogress.org/mission. Accessed September 10, 2020.

Barack Obama.com. 2020. "About President Barack Obama." https://www.barackobama.com/about. Accessed September 9, 2020.

Belknap, Michal. 2005. *The Supreme Court under Earl Warren, 1953–1969.* Columbia: University of South Carolina Press.

Brennan Center.org. 2020. "About Us." https://www.brennancenter.org/about. Accessed September 10, 2020.

Brookhiser, Richard. 2018. *John Marshall: The Man Who Made the Supreme Court.* New York: Basic Books.

Bureau of Justice Statistics.gov. 2020. "About BJS." https://www.ojp.gov/about/offices/bureau-justice-statistics-bjs. Accessed September 10, 2020.

Carmon, Irin, and Shana Knizhnik. 2015. *Notorious RBG: The Life and Times of Ruth Bader Ginsburg.* New York: Dey Street Books.

Caro, Robert. 2012. *The Years of Lyndon Johnson: The Passage of Power.* New York: Knopf.

Cato Institute. 2020. "Mission." https://www.cato.org/mission. Accessed October 28, 2021.

Center for American Progress. 2020. "Mission." https://www.americanprogress.org/Mission. Accessed September 10, 2020.

Center for Individual Rights.org. 2020. "Mission and History." https://www.cir-usa.org/mission/history. Accessed September 11, 2020.

Center for Justice and Democracy.org. 2020. "About the Center for Justice & Democracy." https://www.centerjd .org/about-us. Accessed September 11, 2020.

Center for Study of Law and Religion. 2020. "About the CSLR." http://cslr.law.emory.edu/about. Accessed September 9, 2020.

Chesney-Lind, Meda, and Marc Mauer, eds. 2003. *Invisible Punishment: The Collateral Consequences of Mass Imprisonment.* New York: New Press.

Cole, David. 2016. *Engines of Liberty: The Power of Citizen Activists to Make Constitutional Law.* New York: Basic Books.

Constitution Center.org. 2020. "Mission & History." https:// constitutioncenter.org/about/mission-history. Accessed September 11, 2020.

Cornell.Law.edu. 2020. "About lii." https://www.law.cornell .edu/lii/about/about_lii. Accessed October 28, 2021.

Davis, Michael, and Hunter Clark. 1992. *Thurgood Marshall: Warrior at the Bar, Rebel on the Bench.* New York: Birch Lane Books.

Economic Policy Institute.org. 2020. "About EPI." https:// www.eip.org/about. Accessed September 11, 2020.

Federal Judicial Center.gov. 2020. "About the FJC." https:// www.fjc.gov/about. Accessed September 11, 2020.

Federalist Society.org. 2020. "About Us/Our Background." https://fedsoc.org/about-us#Background. Accessed September 11, 2020.

Gideon v. Wainwright. 2021. https://www.us

Ginsburg, Ruth Bader. 2018. *My Own Words.* New York: Simon and Schuster.

Goldman School of Public Policy.org. 2020. "Robert Reich." https://gspp.berkeley.edu/faculty-and-impact/faculty /robert-reich. Accessed September 13, 2020.

Gould, Lewis. 2016. *The First Modern Clash over Federal Power: Wilson v. Hughes in the Presidential Election of 1916.* Lawrence: University Press on Kansas.

Govtrack.us. 2020. "Sen. William Evarts." https://www .govtrack.us/congress/members/william-evarts/403943. Accessed September 13, 2020.

Guardian.com. 2020. "Profile, Robert Reich." https://www .theguardian.com/profile/robert-reich. Accessed September 14, 2020.

Hagedorn, Sara, and Michael LeMay. 2019. *The American Congress.* Santa Barbara: ABC-CLIO.

Hall, Kermit, and John Patrick. 2006. *The Pursuit of Justice: Supreme Court Decisions That Shaped America.* New York: Oxford University Press.

Heritage.org. 2020. "About Heritage." https://www.heritage. org/about-heritage/mission. Accessed September 9, 2020.

History Central.com. 2021, "Rehnquist biography," https:// www.historycentral.com/Bio/people/Rehnquist.html. Accessed October 28, 2021.

History.com. 2020a. "Marbury v. Madison." https:// www.history.com/topics/marbury-v-madison. Accessed September 9, 2020.

History.com. 2020b. "William Howard Taft." https://www .history.com/topics/us-presidents/william-howard-taft. Accessed September 14, 2020.

History.state.gov. 2020. "William Evarts." https://history .state.gov/department-history/people/evarts-william -maxwell. Accessed September 13, 2020.

Hudson, David L., Jr. 2006. *The Rehnquist Court: Understanding Its Impact and Legacy.* New York: Praeger.

Institute for Justice.org. 2020. "About Us." https://ij.org
/about-us. Accessed September 11, 2020.

Johnson, Herbert. 1998. *The Chief Justiceship of John Marshall,
1801–1835*. Columbia: University of South Carolina Press.

Kanefield, Teri. 2016. *Free to Be Ruth Bader Ginsburg: The
Story of Women and Law*. New York: Amazon Publishing.

Laurence, Helen, and William Miller. 2000. *Academic
Research on the Internet: Options for Scholars and Libraries*.
New York: Routledge.

Law and Economics Center.org, "Mission," https://mason.lec
.org/About. Accessed October 28, 2021.

Law.Cornell.edu. 2021. "Justice Scalia," https://www
.law.cornell.edu/supct/justices/scalia.bio.html. Accessed
October 28, 2021.

Law.Emory.edu. 2020. "Law in Action, Centers and
Programs," http://www.law.emory.edu/centers-and
-programs. Accessed October 29, 2021.

Leahy.Senate.gov. 2020. "About Senator Leahy." https://www
.leahy.senate.gov/about. Accessed September 13, 2020.

LeMay, Michael. 2009. *The Perennial Struggle: Race, Ethnicity,
and Minority Group Relations in the United States*, 3rd ed.
Upper Saddle River, NJ: Prentice-Hall.

LeMay, Michael. 2018. *Religious Freedom in America: A
Reference Handbook*. Santa Barbara, CA: ABC-CLIO.

LeMay, Michael. 2019. *Immigration Reform: A Reference
Handbook*. Santa Barbara: ABC-CLIO.

LeMay, Michael. 2021. *The First Amendment Freedoms: A
Reference Handbook*. Santa Barbara, CA: ABC-CLIO.

LeMay, Michael, and Elliott Barkan, eds. 1999. *U.S.
Immigration and Naturalization Laws and Issues: A
Documentary History*. Westport, CT: Greenwood Press.

Lewis, Anthony. 1989. *Gideon's Trumpet: How One Man, a
Poor Prisoner, Took His Case to the Supreme Court—and*

Changed the Law of the United States. New York: Vintage Books.

Lgraham.senate.gov. 2020. "Lindsey Graham." https://www.lgraham.senate.gov/public/. Accessed September 13, 2020.

Littlefield, Nick, and David Nexon. 2016. *Lion of the Senate*. New York: Simon and Schuster.

Mack, Kenneth. 2012. *Representing the Race: The Creation of the Civil Rights Lawyer*. Cambridge, MA: Harvard University Press.

Marshall, Thurgood, and Mark Tushnet, ed. 2001. *Thurgood Marshall: His Speeches, Writings, Arguments, Opinions, and Reminiscences*. Chicago: Lawrence Hill Books.

Mason Law and Economic Center.org. 2020. "About LEC." https://masonlec.org/about. Accessed September 11, 2020.

Mauer, Marc, and Sabrina Jones. 2013. *Race to Incarcerate*. New York: New Press.

Mayer, Jane. 2016. *Dark Money: The Hidden History of the Billionaires behind the Rise of the Radical Right*. New York: Anchor Books.

Miller, John. 2005. *A Gift of Freedom: How the John M. Olin Foundation Changed America*. New York: Encounter Books.

Murphy, Bruce A. 2003. *Wild Bill: The Legend and Life of William O. Douglas*. New York: Random House.

Nader.org. 2020. "Ralph Nader." https://nader.org. Accessed September 13, 2020.

Newmyer, R. Kent. 2005. *The Supreme Court under Marshall and Taney*. Hoboken, NJ: Wiley-Blackwell.

Newton, Jim. 2006. *Justice for All: Earl Warren and the Nation He Led*. New York: Riverhead Books.

Obermayer, Herman. 2009. *Rehnquist: A Personal Portrait of the Distinguished Chief Justice of the United States*. New York: Oxford University Press.

O'Connor Institute.org. 2021. "Biography," https://
oconnorinstitute.org/civic-programs/oconnor-history
/sandra-day-oconnor-policy-archives-research-library
/biography. Accessed October 28, 2021.

Oyez.org. 2020. "Samuel Chase." https://www.oyez.org
/justices/samuel_chase. Accessed September 13, 2020.

Oyez.org. 2020. "William O. Douglas." https://www.oyez.org
/justices/william_o_douglas. Accessed September 13, 2020.

Oyez.org. 2020. "Ruth Bader Ginsburg." https://www.oyez
.org/justices/ruth_bader_ginsburg. Accessed September 13,
2020.

Oyez.org. 2020. "Charles E. Hughes." https://www.oyez.org
/justices/charles_e_hughes. Accessed September 13, 2020.

Oyez.org. 2020. "William H. Rehnquist." https://www.oyez
.org/justices/william_h_rehnquist. Accessed September 13,
2020.

Oyez.org. 2020. "Roger B. Taney." https://www.oyez.org
/justices/roger_b_taney. Accessed September 14, 2020.

Oyez.org. 2020. "Thurgood Marshall." https://www.oyez.org
/justices/thurgood_marshall. Accessed September 14, 2020.

Oyez.org. 2020. "Earl Warren." https://www.oyez.org
/justices/earl_warren. Accessed September 14, 2020.

Pew Research Center. 2020. "Politics & Policy." https://www
.pewresearch.org/politics. Accessed September 10, 2020.

Powe, Lucas. 2000. *The Warren Court and American Politics.*
Cambridge, MA: Belknap Press/Harvard University Press.

Rawn, James, Jr. 2010. *Root and Branch: Charles Hamilton
Houston, Thurgood Marshall, and the Struggle to End
Segregation.* New York: Bloomsbury Press.

RobertReich.org. 2020. https://robertreich.org/. Accessed
September 14, 2020.

Schwartz, Herman. 2003. *The Rehnquist Court: Judicial
Activism of the Right.* New York: Hill and Wang.

Senate Judiciary Committee.gov. 2020. "History." https:// www.judiciary.senate.gov/about/history. Accessed September 11, 2020.

The Sentencing Project.org. 2021. "About-us." https://www .sentencingproject.org/about-us. Accessed September 11, 2020.

Simon, James. 2003. *What Kind of Nation: Thomas Jefferson, John Marshall, and the Epic Struggle to Create a United States.* New York: Simon and Schuster.

Southern Poverty Law Center.org. 2020. "Our History." https://www.splcenter.org/about-us/our-history. Accessed September 11, 2020.

Trinkle, Dennis, and Scott Merriman. 2001. *The History Highway: A 21st Century Guide to Internet Resources.* Armonk, NY: M. E. Sharpe.

Trump.com. 2020. "Donald J. Trump." http://www.trump .com/biography. Accessed September 9, 2020.

Tushnet, Mark. 1994. *Making Civil Rights Law: Thurgood Marshall and the Supreme Court, 1936–1961.* London: Oxford University Press.

Tushnet, Mark. 1996. *The Warren Court in Historical and Political Perspective.* Charlottesville: University of Virginia Press.

Tushnet, Mark. 2005. *A Court Divided: The Rehnquist Court and the Future of Constitutional Law.* New York: W. W. Norton.

Tushnet, Mark. 2008. *Dissent: Great Opposing Opinions in Landmark Supreme Court Cases.* Boston: Beacon Press.

Urofsky, Melvin. 2001. *The Warren Court: Justices, Rulings, and Legacy.* Santa Barbara, CA: ABC-CLIO.

U.S. Courts.gov. 2020a. "About Federal Courts." https:// www.uscourts.gov/about-federal-courts. Accessed September 9, 2020.

U.S. Courts.gov. 2020b. "Gideon v. Wainwright." https://www.uscourts.gov/educationalresources

/educational-activities/facts-and-case-summary-gideon-v
.wainwright. Accessed September 13, 2020.

U.S. Courts.gov. 2020c. "Thurgood Marshall." https://www
.uscourts.gov/educational-resources/educational-activities
/justice-thurgood-marshall-profile-brown-v-board. Accessed
September 14, 2020.

U.S. Supreme Court.gov. 2020d. "Sandra Day O'Connor."
https://www.supremecourt.gov/visiting/sandradayoconnor
.aspx. Accessed September 9, 2020.

U.S. Supreme Court History.org. 2020. "Earl Warren."
https://supremecourthistory.org/history-of-the-court
-timeline-of-the-justices-earl-warren-1953-1969. Accessed
October 28, 2021.

U.S. Department of Justice. 2020. https://www.justice.gov.
Accessed September 9, 2020.

Vera.org. 2020. "Our Mission." https://www.vera.org/about.
Accessed September 12, 2020.

Vile, John, ed. 2003. *Great American Judges: An Encyclopedia.*
Santa Barbara, CA: ABC-CLIO.

Wainwright, Susan. 2019. *In Defense of Justice: The
Greatest Dissents of Ruth Bader Ginsburg.* Fairhope, AL:
Mockingbird Press.

Warren, Earl. 1977. *The Memoirs of Earl Warren.* Garden City,
NY: Doubleday.

White House.gov. 2020. "President Obama." https://www
.whitehouse.gov/about-the-white-house/presidents/barack
-obama. Accessed October 28, 2021.

White House.gov. 2020. "President William Howard Taft."
https://www.whitehouse.gov/about-the-white-house
/presidents/william-howard-taft. Accessed September 14,
2020.

Woods, Randall. 2006. *LBJ: Architect of American Ambition.*
New York: Free Press.

Young, Louise, and Ralph Young. 1989. *In the Public Interest: The League of Women Voters, 1920–1970*. Westport, CT: Greenwood Press.

Zentner, Scot, and Michael LeMay. 2020. *Party and Nation: Immigration and Regime Politics in American History*. Lanham, MD: Lexington Books.

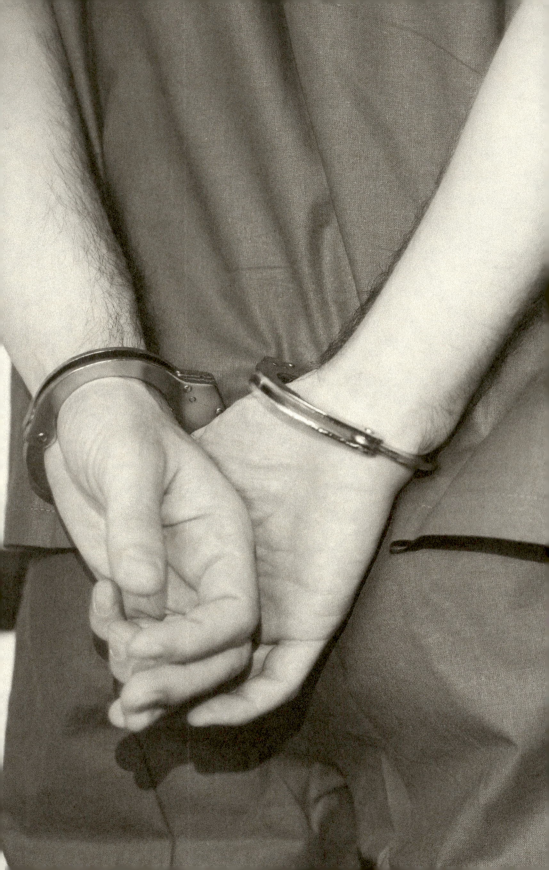

5 Data and Documents

Introduction

This chapter presents five figures (a map and four graphs) that offer the reader insight into the American judicial system. The figures section is followed by six tables of data that detail aspects of the judicial system at both the state and federal levels. The tables section is followed by excerpts from ten chronologically arranged documents spanning from 1789 to 2019. The documents synthesize the history of the American judicial system as evidenced in the Constitution, in laws enacted by the U.S. Congress, in landmark Supreme Court decisions, and in a model state government judicial nonpartisan selection plan.

Data

The figures section begins with a map that depicts the geographical boundaries for the ninety-four district courts of original jurisdiction, and the thirteen federal circuit courts of appeals. Figure 5.2 presents a flowchart for the organization of the New York state judicial system, one of the largest and more complex of the fifty state systems. Figure 5.3 details the Louisiana state court system, another complex state system. Figure 5.4 presents a line graph on the race and ethnicity of persons incarcerated, by the rate of federal imprisonment per 100,000 residents. Figure 5.5 depicts in comparative format the likelihood that a person born in 2001 will be imprisoned during their lifetime, depending on gender, race, and ethnicity.

Prisoner with handcuffs in a cell. The United States leads the world in incarceration as a percentage of its total population. (Sandra Dragojlovic /Dreamstime.com)

Figure 5.1 Map of the Geographic Boundaries for U.S. District Courts and Circuit Courts of Appeals

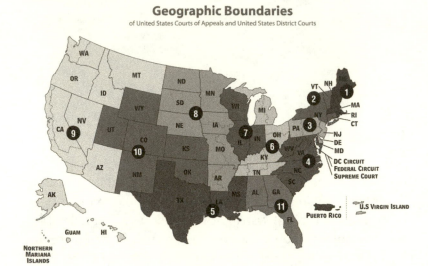

Source: https://www.uscourts.gov/sites/default/files/u.s._federal_courts_circuit_map-1.pdf.

Figure 5.2 New York State Judicial System Flowchart

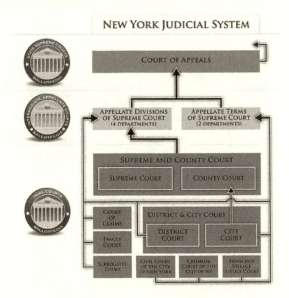

Source: https://nycourts.gov/courts/structure.shtml.

Figure 5.3 Louisiana Courts Structure

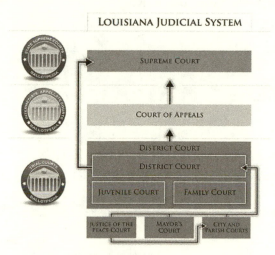

Source: https://cdn.ballotpedia.org/images/9/94/Louisiana_State_Court_Flow
_Chart.png.

**Figure 5.4 Line Graph of the Combined State and Federal Imprisonment
Rates per 100,000 Residents, by Race and Ethnicity, 2008–2018**

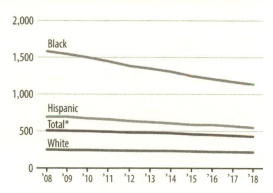

Note: Rates are based on prisoners sentenced to serve more than one year in
state or federal prison. See Table 5 for rates from 2008 to 2018. *Includes all
races, including those not shown separately in the figure.

Source: Bureau of Justice Statistics, National Prisoner Statistics, 2008–2018.

Figure 5.5 Lifetime Likelihood of Imprisonment for Persons Born in 2001; White, Black, Latinx; Men and Women

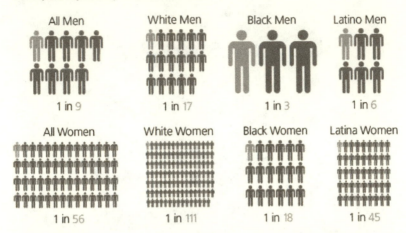

| All Men | White Men | Black Men | Latino Men |
| 1 in 9 | 1 in 17 | 1 in 3 | 1 in 6 |

| All Women | White Women | Black Women | Latina Women |
| 1 in 56 | 1 in 111 | 1 in 18 | 1 in 45 |

Source: The Sentencing Project, figure created from Bonczar, T. 2003. *Prevalence of Imprisonment in the U.S. Population, 1974–2001*. https://bjs.ojp.gov/content/pub/pdf/piusp01.pdf

Table 5.1. Year States Were Admitted to the Union, by Year Admitted

Table 5.1 lists, in alphabetical order, the fifty states and the year in which they were admitted to the United States of America, which is also the year in which each state established its initial state judicial court system. The earlier the year a state joined the union, the more likely it is to have later amended the structure of its court system, especially with regard to how judges are selected for the various levels of state and local courts.

Table 5.1

State	Admitted
ALABAMA	1819
ALASKA	1959
ARIZONA	1912
ARKANSAS	1836
CALIFORNIA	1850
COLORADO	1876

Table 5.1   (*continued*)

State	Admitted
CONNECTICUT	1788
DELAWARE	1787
FLORIDA	1845
GEORGIA	1788
HAWAII	1959
IDAHO	1890
ILLINOIS	1818
INDIANA	1816
IOWA	1846
KANSAS	1861
KENTUCKY	1792
LOUISIANA	1812
MAINE	1820
MARYLAND	1788
MASSACHUSETTS	1788
VERMONT	1790
MICHIGAN	1837
MINNESOTA	1858
MISSISSIPPI	1817
MISSOURI	1821
MONTANA	1889
NEBRASKA	1867
NEVADA	1864
NEW HAMPSHIRE	1788
NEW JERSEY	1787
NEW MEXICO	1912
NEW YORK	1788
NORTH CAROLINA	1789
NORTH DAKOTA	1889
WASHINGTON	1889

(*continued*)

Table 5.1   *(continued)*

State	Admitted
OHIO	1803
OKLAHOMA	1907
OREGON	1859
PENNSYLVANIA	1787
RHODE ISLAND	1790
SOUTH CAROLINA	1788
SOUTH DAKOTA	1889
TENNESSEE	1796
TEXAS	1845
UTAH	1896
VIRGINIA	1788
WEST VIRGINIA	1863
WISCONSIN	1848
WYOMING	1890

Source: https://www.unitedstatesnow.org/when-were-individual-states-admitted-to-the-us.htm

Table 5.2. Number of States Using Assorted Methods of Judicial Selection

Table 5.2 presents the number of states using assorted methods for selecting their judges to serve on statewide or local courts by level of state court.

Table 5.2

Type of Method Used	Supreme Court	Trial Courts, General	Trial Courts, Limited
Partisan election	9	8	14
Partisan, then retention	1	4	0
Nonpartisan election	13	17	12
Nomination by governor (no commission)	2	2	2

Table 5.2 *(continued)*

Type of Method Used	Supreme Court	Trial Courts, General	Trial Courts, Limited
Nomination by governor, with commission/ retention	15	10	3
Selection by legislature	4	3	1
Selection by judges/higher court	0	0	2
Other/Variations methods	8	8	15

Source: Table by author. Data from National Center for State Courts. https://judicialselection.us/judicial_selection/methods/selection_of_judges.cfm. Accessed September 7, 2020.

Table 5.3. Federal Judges Impeached, 1804–2010

Table 5.3 details the federal judges who were impeached during the years 1804 to 2010, including the court on which they served and the results of the impeachment process: whether they were acquitted in their U.S. Senate trial, resigned before a Senate trial, or were tried in the Senate, found guilty, and removed from the bench.

Table 5.3

Name of Justice	Federal Court Served On	Result of Impeachment
Pickering, John	District Court for New Hampshire	Convicted, removed 1804
Chase, Samuel	Associate Justice, Supreme Court	Acquitted, 1805
Peck, James	District Court for Missouri	Acquitted, 1831
Humphreys, West H.	District Court, Tennessee	Convicted, removed 1862
Delahay, Mark W.	District Court for Kansas	Resigned before trial, 1873
Swayne, Charles	District for Northern Florida	Acquitted, 1905

(continued)

Table 5.3   *(continued)*

Name of Justice	Federal Court Served On	Result of Impeachment
Archbald, Robert W.	U.S. Court of Appeals, Third Circuit	Convicted, removed, 1913
English, George W.	District Court, Eastern Illinois	Resigned, 1926
Louderback, Harold	District Court, Northern California	Acquitted, 1933
Ritter, Halsted L.	District Court, Southern Florida	Convicted, removed 1936
Claiborne, Harry E.	District Court for Nevada	Convicted, removed 1986
Hastings, Alice L.	District Court, Southern Florida	Convicted, removed 1989
Nixon, Walter L.	District Court for Southern Mississippi	Convicted, removed 1989
Kent, Samuel	District Court for Southern Texas	Dismissed by Senate
Porteous, G. Thomas	District Court for Eastern Louisiana	Convicted, removed 2010

Source: Table by author. Data from https://www.fjc.gov/history/judges/impeachment-federal-judges. Accessed September 27, 2020.

Table 5.4. Federal Judicial Nominees by Rate Not Qualified by ABA, 1989 to 2019

Table 5.4 lists the judicial nominees to the federal bench who were assessed as "not qualified" by the American Bar Association's rating system, the federal court for which they were nominated, the president who nominated them, and whether they were nonetheless confirmed by the U.S. Senate or withdrew their names from the nomination process. As shown in the data, the majority of judges nominated to the federal bench were confirmed despite the "not qualified" rating by the ABA. It illustrates that political party affiliation considerations weigh more heavily in the appointment process than does the rating for professional qualification to serve on the federal bench by the ABA.

Table 5.4

Name	Court	President	Result of Process
Williams, Alexander Jr.	District-Maryland	Clinton	Confirmed, 1993
Greer, Bruce	Southern District, Florida	Clinton	Withdrawn
Hamilton, David	Southern District, Indiana	Clinton	Confirmed, 1994
Katz, David	Northern District, Ohio	Clinton	Confirmed, 1994
Ryan, Daniel Patrick	Eastern District, Michigan	G. W. Bush	Withdrawn
Bunning, David	Eastern District, Kentucky	G. W. Bush	Confirmed, 2002
Irizarry, Dora	Eastern District, New York	G. W. Bush	Confirmed, 2004
Rohlfing, Frederick	District of Hawaii	G. W. Bush	Withdrawn
Van Tatenhove, Gregory	Eastern District, Kentucky	G. W. Bush	Confirmed, 2005
Wallace, Michael B.	Fifth Circuit Appeals	G. W. Bush	Withdrawn
Benitez, Roger	Southern District, California	G. W. Bush	Confirmed, 2004
Bryant, Vanessa	District of Connecticut	G. W. Bush	Confirmed, 2007
Talley, Brett	Middle District, Alabama	Trump	Withdrawn
Goodwin, Charles B.	Western District, Oklahoma	Trump	Confirmed, 2018
Teeter, Holly L.	District of Kansas	Trump	Confirmed, 2018
O'Connor, John	N.E.W. District, Oklahoma	Trump	Withdrawn
Kobes, Jonathan	Eighth Circuit Ct. of Appeals	Trump	Confirmed, 2018
Walker, Justin	Western Kentucky	Trump	Confirmed, 2019
Grasz, Steven	Eighth Circuit Ct. of Appeals	Trump	Confirmed, 2017
Van Dyke, Lawrence	Ninth Circuit Ct. of Appeals	Trump	Confirmed, 2019
Pityk, Sarah	Eastern District, Missouri	Trump	Confirmed, 2019

Source: Table by Author. Data from https://ballotpedia.org/ABA_ratings_during_Trump-administration. Accessed September 3, 2020.

Table 5.5. Chief Justices of the U.S. Supreme Court

Table 5.5 lists the chief justices of the United States Supreme Court, the years they served in that office, and the name of the U.S. president who appointed them as chief justice. The nominating president who selected the most chief justices of the U.S. Supreme Court was President George Washington, who during the eight years of his two terms was able to nominate and see confirmed three of his selections as chief justice.

Table 5.5

Name of Chief Justice	Years Served	Appointed by President
Jay, John	1789–1795	George Washington
Rutledge, John	1795–1796	George Washington
Ellsworth, Oliver	1796–1800	George Washington
Marshall, John	1801–1835	John Adams
Taney, Roger B.	1836–1864	Andrew Jackson
Chase, Salmon	1864–1873	Abraham Lincoln
Waite, Morrison	1874–1888	Ulysses Grant
Fuller, Melville	1888–1910	Grover Cleveland
White, Edward	1910–1921	William H. Taft
Taft, William Howard	1921–1930	Warren G. Harding
Hughes, Charles Evans	1930–1941	Herbert Hoover
Stone, Harlan Fiske	1941–1946	Franklin D. Roosevelt
Vinson, Fred Moore	1946–1953	Harry S. Truman
Warren, Earl	1953–1969	Dwight D. Eisenhower
Burger, Warren Earl	1969–1986	Richard M. Nixon
Rehnquist, William H.	1986–2005	Ronald Reagan
Roberts, John G., Jr.	2005–	George W. Bush

Source: Table by author. Data from https://www.supremecourt.gov/about/members
_text.aspx. Accessed August 4, 2020.

Table 5.6. Methods of Judicial Selection in State Court Systems

Table 5.6 lists the states that use a particular method to select their judges for a particular level of bench. It shows the increasing popularity of using some variation of the "Missouri Plan," in which judges are selected from a list provided by a judicial nomination commission followed by a retention election by voters. Most retention elections are held after a year or two of service on the bench before the judge runs (unopposed) in the retention election. When voters opt not to retain a judge, no opponent is immediately selected. In the case of a failed vote of retention, the appointment process starts all over with a new judicial nominee from the list submitted to the governor or state legislature, who is then appointed, and after a year or two, a new retention election is held.

Table 5.6

Partisan Election for All or Most Judges—Eight States:

Alabama, Arkansas, Connecticut, Illinois, Louisiana, Pennsylvania, Tennessee, Texas

Nonpartisan Elections for All Judges—Thirteen States:

Idaho, Kentucky, Michigan, Minnesota, Mississippi, Montana, Nevada, North Carolina, North Dakota, Ohio, Oklahoma, Washington, West Virginia

Mixed Merit System of Appointments (Modified Missouri Plan)—Twenty-One States:

Twelve States and D.C. Use Gubernatorial or Legislature Appointment and Nominating Commission Followed by a Retention Election:

Alaska, Colorado, Connecticut, Delaware, D.C., Hawaii, Iowa, Maryland, Nebraska, Rhode Island, Vermont, Wyoming

Nine States Use Commission for Some Judges (Appellate, Supreme Court):

Arizona, Florida, Indiana, Kansas, Missouri, New York, Oklahoma, South Dakota, Tennessee

Eight States Use Commission and Gubernatorial Appointment Only for Vacancies between Elections:

Alabama, Idaho, Kentucky, Montana, Nevada, New Mexico, North Dakota, West Virginia

Source: Table by author. Data from Denver University report, https://iaals .du.edu/judicial-nominating-commission-states. 2021. Accessed July 18, 2021.

Documents

Document 5.1: Article III, the Constitution of the United States

Document 5.1 presents Article III of the U.S. Constitution. The article, in its three sections, establishes the judicial system of the federal level of government. It authorizes the U.S. Congress to further establish by law lower-level federal courts, specifies some of the original jurisdiction of the Supreme Court, and authorizes the Congress to enact laws to further define the jurisdiction of the various "lower" courts of the federal system. The document retains the spelling, use of capitalization, and the punctuation used in the Constitution.

Section 1. The judicial Power of the United States shall be vested in one supreme Court, and in such inferior Courts as the Congress may from time to time ordain and establish. The Judges both of the supreme and inferior Courts, shall hold their Offices during good Behavior, and shall, at stated Times, receive for their Services a Compensation, which shall not be diminished during their Continuance in Office.

Section 2. The judicial Power shall extend to all Cases in Law and Equity, arising under this Constitution, the Laws of the United States, and Treaties made, or which shall be made, under their Authority;—to all Cases, affecting Ambassadors, other public Ministers and Consuls;—to all Cases of admiralty and maritime jurisdiction;—to Controversies in which the United States shall be a Party;—to Controversies between two or more States;—between a State and Citizens of another State;—between Citizens of different States;—between Citizens of the same State claiming Lands under Grants of different States; and between a State, or the Citizens thereof, and foreign States, Citizens, or Subjects.

In all Cases affecting Ambassadors, other public Ministers and Consuls, and those in which a State shall be Party, the supreme Court shall have original Jurisdiction. In all the other

Cases before mentioned, the supreme Court shall have appellate Jurisdiction, both as to Law and Fact, with such Exceptions, and under such Regulations as the Congress shall make.

The Trial of all Crimes, except in Cases of Impeachment, shall be by Jury, and such Trial shall be held in the State where the said Crimes shall have been committed; but when not committed within any State, the Trial shall be at such Place or Places as the Congress may by Law have directed.

Section 3. Treason against the United States, shall consist only in levying War against them, or in adhering to their Enemies, giving them Aid and Comfort. No Person shall be convicted of Treason unless on the Testimony of two Witnesses to the same overt Act, or on Confession in open Court.

The Congress shall have the power to declare the Punishment of Treason, but no Attainder of Treason shall work Corruption of Blood, or Forfeiture except during the Life of the Person attainted.

Source: U.S. Constitution, art. 3, sec. 1–3.

Document 5.2: Excerpts from the Judiciary Act of 1789

Document 5.2 presents excerpts from the Judiciary Act of 1789, wherein the U.S. Congress established the judicial courts. This document presents ten sections, in full or in part, of the act's thirty-five total sections. They detail the basic structure of the district and appellate courts as originally established. Numerous subsequent laws added more courts, as the nation expanded its territory, created special jurisdiction courts, modified the number of justices on the Supreme Court or lower courts, and modified their jurisdiction.

An Act to Establish the Judicial Courts of the United States

Section 1: *Be it enacted by the Senate and the House of Representatives of the United States of America in Congress assembled.* That the supreme court of the United States shall consist of a chief justice and five associate justices, any four of whom shall be a quorum, and shall hold annually at the seat of government two sessions, the one commencing the first Monday of February, and the other the first Monday of August. That the associate justices shall have precedence according to the date of their commission, or when the commissions of two or more of them bear date on the same day, according to their respective ages.

Sec. 2. *And be it further enacted,* That the United States shall be, and they are hereby divided into thirteen districts, to be limited and called as follows, to wit: one to consist of that part of the State of Massachusetts which lies easterly of the State of New Hampshire, and to be called Maine District; one to consist of the State of New Hampshire, and to be called the New Hampshire District; one to consist of the remaining part of the State of Massachusetts, and to be called Massachusetts district; one to consist of the State of Connecticut, and to be called Connecticut District; one to consist of the State of New York, and to be called the New York District; one to consist of the State of New Jersey, and to be called New Jersey District; one to consist of the State of Pennsylvania, and to be called Pennsylvania District; one to consist of the State of Delaware, and to be called Delaware District; one to consist of the State of Maryland, and to be called Maryland District; one to consist of the State of Virginia, except that part called the District of Kentucky, and to be called Virginia District; one to consist of the remaining part of the State of Virginia, and to be called Kentucky District; one to consist of the State of South Carolina, and to be called South Carolina District; and one to consist of the State of Georgia, and to be called Georgia District.

Sec. 3. *And be it further enacted,* That they be a court called a District Court, in each of the afore mentioned districts, to consist of one judge, who shall reside in the district for which he is appointed, and shall be called a District Judge, and shall hold annually four sessions, the first of which to commence as follows, to wit: in the districts of New York and New Jersey on the first, in the district of Pennsylvania on the second, in the district of Connecticut on the third, and in the district of Delaware on the fourth, Tuesdays of November next; in the districts of Massachusetts, of Maine, and of Maryland, on the first, in the district of Georgia on the second, and in the districts of New Hampshire, of Virginia, and of Kentucky, on the third Tuesday of December next; and that the District Judge shall have the power to hold special courts at his discretion. That the stated District Court shall be held at the places following, to wit: in the district of Maine, at Portland and Pownalsborough in the district of New Hampshire, at Exeter and Portsmouth alternately, beginning at the first; in the district of Massachusetts, at Boston and Salem alternately, beginning at the first; in the district of Connecticut, alternately at Hartford and New Haven, beginning at the first; in the district of New York, at New York; in the district of New Jersey, alternately at New Brunswick and Burlington, beginning at the first; in the district of Pennsylvania, at Philadelphia and York Town alternately, beginning at the first; in the district of Delaware, alternately at Newcastle and Dover, beginning at the first; in the district of Maryland, alternately at Baltimore and Easton, beginning at the first; in the district of Virginia, alternately at Richmond and Williamsburgh, beginning at the first; in the district of Kentucky, at Harrodsburgh; in the district of South Carolina, at Charleston; and in the district of Georgia, alternately at Savannah and Augusta, beginning at the first; and that the special court shall be held at the same place in each district as the stated courts, or in districts that have two, at either of them, in the discretion of the judge, or at such place in the district, as the nature of the business and his discretion shall direct. And that in the districts that have but one place for holding the District Court, the records thereof shall be kept at that place, and in districts that have two, at that place in each district which the judge shall appoint. . . .

Sec. 7. *And be it [further] enacted.* That the Supreme Court, and the district courts shall have power to appoint clerks for their respective courts, and that the clerk for each district shall be clerk also of the circuit court in such district, and each of the said clerks shall, before he enters upon the execution of his office, take the following oath or affirmation, to wit: "I, A.B., being appointed clerk of, do solemnly swear, or affirm, that I will truly and faithfully enter and record at the orders, decrees, judgments and proceedings of the said court, and that I will faithfully and impartially discharge and perform all the duties of my said office, according to the best of my abilities and understanding. So help me God." Which words, so help me God, shall be omitted, in all cases, where an affirmation is admitted instead of an oath, and the said clerks shall also severally give bond, with sufficient sureties, (to be approved of by the Supreme and district courts respectively) to the United States, in the sum of two thousand dollars, faithfully to discharge the duties of his office, and seasonably to record the decrees, judgments and determinations of the court of which he is clerk. . . .

Sec. 9. *And be it further enacted.* That the district courts shall have, exclusively of the courts of the several States, cognizance of all crimes and offenses that shall be cognizable under the authority of the United States, committed within their respective districts, or upon the high seas, where no other punishment than whipping, not exceeding thirty stripes, a fine not exceeding one hundred dollars, or a term of imprisonment not exceeding six months, is to be inflicted; and shall also have exclusive original cognizance of all civil causes of admiralty and maritime jurisdiction, including all seizures under laws of impost, navigation or trade of the United States, where the seizures are made, on waters which are navigable from the sea by vessels of ten or more tons burden, within their respective districts as well as upon the high seas; saving to suitors, in all cases, the right of a common law remedy, where the common law is competent to give it, and shall also have exclusive cognizance of all seizures on land, or other waters than as aforesaid, made, and of all suits for penalties and forfeitures incurred, under the laws of the United States. And shall also have cognizance, concurrent with the courts of the several States, or the circuit courts, as the cause may be, of all causes where an alien sues for a tort only in violation of the laws of nations or a treaty of the United States. And shall also have cognizance, concurrent as last mentioned, of all suits at common law where the United States sue, and the matter in dispute amounts, exclusive of costs, to the sum or value of one hundred dollars. And shall also have jurisdiction exclusively of the courts of the several States, of all suits against consuls or vice-consuls, except for offences above the description aforesaid. And the trial of issues in fact, in the district courts, in all causes except civil causes of admiralty and maritime jurisdiction, shall be by jury. . . .

Sec. 11. *And be it further enacted.* That the circuit courts shall have original cognizance, concurrent with the courts of the several States, of all suits of a civil nature at common law or in equity, where the matter in dispute exceeds, exclusive of costs, the sum or value of five hundred dollars, and the United States are plaintiffs, or petitioners; or an alien is a party, or the suit is between a citizen of the State where the suit is brought, and a citizen of another State. And shall have exclusive cognizance of all crimes and offences cognizable under the authority of the United States, except where this Act otherwise provides, or the laws to the United States shall otherwise direct, and concurrent jurisdiction with the district courts of the crimes and offenses cognizable therein. But no person shall be arrested in one district for trial in another, in any civil action before a circuit or district court. And no civil suit shall be brought before either of said courts against an inhabitant of the United States by any original process in any other district than that whereof he is an inhabitant, or in which he shall be found at the time of serving the writ, nor shall any district or circuit court have cognizance of any suit to recover the contents of any promissory note or other shoes in action in favour of an assignee, unless a suit might have been prosecuted in such court to recover the said contents if not assignment had been made, except in cases of foreign bills of exchange. And the circuit courts shall also have appellate jurisdiction from the district courts under the regulations and restriction herein after provided. . . .

Sec. 13. *And be it further enacted*. That the Supreme Court shall have exclusive jurisdiction of all controversies of a civil nature, where a state is a party, except between a state and its citizens, and except also between a state and citizens of other states, or aliens, in which latter case it shall have original but not exclusive jurisdiction. And shall have exclusively all such jurisdiction of suits or proceedings against ambassadors, or other public ministers, or their domestics, or domestic servants, as a court of law can have or exercise consistently with the law of nations, and original but not exclusive jurisdiction of all suits brought by ambassadors, or other public ministers, or in which a consul or vice consul shall be a party. And the trial of issues in fact in the Supreme Court, in all actions at law against citizens of the United States, shall be by jury. The Supreme Court shall also have appellate jurisdiction from the circuit courts and courts of the several states, in the cases herein after specially provided for, and shall have power to issue with a writ of prohibition to the district courts, when proceeding as courts of admiralty and maritime jurisdiction, and writs of mandamus, in cases warranted by the principles and usage of law, to any courts appointed, or persons holding office, under the authority of the United States. . . .

Sec. 29. *And be it further enacted*. That in cases punishable with death, the trial shall be had in the county where the offense was committed, or where that cannot be done without great inconvenience, twelve petit jurors shall be summoned from thence. And jurors in all cases to serve in the courts of the United States shall be designated by lot or otherwise in each State respectively, according to the mode of forming juries therein now practiced, so far as the laws of the same shall render such designation practicable by the courts or marshals of the United States; and the jurors shall have the same qualifications as are requisite for jurors by the laws of the State of which they are citizens, to serve in the highest courts of law of such State, and shall be returned as there shall be occasion for them, from such parts of the district from time to time as the court shall direct, so as shall be most favourable to an impartial trial, and so as not to incur an unnecessary expense, or unduly to burden the citizens of any part of the district with such services. . . .

Sec. 34. *And be it further enacted.* That the laws of the several states, except where the constitution, treaties or statutes of the United States shall otherwise require or provide, shall be regarded as rules of decision in trials at common law in the courts of the United States in cases where they apply.

Sec. 35. *And be it further enacted.* That in all courts of the United States, the parties may plead and manage their own causes personally or by assistance of such counsel or attorney at law as by the rules of the said courts respectively shall be permitted to manage and conduct causes therein. And there shall be appointed in each district a meet person learned in the law to act as an attorney for the United States in such district, who shall be sworn or affirmed to the faithful execution of the office, whose duty it shall be to prosecute in such district all delinquents for crimes and offences, cognizable under the authority of the United States, and all civil actions in which the United States shall be concerned, except before the supreme court in the district in which court shall be holden. And he shall receive as compensation for his services such fees as shall be taxed therefor in the respective courts before which the suits or prosecution shall be. And there shall be appointed a meet person, learned in the law, to act as attorney-general for the United States, who shall be sworn or affirmed to a faithful execution of the office, whose duty it shall be to prosecute and conduct all suits in the Supreme Court in which the United States shall be concerned, and to give the advice and opinion upon questions of law when required by the President of the United States, or when requested by the heads of any of the departments, touching any matters that may concern their departments, and shall receive such compensation for his services as shall by law be provided.

Approved, September 24, 1789.

Source: *Judiciary Act of 1789, U.S. Statutes at Large* 1 (1789): 73.

Document 5.3: Excerpts from *Dred Scott v. Sandford* (1857)

Document 5.3 presents excerpts from the landmark case Dred Scott v. Sandford *(1857). In its ruling, the majority opinion written by Chief Justice Roger Taney, the Supreme Court held that the Bill of Rights limited congressional action in the territories. This decision, which essentially permitted slavery in the territories and in new states, infuriated abolitionists, opened new fronts in the escalating battle over slavery, and pushed the United States ever closer to civil war.*

The Territory being a part of the United States, the Government and the citizen both enter it under the authority of the Constitution, with their respective rights defined and marked out, and the Federal Government can exercise no power over his person or property, beyond what that instrument confers, nor lawfully deny any right which it has reserved. A reference to a few of the provisions of the Constitution will illustrate this proposition.

For example, no one, we presume, will contend that Congress can make any law in a Territory respecting the establishment of religion, or the free exercise thereof, or abridging the freedom of speech or of the press, or the right of the people of the Territory peaceably to assemble, and to petition the Government for redress of grievances.

Nor can Congress deny to the people the right to keep and bear arms, nor the right to trial by jury, nor compel any one to be a witness against himself in a criminal proceeding. These powers, and others, in relation to rights of persons, which it is not necessary herein to enumerate, are, in express and positive terms, denied to the General Government; and the rights of private property have been guarded with equal care. Thus, the rights of property are untied with the rights of person and placed on the same ground by the fifth amendment to the Constitution, which provides that no person shall be deprived of life, liberty, and property, without due process of law. And an act of Congress which deprives a citizen of the United States of his liberty or property, merely because he came himself or brought his property into a particular Territory of the United States, and who had committed no offence against the laws, could hardly be dignified with the name of due process of law . . . [Earlier in the opinion, in holding that blacks generally could not be U.S. citizens, the court said:]

It cannot be supposed that [the original thirteen States] intended to secure to [blacks] rights, and privileges, and rank, in the new political body throughout the Union, which every one of them denied within the limits of its own dominion. More especially, it cannot be believed that the large slaveholding States regarded them as included in the word citizens, would have consented to a Constitution which might compel them to receive them in that character from another State. For if they were so received, and entitled to the privileges and immunities of citizens, it would exempt them from the operation of the special laws and from the police regulations which they considered to be necessary for their own safety.

It would give to persons of the negro race, who were recognized as citizens in any one State of the Union, the right to enter every other State whenever they pleased, singly or in companies, without pass or passport, and without obstruction, to sojourn there as long as they pleased, to go where they pleased at every hour of the day or night without molestation, unless they committed some violation of law for which a white man could be punished; and it would give them the full liberty of speech in public and in private upon all subjects upon which its own citizens might speak; to hold public meetings upon political affairs, and to keep and carry arms wherever they went.

And all of this would be done in the face of the subject race of the same color, both free and slaves, and inevitably producing discontent and insubordination among them, and endangering the peace and safety of the State.

Source: *Dred Scott v. Sandford*, 60 U.S. 393 (1857).

Document 5.4: Judiciary Act of 1869

Document 5.4 presents, in full, the Judiciary Act of April 10, 1869, also known as the Circuit Judges Act of 1869. It reflected the increased business of the Supreme Court after the Civil War, and it amended the Judiciary Act of 1790 by changing the number of justices of the Supreme Court to nine, amending the nine existing circuits, and appointing a circuit judge for the new circuits. It specifies the location of the courts and salaries of the judges and clerks, and the jurisdiction of the courts, expanding the number to nine, and authorizing the president to appoint judges to fill any vacancies.

Be it enacted by the Senate and House of Representatives of the United States of America in Congress assembled. That the Supreme Court of the United States shall hereafter consist of the Chief Justice of the United States and eight associate justices, any six of whom shall constitute a quorum; and for the purposes of this act, there shall be appointed an additional associate justice of said court.

Sec. 2. *And be it further enacted.* That for each of the nine existing judicial circuits there shall be appointed a circuit judge, who shall reside in his circuit, and shall possess the same power and jurisdiction therein as the justices of the Supreme Court allotted to the circuit. The circuit courts in each circuit shall be held by the justice of the Supreme Court allotted to the circuit, or by the circuit judge of the circuit, or by the district judge of the district sitting alone, or by the justice of the Supreme Court and circuit judge sitting together, in which case the justice of the Supreme Court shall preside, or in the absence of either of them by the others, (who shall preside,) and the district judge. And such courts may be held at the same time in the different districts of the same circuits, and cases may be heard and tried by each of the judges holding any such court siting apart by the direction of the presiding justice or judge, who shall designate the business to be done by each. The circuit judges shall each receive an annual salary of five thousand dollars.

Sec. 3. *And be it further enacted.* That nothing in this act shall affect the powers of the justices of the Supreme Court as judges of the circuit court, except in the appointment of clerks of the circuit courts, who in each circuit shall be appointed by the circuit judge of that circuit, and the clerks of the district courts shall be appointed by the judges thereof respectively; *Provided,* That the present clerks of said courts shall continue in office till other appointments be made in their place, or they be otherwise removed.

Sec. 4. *And be it further enacted,* That it shall be the duty of the Chief Justice and of each justice of the Supreme Court to attend at least one term of the circuit court in each district of his circuit during every period of two years.

Sec. 5. *And be it further enacted,* That any judge of any court of the United States, who, having held his commission as such at least ten years, shall thereafter, during the residue of his natural life, receive the same salary which was by law payable to him at the time of his resignation.

Sec. 6. *And be it further enacted,* That this act shall take effect on the first Monday of December, eighteen hundred and sixty-nine.

Approved, April 10, 1869.

Source: *Judiciary Act of 1869, U.S. Statutes at Large* 16 (1869): 44.

Document 5.5: Excerpts from *Miller v. Texas* (1894)

Document 5.5 excerpts an 1894 Supreme Court decision, Miller v. Texas, *in which the Court stated that the doctrine of incorporation did not apply to Second Amendment gun ownership rights in the state of Texas, holding that the amendment only limits the federal government, not a state government. It was the first case in which the defendant brought the Fourteenth Amendment into play as well as his Second Amendment rights. Associate Justice Henry B. Brown wrote the majority opinion in the case.*

In his motion for a rehearing, however, the defendant claimed that the law of the state of Texas forbidding the carrying of weapons, and authorizing the arrest, without warrant, of any person violating such law, under which certain questions arose upon the trial of the case, was in conflict with the second and fourth amendments to the constitution of the United States, one of which provides that the right of the people to keep and bear arms shall not be infringed, and the other which protects the people against unreasonable search and seizure.

We have examined the record in vain, however, to find where the defendant was denied the benefit of any of these provisions, and, even if he were, it is well settled that the restrictions of these amendments operate only upon the federal power and have no reference whatever to proceedings in state courts. And if the fourteenth amendment limited the power of the states as to such rights, as pertaining to citizens of the United States, we think it was fatal to this claim that it was not set up in the trial court.

Source: *Miller v. Texas.* 153 U.S. 535 (1894).

Document 5.6: The Nonpartisan Court Plan (Missouri Plan)

Document 5.6 presents the 1940 Nonpartisan Court Plan, more commonly known as the Missouri Plan. It has served as a national model for the selection of judges and has been adopted in some fashion by more than thirty other states since it was first unveiled. The Missouri Plan came about in response to widespread public dissatisfaction with the increasing role of politics in judicial selection and judicial decision-making. By the 1930s, judges were seen as being plagued by outside influences due to the political aspects of the election process, and court dockets were congested due to the time judges spent campaigning. In November 1940, voters in Missouri amended the state constitution by adopting the "Nonpartisan Selection of Judges Court Plan," which had been placed on the ballot by initiative petition. Adoption of the initiative resulted from a public backlash against widespread abuses of the judicial system by "Boss Tom" Pendergast's political machine in Kansas City, and by the political control exhibited by ward bosses in St. Louis.

The nonpartisan plan provides for the selection of judges based on merit rather than on political affiliation. Initially, the nonpartisan plan applied to judges of the Supreme Court; the court of appeals; the circuit, criminal corrections, and probate courts of St. Louis County; and three years later, voters extended the plan to judges in Clay and Platte counties. These changes are reflected in the Missouri Constitution, as amended in 1976. The Kansas City Charter extends the nonpartisan selection plan to Kansas City municipal court judges, as well. Under the constitution, other judicial circuits may adopt the plan upon approval of a majority of voters in the circuit. Most recently, in November 2008, Greene County voted to extend the nonpartisan plan to its judges.

Nonpartisan Judicial Commissions under the Plan

Under the Missouri Nonpartisan Court Plan, a nonpartisan judicial commission reviews applications, interviews candidates, and selects a judicial panel. For the Supreme Court and Courts of Appeals, the Appellate Judicial Commission makes the selection. It is composed of three lawyers elected by the lawyers of the Missouri Bar (the organization of all lawyers licensed in this state), three citizens selected by the governor, and the chief justice who serves as chair. Each of the geographic districts of the Court of Appeals must be represented by one lawyer and one citizen member on the Appellate Judicial Commission. Each of the circuit courts in Clay, Greene, Jackson, Platte and St. Louis counties and St. Louis city has its own circuit judicial commission. These commissions are composed of the chief judge of the court of appeals district in which the circuit is located, plus two lawyers elected by the bar and two citizens selected by the governor. All of the lawyers and citizens must live within the circuit for which they serve the judicial commission.

Filling Judicial Vacancies under the Nonpartisan Court Plan

Regardless of the commission handling the applications, the constitutional process of filling a judicial vacancy is the same. With any vacancy, the appropriate commission reviews applications of lawyers who wish to join the court and interviews the applicants. It then submits the names of three qualified candidates—called the "panel" of candidates—to the Missouri governor. Normally, the governor will interview the three candidates and review their backgrounds before selecting one for the vacancy. If the governor does not appoint one of the three panelists within 60 days of submission, the commission selects one of the three panelists to fill the vacancy.

The People Retain a Say over Nonpartisan Court Judges

The nonpartisan plan also gives the voters a chance to have a say in the retention of judges selected under the plan. Once a judge has served in office for at least one year, that judge must stand for a retention election at the next general election. The judge's name is placed on a separate judicial ballot, without party designation, and voters decide whether to retain the judge based on his or her judicial record. A judge must receive a majority of votes to be retained for a full term of office. The purpose of this vote is to provide another accountability mechanism of the nonpartisan plan to ensure quality judges. If a judge retires or resigns during or at the end of his or her term, a vacancy is created, which will be filled under the Missouri Nonpartisan Court Plan as described above. . . . The success of the plan in selecting qualified judges is evident from the fact that, since its adoption, the public has not voted any appellate judge out of office, and only four trial judges have been voted out of office. . . .

Source: "The Nonpartisan Court Plan." https://www.courts .mo.gov/page.jsp?od=297. Accessed September 18, 2020.

Document 5.7: Excerpts from the Legal Services Corporation Act of 1974

Document 5.7 excerpts the 1974 federal act (42 U.S. C. 2996) that amended the Economic Opportunity Act of 1964. Specifically, the Legal Services Corporation Act provided for the transfer of the legal services program of the Office of Economic Opportunity to a semi-independent government corporation, the Legal Services Corporation. It is designed to provide equal access to legal assistance to the U.S. system of justice for those otherwise unable to afford adequate legal counsel in noncriminal proceedings. An Act to amend the Economic Opportunity Act of 1964 to provide for the transfer of the legal services program of the Office of Economic Opportunity to a Legal Services Corporation, and for other purposes.

Section 1. *Be it enacted by the Senate and the House of Representatives of the United States of America in Congress assembled,* That this Act may be cited as the Legal Services Corporation Act of 1974.

Sec. 2. The Economic Opportunity Act of 1964 is amended by adding at the end thereof the following new title:

TITLE X. LEGAL SERVICES CORPORATION ACT

STATEMENT OF FINDINGS AND DECLARATION OF PURPOSE

Sec. 1001. The Congress finds and declares that—

(1) there is a need to provide equal access to the system of justice in our Nation for individuals who seek redress of grievances;

(2) there is a need to provide high quality legal assistance to those who would be otherwise unable to afford adequate legal counsel and to continue the present vital legal services program;

(3) providing legal assistance to those who face an economic barrier to adequate counsel will serve best the ends of justice and assist in improving opportunities for low-income persons consistent with the purposes of this Act;

(4) for many of our citizens, the availability of legal services has reaffirmed faith in our government and laws;

(5) to preserve its strength, the legal services program must be kept free from the influence of or use by it of political pressure; and

(6) attorneys providing legal assistance must have full freedom to protect the best interest of their clients in keeping with the Code of Professional Responsibility, the Cannons of Ethics, and the high standards of the legal profession . . .

ESTABLISHMENT OF CORPORATION

Sec. 1003. (a). There is established in the District of Columbia a private non-membership nonprofit corporation, which shall be known as the Legal Services Corporation, for the purpose of providing financial support for legal assistance in noncriminal proceedings or matters to persons financially unable to afford legal assistance.

(b) The Corporation shall maintain its principal office in the District of Columbia and shall maintain therein a designated agent to accept service of process for the Corporation. . . .

GOVERNING BODY

Sec. 1004. (a). The Corporation shall have a Board of Directors consisting of eleven voting members appointed by the President, by and with the advice and consent of the Senate, no more than six of whom shall be of the same political party. A majority of members shall be members of the bar of the highest court of any State, and none shall be a full-time employee of the United States. . . .

(b) The term of office of each member of the Board shall be three years, except that five of the members first appointed, as designated by the President at the time of appointment, shall serve for a term of two years. Each member of the Board shall continue to serve until the successor to such member has been appointed and qualified. . . .

(c) The members of the Board shall not, by reason of such membership, be deemed officers or employees of the United States.

(d) The President shall select from among the voting members of the Board a chairman, who shall serve for a term of three years. Thereafter the Board shall annually elect a chairman from among its voting members.

(e) A member of the Board may be removed by a vote of seven members for malfeasance in office or for persistent neglect of or inability to discharge duties, or for offenses involving moral turpitude, and for no other cause. . . .

(h) The Board shall meet at least four times during each calendar year.

Sec. 1005. (a). The Board shall appoint the president of the Corporation, who shall be a member of the bar of the highest court of a State and shall be a non-voting ex-officio member of the Board, and such other officers as the Board determines are necessary. No officer of the Corporation may receive any salary or other compensation for services from any source other than the Corporation during his period of employment by the Corporation, except as authorized by the Board. All officers shall serve at the pleasure of the Board.

(2) No political test or political qualifications shall be used in selecting, appointing, promoting, or taking any other personnel action with respect to any officer, agent, or employee of the Corporation or of any recipient, or in selecting or monitoring any grantee, contractor, or person or entity receiving financial assistance under this title . . .

POWERS, DUTIES, AND LIMITATIONS

Sec. 1006 (a). To the extent consistent with the provisions of this title, the Corporation shall exercise the powers conferred upon a nonprofit corporation by the District of Columbia Nonprofit Corporation Act (except for section 1005(o) of title 29 of the District of Columbia Code). In addition, the Corporation is authorized—

(1)(A) to provide financial assistance to qualified programs furnishing legal assistance to eligible clients, and to make grants to and contracts with—

(i)   individuals, partnerships, firms, corporations, and non-profit organizations, and

(ii) State and local governments (only upon application by an appropriate State or local agency or institution and upon a special determination by the Board that the arrangements to be made by such an agency or institution will provide services which will not be provided adequately through nongovernmental arrangements), for the purpose of providing legal assistance to eligible clients under this title . . .

Source: *The Legal Services Corporation Act as Amended*, U.S. Code 42 (1974) § 2996 et seq.

Document 5.8: Excerpts from *United States v. Verdugo-Urquidez* (1990)

Document 5.8 excerpts a ruling of the U.S. Supreme Court in United States v. Verdugo-Urquidez *(1990). The question in the case was whether the Fourth Amendment protected foreign citizens on foreign soil from unreasonable searches or applied only to U.S. soil or U.S. residents. The 6-3 majority opinion in the case was written by Chief Justice William Rehnquist, joined by justices White, O'Connor, Scalia, Kennedy, and Stevens. The dissents were by justices Brennan, Marshall, and Blackmun. The majority opinion illustrates the impact of the conservative ideological perspective of a majority of justices under Chief Justice Rehnquist. Since it held that Fourth Amendment protections applied only to citizens, not to persons resident in a state, it set a precedent impacting search and seizure doctrine on states thereafter, and effectively limited Fourth Amendment protections to American citizens.*

For the purposes of this case, therefore, if there were a constitutional violation, it occurred solely in Mexico. . . . The Fourth Amendment provides: "The right of the people to be secure in their persons, houses, papers, and effects, against unreasonable searches and seizures, shall not be violated, and no Warrants shall issue, but upon probable cause, supported by Oath or affirmation, and particularly describing the place to be searched, and the persons or things to be seized." That text, by contrast with the Fifth and Sixth Amendments, extends to reach only to "the people."

Contrary to the suggestion of amici curiae that the framers used this phrase "simply to avoid [an] awkward rhetorical redundancy," "the people" seems to have been a term of art employed in select parts of the Constitution. The Preamble declares that the Constitution is ordained and established by "the People of the United States." The Second Amendment protects "the right of the people to keep and bear Arms," and the Ninth and Tenth Amendments provide that certain rights and powers are retained by and reserved to "the people." See also U.S. Constitution Amendment 1 ("Congress shall make no law . . . abridging . . . the right of the people peaceably to assemble"); Art I, paragraph 2, cl.1 ("The House of Representatives shall be composed of Members chosen every second year by the People of the several States.").

While this textual exegesis is by no means conclusive, it suggests that "the people" protected by the Fourth Amendment, and by the First and Second Amendments, and to whom rights and powers are reserved in the Ninth and Tenth Amendments, refers to a class of persons who are part of a national community or who have otherwise developed sufficient connection with this country to be considered part of that community.

Source: *United States v. Verdugo-Urquidez*, 494 U.S. 259 (1990).

Document 5.9: Excerpts from *Arizona Christian School Tuition Organization v. Winn et al.* (2011)

Tax law and the use by a state government aiding a private Christian school by means of a tax credit were at issue in an Arizona case brought to the Supreme Court based on a challenge on grounds that it violated the establishment clause of the First Amendment. Document 5.9 presents a summary of the case of Arizona Christian School Tuition Organization v. Winn, et al. This case is a good illustration of the Supreme Court supervising, by judicial review, a state law and a federal court of appeals decision but doing so on the narrowest "technical" basis, in this case whether the plaintiff had the standing to sue. It also illustrates the Supreme Court's use of precedent set in an earlier decision to guide the decision in this case. The Supreme Court's 5-4 decision reversed the ruling of the court of appeals. The Supreme Court ruled that the plaintiffs lacked standing to bring suit based on the difference between a law that granted a tax credit as opposed to a law involving a tax expenditure.

Respondents, Arizona taxpayers, sued petitioner, Director of the State Department of Revenue, challenging Arizona Revised Statute Ann. 43-1089, on Establishment grounds. The Arizona law gives tax credits for contributions to provide scholarships to students attending private schools, including religious schools. Petitioner, Arizona Christian School Tuition Organization and others later intervened. The District Court dismissed the suit for failure to stake a claim (having standing to sue). Reversing, the Ninth Circuit Court held that the respondents had standing as taxpayers under *Flast v. Cohen (392 U.S. 83)* and had stated an Establishment Clause claim.

Held:

(1) Because respondents challenge a tax credit as opposed to a government expenditure, they lack Article III standing under *Flast v. Cohen.* . . . Article III vests the Federal judiciary the "Power" to resolve "Cases" and

"Controversies." To obtain a ruling on the merits in federal court, a plaintiff must assert more than just the "generalized interest of all citizens in constitutional governance". . . . Instead, the plaintiff must establish standing, which required "an injury in fact," "a causal connection between the injury and the conduct complained of," and a conclusion that it is "likely," as opposed to merely "speculative," that the injury will be "redressed by a favorable decision."

(b) In general, the mere fact that someone is a taxpayer doesn't provide standing to seek relief in a federal court.

(c) Respondents' suit does not fall within the narrow exception to the rule against taxpayer standing established in *Flast v. Cohen*. . . . To have standing under Flast, taxpayers must show (1) a "logical link" between the plaintiff's taxpayer status and "the type of legislative enactment attacked," and (2) "a nexus" between such taxpayer status and the "precise nature of the constitutional infringement alleged" . . .

(d) Respondents' contrary position—the Arizonians benefit from the tax credit in effect are paying their state income tax to STOs—assumes that all income is government property, even if it has not come into the tax collector's hands. That premise has no basis in standing jurisprudence.

562 F.3d 1002, reversed.

Justice Anthony Kennedy delivered the opinion of the Court, in which justices Roberts, Scalia, Thomas, and Alito joined. Justice Elena Kagan filed a dissenting opinion, in which justices Ginsburg, Breyer, and Sotomayor joined.

Source: *Arizona Christian School Tuition Organization v. Winn*, 563 U.S. 125 (2011).

Document 5.10: Description of the Judicial Conduct and Disability Act of 1980, Amended March 12, 2019

Because federal judges are appointed for life, and the process for removing a judge through impeachment is complex, difficult, and rather rarely used successfully, Congress enacted a law in 1980 that provides for the removal of a judge for misconduct or by reason of a disability short of the impeachment process. Document 5.10 provides an official court description of the Judicial Conduct and Disability Act of 1980, as amended in March 2019. As noted in the document, the act allows anyone to file a complaint alleging a federal judge has committed misconduct or has a disability.

The Judicial Conduct and Disability Act of 1980 (28 U.S.C. 351) establishes a process by which any person can file a complaint alleging a federal judge has engaged in "conduct prejudicial to the effective and expeditious administration of the business of the courts," or has become, by reason of mental or physical disability, "unable to discharge the duties" of the judicial office. The Rules for Judicial Conduct and Judicial Disability Proceedings, as amended on March 12, 2019, provide mandatory and nationally uniform provisions governing the substantive and procedural aspects of misconduct and disability proceedings under the Judicial Conduct and Disability Act. The judicial conduct and disability review process cannot be used to challenge the correctness of a judge's decision in a case. A judicial decision that is unfavorable to a litigant does not alone establish misconduct or disability.

Source: United States Courts.gov at: https://www.uscourts .gov/judges-judgeships/judicial-conduct-and-disability. Accessed September 17, 2020.

Introduction

This chapter lists and briefly annotates major sources of information that the reader is encouraged to consult for further research and study on this topic. It begins with print resources, first citing and annotating a selection of scholarly books related to the U.S. court system and American jurisprudence, then listing major scholarly journals that publish original research articles and book reviews on America's courts and legal system. It also provides an extensive rundown of noteworthy online resources that the reader is encouraged to consult. The chapter concludes with an annotated descriptions of two feature-length documentary films.

Print Resources

Books

Ackerman, Bruce, ed. 2002. *Bush v. Gore: The Question of Legitimacy.* New Haven, CT: Yale University Press.

> Ackerman's book brings together a collection of prominent legal scholars to examine the larger questions raised by *Bush v. Gore* and the U.S. Supreme Court's decision to intervene in the case. Ackerman asks if the Court violated the rule of law and examines whether the decision inaugurated an era of hyper-politicized jurisprudence.

The Supreme Court building in Washington, D.C. Its architecture reflects a Greek temple, and it is a symbol of the federal judicial system. (Richie Lomba/Dreamstime.com)

Alley, Robert. 1999. *The Constitution and Religion: Leading Supreme Court Cases on Church and State*. Amherst, NY: Prometheus Press.

> An excellent collection of essays that chronicle the most important church-state–related cases over the past three decades. It concerns prayer in state legislatures, the Pledge of Allegiance, displays of the Ten Commandments in public buildings, religious displays on public property, school prayers, use of vouchers for religious schools, and religion in science classes. It exemplifies the critically important role that the American judicial system, at all levels, plays in determining the complex relationship of church and state in the politics of the United States.

Avery, Michael, and Danielle McLaughlin. 2013. *The Federalist Society: How Conservatives Took the Law Back from Liberals*. Nashville, TN: Vanderbilt University Press.

> This book explains how the Federalist Society rose to its present-day status and position of influence in Republican presidential administrations. It covers the group's influence in federal judicial selection and on conservative ideology with respect to the major issues of constitutional law. It traces how Society ideas about originalism came to dominate the legal landscape.

Bach, Amy. 2010. *Ordinary Justice: How America Holds Court*. New York: Henry Holt.

> Bach, a lawyer and a journalist, investigated widespread courtroom failures and argues that the "assembly-line" approach to justice rewards mediocre advocacy and bypasses due process. She describes the failures of the public defender system to adequately represent their clients, addresses the bail system and its faults, and criticizes prosecutors for failing to pursue cases. Bach's book contends that the judicial system is impacted by a club-like legal culture of compromise and details the tragic

consequences that result from the rules by which lawyers play rather than the rule of law. Bach suggests new methods of checks and balances as a first and necessary step for reforming the judicial system.

Baker, Jean. 2004. *Women and the U.S. Constitution, 1776– 1920.* Washington, DC: American Historical Association.
Baker looks at how women were marginalized in the Constitution, and how women's rights activists pushed to change that—an effort that culminated with passage of a constitutional amendment granting women the vote in 1920.

Barton, Benjamin H. 2010. *The Lawyer-Judge Bias in the American Legal System.* New York: Cambridge University Press.
Barton argues persuasively that lawyer-judges favor the legal profession, and that their bias has far-reaching and deleterious effects on American law. He argues that the bias occurs regardless of the political party affiliation, race, or gender of the judges. He provides a theoretical explanation for the bias, and uses case law from diverse areas, such as legal ethics, criminal procedure, constitutional law, torts, evidence, and the business of law as a springboard for suggesting possible reforms.

Barton, Benjamin H., and Stephanos Bibas. 2017. *Rebooting Justice: More Technology, Fewer Lawyers, and the Future of Law.* New York: Encounter Books.
Barton and Bibas argue that our laws are too complex, and that legal advice is too expensive. They examine both criminal and civil law and the maze of technical procedures and rules. They offer a novel response to an age-old problem, using technology and procedural innovations designed to simplify the legal process and streamline complex procedures. They argue that the American judicial system needs a cheaper and faster justice system to control costs.

Baum, Lawrence, David Klein, and Matthew Streb. 2017. *The Battle for the Court: Interest Groups, Judicial Elections, and Public Policy.* Charlottesville: University of Virginia Press.

This book presents a systematic investigation of the effects of interest group involvement in the election of judges. The authors focus on personal-injury law to detail how interest groups mobilize a response to unfavorable decisions in state supreme court cases. They detail how interest groups influence the outcomes of state supreme court elections, and how those outcomes, in turn, can reshape public policy. The innovative book traces several decades' worth of new data on campaign activity, voting behavior, and judicial policymaking in Ohio to exemplify the relations among interest groups, elections, and judicial policy.

Bedell, Kenneth B. 2017. *Realizing the Civil Rights Dream: Diagnosing and Treating American Racism.* Santa Barbara, CA: Praeger.

Bedell makes the case that by adopting a larger perspective about the role of racism in preserving social, cultural, economic, and political institutions and practices, Americans can better understand why it has been so difficult to fulfill the promises of the 1960s civil rights movement. He uses sociological theories to explain why racism is still so prevalent in the United States. He concludes with identifying steps necessary to overcome racism.

Belknap, Michal. 2005. *The Supreme Court under Earl Warren, 1954–1969.* Columbia: University of South Carolina Press.

Belknap recounts the eventful history of the Warren Court and its controversial decisions, which are still hotly debated today. He draws on internal memoranda as well as published opinions of the justices to reveal the philosophical debates and the personality conflicts behind the Court's major decisions. He places them in their political and social context.

Bharara, Preet. 2019. *Doing Justice: A Prosecutor's Thoughts on Crime, Punishment, and the Rule of Law.* New York: Knopf.

> Bharara presents an important overview of the way the justice system in the United States works. He uses case histories as well as his own compelling personal experiences to describe what is needed to achieve justice within American society.

Biskupic, Joan. 2019. *The Chief: The Life and Turbulent Times of Chief Justice John Roberts.* New York: Basic Books.

> Biskupic provides an incisive biography of Chief Justice John Roberts and examines his most consequential decisions to date. Biskupic contends that Roberts is torn between two often divergent priorities: to carry out a conservative agenda, and to protect the Court's image and his own place in history. She argues that those commitments have fostered distrust among his colleagues and have had major consequences for the law. Her book illustrates the making of justice and the drama that often swirls around the nation's highest court.

Bucerius, Sandra M., and Michael Tonry, eds. 2014. *The Oxford Handbook of Ethnicity, Crime, and Immigration.* New York: Oxford University Press.

> This book is a major examination and synthesis of the literature on immigration and crime, ethnicity and crime, and race and crime for the United States and other countries. Individual chapters provide in-depth overviews of such topics as juvenile incarceration, homicide, urban violence, and social exclusion. The book provides comprehensive analyses of legal and illegal immigration, ethnic and race relations, and crime in the United States and elsewhere by leading scholars from sociology, criminology, law, psychology, geography, and political science. It shows, for example, that a defendant's race and ethnicity affect decisions regarding bail, charging, plea bargaining,

and sentencing. It demonstrates that inequities exist and persist at all stages in court processing, the most compelling in capital sentencing.

Buenger, Michael, and Paul J. De Muniz. 2015. *American Judicial Power: The State Court Perspective.* Cheltenham, UK: Edward Elgar Publishing.

The authors provide an accessible and illuminating overview of state courts and their functions in the American judicial system. They argue that the study of the judicial system is typically skewed toward the federal court system and neglects the importance of the state courts. They examine the wide and distinctive powers exercised by state courts and their role in administering the bulk of the nation's justice system. The book is a groundbreaking examination of critical topics relevant to state courts. The book compares the history of American state courts and the judicial selection process used for state courts. They describe the unique role played by state courts and the varying structure of state courts. The authors focus on the relationship between state judicial power and state legislative power and emphasize the challenges facing state courts. Their analysis of state courts and their powers provide interesting insights for students of constitutional law.

Burbank, Stephen B., and Barry Friedman, eds. 2002. *Judicial Independence at the Crossroads: An Interdisciplinary Approach.* Thousand Oaks, CA: Sage.

This book is based on a conference of assorted scholars of judges and the courts from the disciplines of economics, history, law, political science, and sociology. It is a fine collection of essays that reflect the various disciplinary perspectives of the contributors. It raises important questions about the concept of judicial independence, how it changed over time and why, its status today, and how it can be protected. It exemplifies the scholarship promoted by the American Judicature Society.

Campbell, Nedra B. 2003. *More Justice, More Peace: The Black Person's Guide to the American Legal System.* Chicago: Chicago Review Press.

This book provides legal information for activists to demand those in power to respect and honor their rights, no matter how difficult the situation. It shows how the legal system was created by white men for white men, and how it fails to reflect the values and interests of Black men and women. Yet it shows how activists of color can still use this imperfect system to their advantage to exercise their rights.

Carmon, Irin, and Shana Knishnik. 2015. *Notorious RBG: The Life and Times of Ruth Bader Ginsburg.* New York: Dey Street Books/HarperCollins.

The authors draw an intimate look at Associate Justice Ruth Bader Ginsburg through interviews, reported narrative, annotated dissents, and archival documents. The book brings to life the story of a woman who transcended generational divides over the struggle for gender equality and civil rights and had a significant impact on the American judicial system throughout her storied career.

Carp, Robert A., Ronald Stidham, Kenneth Manning, and Lisa Holmes. 2019. *Judicial Process in America*, 11th ed. Washington, DC: Congressional Quarterly Press.

This classic text presents a comprehensive overview of the American judiciary. This eleventh edition examines recent Supreme Court rulings on same-sex marriage, healthcare subsidies, and discusses the impact of having three women justices on the Court. The book also analyzes the policymaking role of state courts and uses original data to study the decision-making behavior of trial judges seated during the Obama administration.

Chemerinsky, Erwin. 2014. *The Case against the Supreme Court.* New York: Penguin.

>An eminent constitutional scholar presents a hard-hitting analysis of the Supreme Court over its more than 200-year history. He argues that the Supreme Court has often failed at its most important tasks at its most important moments.

Chemerinsky, Erwin. 2017. *Constitutional Law: Principles and Policies*, 6th ed. New York: Wolters Kluwer.

>This treatise on constitutional law identifies the underlying policy issues in each area of constitutional law. It provides thorough coverage of such critical topics as standing, congressional power, presidential power, school desegregation, abortion, voting rights, and freedom of speech and religion.

Coan, Andrew. 2019. *Rationing the Constitution: How Judicial Capacity Shapes Supreme Court Decision-Making.* Cambridge, MA: Harvard University Press.

>Coan examines Supreme Court decision-making and explains how the judicial caseload shapes constitutional law and the role of the high court in American society. He demonstrates how having only a few constitutional issues arising in any given year is essential to understanding how the U.S. Supreme Court makes constitutional law. Coan argues that the structural organization of the judiciary and widely shared professional norms affect and limit the capacity of the Supreme Court to review lower-court decisions. The book examines the effects of federalism, the separation of powers, and individual rights, and how those constrain the Court and provide strong pressure to adopt hard-edged categorical rules, or to defer to the political process, or both. The book shows the profound implications of this constraint on constitutional law. Coan argues that the substantially constrained Court's

judicial capacity works to overrule democratic majorities. It depicts the U.S. Supreme Court as more of a David rather than a Goliath.

Cole, David. 2010. *No Equal Justice: Race and Class in the American Criminal Justice System*. New York: New Press.

Cole argues that despite the promise of equal treatment before the law, the administration of criminal law is predicated on the exploitation of inequality. He argues that reforms have either ignored inequality in the system or failed to address its various manifestations. He asserts that without race and class disparities the policy of mass incarceration pursued over the past two decades would not be affordable, and the privileged would not have the same level of constitutional protection of their liberties as they currently enjoy.

Corley, Pamela, Artemus Ward, and Wendy Martinek. 2015. *American Judicial Process: Myth and Reality in Law and Courts*. New York: Routledge.

This general introductory text covers the major institutions, actors, and processes that comprise the U.S. judicial system. The text is grounded in empirical social science terms, and it identifies popular myths about the structure and process of American law and courts. It details and contrasts those myths with the reality of what takes place.

Crowe, Justin. 2012. *Building the Judiciary: Law, Courts, and the Politics of Institutional Development*. Princeton, NJ: University of Princeton Press.

Crowe discusses the causes and consequences of judicial institutional building in the United States from 1789 to 2000. He explains why and how the federal judiciary became independent, autonomous, and powerful. Crowe develops a useful theory to explain why political actors seek to build the judiciary. The book's discussion ranges from substantive policy to partisan and electoral politics. He covers judicial performance and reforms using a series of case studies and provides contextual understanding of the various historical eras.

Cushman, Clare. 2001. *Supreme Court Decisions and Women's Rights*. Washington, DC: Congressional Quarterly Press.
Cushman's book examines a range of hot-button women's issues before the Supreme Court from the nineteenth century to *Roe v. Wade* (1973). It features more than one hundred cases, as well as biographies of important figures. It is a complete study of all the important issues and movements involving gender bias and shows that gender bias is worst for women of color.

Decker, Scott H., and Kevin A. Wright, eds. 2005. *Criminology and Public Policy*, 2nd ed. Philadelphia: Temple University Press.
The editors provide a collection of eighteen essays by leading scholars that examine both theory and practice in criminology and public policy, and how they interact across a wide range of key problems in the U.S. criminal justice system. Among the major topics the essays cover are racial and environmental concerns, gun control, rates of recidivism among racial and ethnic populations, the use of force by police, the prevalence of mass incarceration, and racial and ethnic disparity in sentencing.

Douglas, Todd. 2017. *The Police in a Free Society: Safeguarding Rights while Enforcing the Law*. Santa Barbara, CA: Praeger.
Douglas offers a detailed look at the evolution of American police, examining how officers moved from their first role as peacekeepers and guardians of citizen rights to acting primarily as "law enforcement officers." The book reveals realities and myths about police in American society and what can—and cannot—be done to improve police relations with the public.

Epstein, Lee, William Landes, and Richard Posner. 2013. *The Behavior of Federal Judges: A Theoretical and Empirical Study of Rational Choice.* Cambridge, MA: Harvard University Press.

In this innovative book, a political scientist, an economist, and a judge work together to construct a unified theory of judicial decision-making. It tests hypotheses of the theory using statistical methodology. It covers federal judicial decision-making at the federal district, circuit, and Supreme Court levels. The authors use a labor-market rational choice model and contend that it explains judicial behavior better than does the traditional "legalist" theory. They show that ideology does figure into decision-making at all three levels, but that its influence diminishes as one goes down the judicial hierarchy. It demonstrates that federal judges are not just robots or politicians in judicial robes.

Geyh, Charles G. 2009. *When Courts and Congress Collide: The Struggle for Control of America's Judicial System.* Ann Arbor: University of Michigan Press.

Geyh's book offers a study of judicial independence that reflects the author's broad and deep experience with both the judicial and legislative branches. Geyh incorporates insights from law, history, and political science. The book is a sweeping analysis of the relationship between Congress and the federal courts. Geyh distinguishes between direct methods Congress could use to curb the courts, such as impeaching uncooperative judges, or gerrymandering their jurisdiction, or slashing judicial budgets; and indirect methods, such as blocking the appointments of ideologically unacceptable nominees. He shows that the Congress rarely uses direct methods. The book stresses the balance is governed by a "dynamic equilibrium," a constant give-and-take between congressional desire to control the judiciary and respect for historical norms of judicial independence.

Gibney, Bruce Cameron. 2019. *The Nonsense Factory: The Making and Breaking of the American Legal System.* New York and Boston: Hachette Books.

> In this stinging rebuke of the legal system, Gibney contends that our courts conduct hardly any trials, the correctional system fails to correct, and the rise of mandatory arbitration has ushered in a system of "privatized" justice. Legislators do not follow their own rules for rulemaking, and the rule of law mutates into a nearly perpetual state of emergency. Gibney argues that the legal system is becoming an incomprehensible farce. He shows that over the past seventy years the legal system has confused quantity with quality and might with legitimacy. His book argues that the legal system staggers on by excusing itself from the very commands it insists the rest of society obey. He argues that the legal system leaves Americans at the mercy of arbitrary power. He argues that what is typically portrayed as isolated mistakes or the work of bad actors such as police misconduct, prosecutorial over-reach, or outrages of an imperial presidency are in fact the consequences of the law's descent into lawlessness. The book is a comprehensive overview of the entire legal system, from the grandeur of constitutional theory to the squalid workings of Congress and concludes the book with several options for reform.

Ginsburg, Ruth Bader, with Mary Hartnett and Wendy W. Williams. 2016. *My Own Words.* New York: Simon and Schuster.

> This is a witty, engaging, serious, and playful collection of Ginsburg's writings and speeches covering a wide range of topics. She demonstrates the value of looking beyond U.S. shores when interpreting the Constitution. It is a fascinating glimpse into the life of one of America's most influential women and jurists.

Hale, Dennis. 2016. *The Jury in America: Triumph and Decline.* Lawrence: University Press of Kansas.

> Hale's book is a thorough examination of the jury system, from its English common law origins to colonial times and on up to modern and postmodern periods. It deftly combines history, political science, and law to assess the significance of the jury in American life and politics. It helps the reader better understand the legal and cultural history of the United States and how that history shaped juries. It discusses how jurors are chosen, how evidence gets presented and weighed, and how juries deliberate and reach decisions.

Hall, Kermit, and James Ely, eds. 2009. *The Oxford Guide to United States Supreme Court Decisions.* New York: Oxford University Press.

> The editors offer a collection of insightful accounts by eminent legal scholars of landmark cases before the Supreme Court, from *Marbury v. Madison* to the Dred Scott decision, to *Brown v. Board of Education* and *Roe v. Wade.* It includes more than 400 cases, including more than fifty new landmark rulings, such as *Gonzales v. Planned Parenthood.*

Head, Tom. 2009. *Civil Liberties: A Beginner's Guide.* London: Oneworld Publications.

> This book weaves history, philosophy, and practical advice for activists in a thought-provoking guide to civil liberties. It demonstrates the complex impact of the American judicial system on civil liberties and the problems that activists face in trying to reform it.

Hollis-Brusky, Amanda. 2015. *Ideas with Consequences: The Federalist Society and the Conservative Counterrevolution.* New York: Oxford University Press.

> The author traces how the Federalist Society built its network of power and influence among lawyers, judges,

scholars, and political party activists to successfully shift American constitutional law to the political right. It is rich in detail and thoroughly researched. It illuminates the Society's role in shaping legal doctrine in the Supreme Court.

Howard, J. Woodford, Jr. 2014. *Courts of Appeal in the Federal Judicial System: A Study of the Second, Fifth, and District of Columbia Circuits.* Princeton, NJ: Princeton University Press.

Howard examines three key aspects of the unifying versus decentralization and regionalization of federal law arising out of the appellate court system. He addresses what binds the federal courts into a judicial system. He examines what controls the discretion of judges in law and policymaking. He considers how quality judicial decisions can be maintained under heavy-volume pressure. He specifically studies the federal courts of appeal of the Second, Fifth, and District of Columbia Circuits.

Howard, Philip K. 2014. *The Rule of Nobody: Saving America from Dead Laws and Broken Government.* New York: W. W. Norton.

Howard's book argues that the federal government is sinking into legal quicksand, beyond the power of those supposedly in charge of the system. Howard argues for the need to prune away obsolete laws and to chop away a bloated bureaucracy. He details administrative regulatory law as a nearly impenetrable web of prohibitions and specifications hamstringing everyone. He shows how dense regulations hamper effective regulatory oversight. Howard's ideology is that of common sense and a sense of urgency to address the problems of the legal system.

Hudson, David L., Jr. 2015. *Teen Legal Rights*, 3rd ed. Santa Barbara, CA: Greenwood Press.

Hudson's book examines all aspects of teens' legal rights—at school, work, and home. It simplifies the laws, rights, and constitutional implications affecting teens today to help them better understand the limitations on their rights within the judicial system.

Issacharoff, Samuel, Pamela Karlan, Richard Pildes, and Nathaniel Persily. 2016. *The Law of Democracy: Legal Structure of the Political Process*, 5th ed. New York: Foundation Press.
>   This book offers a systematic account of the legal construction of American democracy. It covers the Voting Rights Act, campaign finance, and political corruption issues. It examines the struggle over gerrymandering, the relationship of the states to political parties, and the tensions between majority rule and minority rights.

Johnson, Anthony. 2017. *America's Corrupt and Discriminating Judicial System against Black, Hispanics, Females, and Low-Income Americans.* New York: Scribner.
>   The title of Anthony Johnson's brief book tells it all. It is promoted as a guide to Black, Hispanic, female, and low-income Americans to inform them of proven methods to successfully oppose the racial, gender, and status discriminatory practices that the author argues are endemic and thoroughly prevalent in both the civil and criminal judicial systems.

Jonakait, Randolph N. 2008. *The American Jury System.* New Haven, CT: Yale University Press.
>   The author, a constitutional law expert, examines the American jury system and describes the historical and social pressures driving the development of the jury system. He contrasts the American system with the legal process in other countries. His book reveals some subtle changes in the popular view of juries, looking at how they are portrayed in the news, media, movies, and books. He discusses empirical data that show how juries operate and what forces influence their decisions in both civil and

criminal cases. He details the important social role that juries play in legitimizing and affirming the justice system more broadly.

Keck, Thomas M. 2004. *The Most Activist Supreme Court in History: The Road to Modern Judicial Conservatism.* Chicago: University of Chicago Press.
    Keck astutely analyzes the Rehnquist Court and how its decisions related to broader trends in American politics and society. It delves into the relationship between constitutional decision-making and the political and social forces that influence the process, as well as the code of conduct that guided America through the growing pains of becoming a truly pluralistic nation.

Koelling, Peter. 2016. *The Improvement of the Administration of Justice.* Washington, DC: American Bar Association.
    Koelling's book is a compendium describing the current condition of the administration of justice. It advocates new directions that the courts can take to make what he argues are essential improvements. The book provides an overview of the various elements of the judicial system. It describes how some aspects have been improved, but also discusses additional recommendations for reform from the perspectives of academics, practitioners, and judges.

Kubicek, Theodore L. 2006. *Adversarial Justice: America's Court System on Trial.* New York: Algora Publishing.
    This book is a strong critique of the adversary system of justice in the United States, which the author demonstrates too often evades truth and makes winning the paramount goal. He links it to attorney–client privileged communication. He advocates abolishing trial and pretrial procedures and evidentiary rules that confuse law enforcement and participants alike. He suggests decreasing the emphasis on confusing evidentiary and technical

matters that have no connection to the guilt or innocence of the accused.

LaFave, Wayne, Jerold Israel, Nancy King, and Orin Kerr. 2017. *Criminal Procedure*, 6th ed. St. Paul, MN: West Publishing.

In this basic text on the topic of criminal procedure, the authors analyze the law governing the major steps in the criminal process from investigation to post-appeal collateral attacks. They emphasize the basic issues in the law and the judicial literature. The book covers leading Supreme Court case opinions of special importance to criminal procedure.

Landis, James, and Felix Frankfurter. 2017. *The Business of the Supreme Court*. New York: Routledge.

This volume, which analyzes judiciary acts passed between 1789 and 1925, is a reprint of a classic book first published in 1928. It emphasizes the connection between form and substance in American law and illustrates the role of the Supreme Court in approving new laws.

Lazarus, Edward. 2005. *Closed Chambers: The Rise, Fall, and Future of the Modern Supreme Court*. New York: Penguin Press.

Lazarus, a former clerk to Justice Harry Blackmun, offers a searing indictment of the U.S. Supreme Court, which he characterizes as essentially at war with itself, often to the neglect of its constitutional duties. The book is a combination of memoir, history, and legal analysis. It details what takes place behind the closed doors of the Supreme Court, illustrating the personal rivalries, conflicting judicial philosophies, and life experiences of the justices.

Levin, Martin, Daniel DiSalvo, and Martin Shapiro. 2012. *Building Coalitions, Making Policy: The Politics of the Clinton,*

Bush, and Obama Presidencies. Baltimore: John Hopkins University Press.

> This book uses a comparative approach to review the policymaking of the Clinton, Bush, and Obama administrations and their attempts to build coalitions. The book is a fine collection of essays by prominent political scientists. It focuses on the strategies of coalition building to hold a party's base while trying to win over independent voters. It has case studies on such policymaking programs as No Child Left Behind, Social Security privatization, Medicare prescription drug reform, education, immigration reform, environmental policy, judicial politics, and national security.

Long, Carolyn. 2006. *Mapp v. Ohio: Guarding against Unreasonable Searches and Seizures.* Lawrence: University Press of Kansas.

> Long's book provides a comprehensive analysis of the landmark case of *Mapp v. Ohio. Mapp* held that Fourth Amendment protections against unreasonable searches and seizures applied to states and ruled that evidence unconstitutionally obtained could not be used in state criminal prosecutions. The book explores the political turmoil that the decision caused in American politics and jurisprudence. It illustrates the complex and often unexpected ways in which constitutional law influences American history, as the *Mapp* case so clearly did. The book details the remarkable perseverance of Dollree Mapp, whom the book dubs the Rosa Parks of the Fourth Amendment.

Marcus, Maeve, ed. 1992. *Origins of the Federal Judiciary: Essays on the Judiciary Act of 1789.* New York: Oxford University Press.

> Maeve Marcus was the director of the Documentary History Project of the U.S. Supreme Court from 1977 to

2006. This volume presents a collection of essays from legal and political perspectives on the history of the U.S. judiciary and its central role in constitutional interpretation. The essays focus on such topics as the judiciary act and its distinctions between federal and state courts, federal common law, problems of holding dual offices, and perceptions of justice in frontier courts.

Marshall, Thurgood, and Mark Tushnet, ed. 2001. *Thurgood Marshall: His Speeches, Writings, Arguments, Opinions, and Reminiscences.* Chicago: Lawrence Hill Books.
The book uses his speeches, writings, majority and dissenting opinions, and reminiscences to illuminate Justice Marshall and his impact on civil rights law and on American jurisprudence.

Mays, G. Larry, and Laura Woods Fidelie. 2016. *American Courts and the Judicial Process.* New York: Oxford University Press.
The authors provide an overview of the criminal justice system, including details about the structures of the courts found at all levels of the judicial system. It provides an understanding of the complex issues that affect the court system in American politics.

McGuire, Kevin T., ed. 2012. *New Directions in Judicial Politics.* New York: Routledge.
McGuire's book seeks to demystify the courts by offering readers the insights of empirical research that address a variety of questions of critical importance to understanding the complexities of judicial politics. The book offers a set of conclusions about how courts operate and models political research that accounts for the various factors that affect the courts and court operations. It invites critical thinking about the substance of law and courts and how we study judicial politics.

McKenna, Marian. 2002. *Franklin Roosevelt and the Great Constitutional War: The Court-Packing Crisis of 1937*. New York: Fordham University Press.

McKenna presents a critical and revisionist portrayal of President Franklin D. Roosevelt's personal role in initiating a reorganization of the federal judiciary by increasing the number of justices on the U.S. Supreme Court from nine to fifteen. The book details his attempts to give the presidency the power to appoint new justices for every justice over the age of seventy who refused to resign or retire. The book chronicles the case histories and events that led to this so-called "court-packing" crisis. It provides thorough documentation and reasoned criticism.

Melone, Albert P., and Allan Karnes. 2008. *The American Legal System: Perspectives, Politics, Processes, and Policies*, 2nd ed. Lanham, MD: Rowman and Littlefield.

This second edition employs social science concepts to examine the relationships among private law, the business legal environment, and various public law issues. Part I of the book examines the legal system and the origins of law from a political perspective, and details how the judiciary functions in the federal system. Part II contrasts various legal processes in civil, criminal, and equity law. Part III discusses legal norms governing civil and criminal law and the regulation of business. The text uses edited court opinions about thought-provoking controversies and such socially explosive developments as same-sex marriage and the war on terror.

Miller, Mark. 2009. *The View of the Courts from the Hill: Interactions between Congress and the Federal Judiciary*. Charlottesville: University of Virginia Press.

Miller traces the evolution of interactions between Congress and the federal courts. He raises an alarm over congressional interference with judicial independence, which he argues has reached dangerous heights. He attributes the emerging threat of the religious right and conservative members of Congress, who act as their allies and promote their agenda.

Murdoch, Joyce, and Deb Price. 2002. *Courting Justice: Gay Men and Lesbians v. the Supreme Court.* New York: Basic Books.

> This book offers a compelling look at the Supreme Court's handling of gay and lesbian efforts to secure equal legal rights. The authors' interviews of friends, relations, and former clerks to Supreme Court justices provide an inside look at individual rulings. Carefully researched, this work advocates for an inspiring new perspective on the gay rights movement.

Neubauer, David, and Stephen Meinhold. 2009. *Judicial Process: Law, Courts, and Politics in the United States.* Boston: Cengage.

> The authors combine detailed information about the many structures and processes of the American judiciary within a framework of law and politics. The book offers an understanding of courthouse dynamics from an insider's perspective. It details the organization and procedures of the various courts to the application of specific laws. It explores the roles and the impact of the judicial system, its legal rules and underlying assumptions, its history, and its goals. The book presents a balanced look at the role of the judicial system in American politics today.

Newton, Jim. 2006. *Justice for All: Earl Warren and the Nation He Made.* New York: Riverhead Books.

> Newton's book provides a solid biography of Chief Justice Earl Warren. It assesses his impact on the Supreme Court and describes his ultimate legacy on American jurisprudence.

Nussbaum, Martha. 2010. *From Disgust to Humanity: Sexual Orientation and Constitutional Law.* New York: Oxford University Press.

> Nussbaum's book combines rigorous analysis of the leading constitutional cases on sexual orientation with a philosophical reflection about the underlying concepts of privacy, respect, discrimination, and liberty. She discusses issues from nondiscrimination and same-sex marriage to "public sex," and the recent landmark decisions of state and federal courts that are shifting toward what she labels a "humanity-centered" vision.

Obermayer, Herman. 2009. *Rehnquist: A Personal Portrait of the Distinguished Chief Justice of the United States.* New York: Oxford University Press.

> Obermayer, a longtime friend of Chief Justice William Rehnquist, provides a personal tribute to the late chief justice. It is a portrait designed to enhance the legacy of the influential and long serving chief justice.

O'Brien, David M. 2017. *Constitutional Law and Politics: Civil Rights and Civil Liberties*, vol. 2. New York: W. W. Norton.

> O'Brien's book is a solid text that explores the intertwining aspects of law and politics. It discusses the origins of constitutional clauses, covers numerous case opinions, and provides a fuller understanding of constitutional law's strengths and weaknesses.

Ogletree, Charles. 2004. *All Deliberate Speed: Reflections on the First Half-Century of Brown v. Board of Education.* New York: W. W. Norton.

> The author provides a measured blend of personal memoir, exacting legal analysis, and studied insight into the *Brown* case. The book offers an eyewitness account of the legacy of the *Brown* decision and its impact on five decades of race relations in the United States.

Posner, Richard. 2017. *The Federal Judiciary: Strengths and Weaknesses.* Cambridge, MA: Harvard University Press.

Judge Richard Posner offers a tour of the judicial branch of the federal government and argues persuasively that "originalism" is a bankrupt legal philosophy. He provides a critical assessment of Justice Antonin Scalia as the "emperor" of originalism and proposes specific and controversial reforms. The book is an iconoclastic critique of the ideas dearly held by many judges and in academia, taking aim at every sacred legal cow.

Powe, Lucas. 2000. *The Warren Court and American Politics.* Cambridge: Harvard University Press.

Chief Justice Earl Warren led the Supreme Court during its most revolutionary and controversial period in American history. Powe looks at the Supreme Court in a wide view of the political environment to argue the Warren Court functioned as a partner in Kennedy–Johnson liberalism imposing national liberal values on groups that were outliers: the white South, rural America, and areas of Roman Catholic dominance. He offers a learned and lively narrative to discuss more than 200 significant rulings that changed the balance of American legislatures, gradually eliminating anticommunism in domestic security programs, reformed basic criminal procedures, banned school-sponsored prayer, and shaped new law on pornography.

Powell, Sidney K. 2018. *Licensed to Lie: Exposing Corruption in the Department of Justice.* Dallas, TX: Brown Books.

The book promotes itself as an expose, a true story of what it labels as the illegal, strong-arm, and unethical tactics of the Department of Justice and of their pursuit of power. It details how that pursuit touched the FBI, the U.S. Senate, and the White House under two presidents (Bush and Obama). It poses a serious conversation about whether the criminal justice system lives up to its vaunted reputation. The book describes the case of the federal prosecution of Edward Snowden as one of duplicity and heavy-handedness.

Ragsdale, Bruce, ed. 2013. *Debates on the Federal Judiciary: A Documentary History, Volume 1 (of 3), 1787–1875.* Washington, DC: Federal Judiciary Center.

Ragsdale's volume covers key primary documents presenting the debates on the judiciary including: the Constitutional Convention debates of the judiciary, the Ratification debates, the Judiciary Act of 1789, early circuit riding, nonjudicial responsibilities of federal judges, the Judiciary Act of 1801 and its repeal, the impeachment trial of Justice Samuel Chase in 1805, judicial tenure, judicial review and federalism, circuit riding as the nation expanded, the Civil War and the reorganization of the federal judiciary, and the Jurisdiction and Removal Act of 1875.

Rawn, James, Jr. 2010. *Root and Branch: Charles Hamilton Houston, Thurgood Marshall, and the Struggle to End Segregation.* New York: Bloomsbury Press.

James Rawn provides a riveting story of two fiercely dedicated lawyers, Charles Hamilton Houston and Thurgood Marshall, and details their epic fight from county courthouses to the U.S. Supreme Court to advance the goals and dreams of the civil rights movement.

Riehl, Jonathan. 2007. *The Federalist Society and Movement Conservatism: How a Fractious Coalition on the Right Is Changing Constitutional Law and the Way We Talk and Think About It.* Chapel Hill: University of North Carolina Press.

Riehl's book presents an in-depth examination of the Federalist Society and how it became the preeminent organization for conservative and libertarian lawyers. It traces the rise of the Society from the Reagan administration to today, when its participants now number more than 40,000 lawyers, judges, law students, and policymakers.

Robertiello, Gina, ed. 2017. *The Use and Abuse of Police Power in America: Historical Milestones and Current Controversies.* Santa Barbara, CA: ABC-CLIO.
Robertiello's book is a timely investigation of law enforcement and how it carries out its public safety and crime-fighting mandates. It details the evolution of police powers and offers a critical perspective on contemporary trends in law enforcement attitudes and practices.

Rosen, Jeffrey. 2006. *The Most Democratic Branch: How the Courts Serve America.* New York: Oxford University Press.
Rosen argues that from the days of John Marshall to the present, the federal courts have mostly reflected the opinions of the mainstream of American politics. He argues that the Supreme Court is most successful when it defers to the constitutional views of the American people, as reflected by the Congress and the presidency. He argues that on the rare occasions when the Supreme Court departed from the consensus, the results have been a disaster. He examines some of the most important Supreme Court decisions in U.S. history involving racial equality, affirmative action, gay rights, and gay marriage and asserts that the Supreme Court's most criticized decisions have gone against mainstream opinion. Rosen also contends that the Court's most successful decisions, such as *Marbury v. Madison* and *Brown v. Board of Education,* avoided imposing constitutional principles over the wishes of the majority of America. He argues the judiciary system works best when it identifies constitutional principles accepted by the majority and enforces them unequivocally as fundamental law.

Rosen, Jeffrey. 2007. *The Supreme Court: The Personalities and Rivalries That Defined America.* Spokane, WA: Griffin Publishing.

    Rosen reviews the history of the U.S. Supreme Court through the lens of the personal and philosophical rivalries that have transformed the law. His book examines four crucial conflicts: Chief Justice John Marshall and President Thomas Jefferson; post-Civil War justices John Marshall Harlan and Oliver Wendell Holmes; liberal icons justices Hugo Black and William Douglas; and conservative stalwarts justices William Rehnquist and Antonin Scalia. He shows how their rivalry was guided by strong ideology and how the justices cared for the Court as an institution. The book ends with a revealing conversation with Chief Justice John Roberts, and what those views portend for the future of American jurisprudence.

Scheb, John M., II, and Hemant Sharma. 2015. *An Introduction to the American Legal System*, 4th ed. Albany, NY: West/Thomson Learning.

    This basic text provides historical context on many aspects of American law and the legal system. It includes numerous case summaries, discusses several "hot-button" issues, and provides a useful glossary of legal terms.

Schudson, Charles B. 2018. *Independence Corrupted: How American Judges Make Their Decisions.* Madison: University of Wisconsin Press.

    The author, an appellate court judge, provides a behind-the-scenes probe of how judges analyze actual trials and sentencing. His book exposes the financial, personal, and professional pressures that threaten judicial ethics and the vaunted "independence" of courts. He proposes reforms to protect judicial independence and to ensure justice for all.

Schwartz, Herman, ed. 2002. *The Rehnquist Court: Judicial Activism on the Right.* New York: Hill and Wang.

> Schwartz argues persuasively that the Rehnquist Supreme Court was able to effect a dramatic shift to the right and displayed a judicial activism that undermined civil rights and weakened the federal government's ability to address pressing social needs. The book is a collection of seventeen essays provided by leading and distinguished legal scholars. They collectively evaluate the Rehnquist Court's record on many controversial issues.

Shapiro, Ilya. 2020. *Supreme Disorder: Nominations and the Politics of America's Highest Court.* South Lake, TX: Gateway Editions.

> The author, director of the Cato Institute's Center for Constitutional Studies, provides an inside look at the history of fiercely partisan judicial nominations. He discusses various proposed reforms to return the Supreme Court to its constitutional role. He argues that only when the Court rebalances constitutional order, curbs administrative overreach, and returns power back to the states will the bitter partisan battle to control the judiciary end.

Shugerman, Jed H. 2012. *The People's Courts: Pursuing Judicial Independence in America.* Cambridge, MA: Harvard University Press.

> Shugerman traces the history of judicial elections in the United States designed to provide for an independent judiciary to ensure fairness before the law. He covers the history of judicial elections from colonial times to the present. He emphasizes the importance of the separation of powers and limited government but notes that they can become threats to judicial independence. Shugerman calls for reforms to reduce partisan and financial influences on judicial selection. He shows how the U.S. citizens have long been deeply committed to judicial independence, but also how that commitment has, at times, been manipulated by special interests.

Stewart, Chuck. 2018. *Documents of the LGBT Movement.* Santa Barbara: ABC-CLIO.

> Stewart provides a concise yet comprehensive review of the LGBTQ civil rights movement from the earliest days of human society to the present-day United States. He highlights a host of primary documents of the LGBTQ community and also traces key events in the movement across the last seventy years that led to the decriminalization of sodomy laws and to the legalization of same-sex marriage in the United States in 2015.

Strum, Philippa. 2010. *Mendez v. Westminster: School Desegregation and Mexican American Rights.* Lawrence: University Press of Kansas.

> Strum's book provides a detailed and compelling analysis of the lesser-known case of *Mendez v. Westminster* (1947). She documents it as the first successful challenge to segregation (in this case, against Mexican Americans) in education. Strum analyzes the carefully crafted arguments and the use, by the federal district court, of social, psychological, and pedagogical data to demonstrate the cost of segregated education and the damage that it does to Mexican American students. She shows how the arguments crafted for the Mendez case were later used by the NAACP in the *Brown v. Board of Education of Topeka, Kansas* case (1954). She effectively weaves together narrative and analysis as well as personal portraits of the various actors involved in the case to present an even-handed discussion of the arguments used by both sides. It is a highly readable and accessible approach that illuminates the judicial philosophies involved and enlightens the reader to the complexity of the jurisprudence that was brought to bear on the case.

Stuart, Gary L. 2004. *Miranda: The Story of America's Right to Remain Silent.* Tucson: University of Arizona Press.

> Stuart tells the inside story of the *Miranda* case. He unravels its complex history and analyzes the competing social issues

of the case. He assesses its aftermath. Stuart updates the story with the Supreme Court's decision in *Dickerson v. United States* (530 U.S. 428, 2000) that upheld the rule requiring the Miranda warning over a federal statute that would have overturned *Miranda v. Arizona*. He discusses the implications for cases in the wake of the 9/11 attacks. He concludes with offering observations on the Miranda case's impact on law enforcement and the civil rights of the accused.

Surrency, Erwin. 2002. *History of the Federal Courts*. Dobbs Ferry, NY: Oceana Publications.
    Surrency surveys the history of the federal judiciary from 1789 to 1990, examining how it grew in response to historical events and to changes in procedural concepts. He examines the evolution of the various types of federal courts through time and explores nuances of procedures and legal terminology and how they were used; for example, on the use of "circuit court" as trial courts until 1911, and the present meaning of the term today as circuit courts of appeals.

Teles, Steven. 2008. *The Rise of the Conservative Movement: The Battle for Control of the Law*. Princeton, NJ: Princeton University Press.
    Teles examines the rise of the conservative legal movement, using internal documents and interviews with key conservative figures to do so. His book reveals the challenges the Federalist Society's members faced with legal liberalism and emphasizes how its individuals and political entrepreneurs learned by trial and error. He uses materials from the Olin Foundation, the Federalist Society, the Center for Individual Rights, the Institute for Justice, and the Law and Economics Center.

Thomas, Evan. 2019. *First: Sandra Day O'Connor*. New York: Random House.
    Thomas presents an intimate, inspiring, and authoritative biography of Justice Sandra Day O'Connor, the first woman

to serve on the U.S. Supreme Court. The book draws on exclusive interviews and was written with the benefit of unusual access to Justice O'Connor's archives. The book is a vivid and personal portrait of the woman who became one of the most powerful women in America. It traces her career from the Arizona state senate through her service as judge on the Arizona Court of Appeals, her service on the U.S. Supreme Court, and her post-court years.

Toobin, Jeffrey. 2008. *The Nine: Inside the Secret World of the Supreme Court.* New York: Anchor Books.
Toobin's compelling narrative of the U.S. Supreme Court is informative and insightful. He had unusual access to the Supreme Court justices and their clerks. He provides a vivid picture of the Court's recent history and an intimate look at individual justices. He shows how their personalities, judicial philosophies, and personal alliances inform decisions of great consequence to the United States. The book is an absorbing group profile and a compelling look at the power and politics behind the Supreme Court.

Toobin, Jeffrey. 2013. *The Oath: The Obama White House and the Supreme Court.* New York: Anchor Books.
Toobin uses firsthand interviews with justices and their clerks to draw a portrait of the Supreme Court under Chief Justice John Roberts. He covers their major decisions and the judicial philosophies of the justices. His compelling narrative shows that the interplay between different personalities and agendas is often more important than any scholarly argument or historical text. The book also provides a revealing look at the ideological battle between the Obama White House and the Supreme Court.

Tushnet, Mark. 2005. *A Court Divided: The Rehnquist Court and the Future of Constitutional Law.* New York: W. W. Norton and Company.
Tushnet examines the Rehnquist Court, arguing that the Court has always followed election returns. He notes that

the Warren and Burger Courts never got far out of line with the national political consensus. Tushnet shows the Rehnquist Court reflected the 1980s and 1990s and the rise of conservatism. He asserts that the Court followed Congress's lead, striking down several symbols of the New Deal regulatory state even as it sided with more liberal positions at the margins of the social cultural wars—on gay rights, affirmative action, and early-term abortions. As Tushnet notes, in the arena of politics, economic conservatives were winning, and cultural conservatives were losing.

Tushnet, Mark V. 2007. *Out of Range: Why the Constitution Can't End the Battle over Guns.* Oxford and New York: Oxford University Press.

Constitutional scholar Mark Tushnet takes on the vexing question of guns and the Constitution, examining competing interpretations of the Second Amendment. On balance, Tushnet supports a view that allows for greater government regulation. He shows how the dispute over guns has become part of the culture war and concludes that reaching a broad consensus on the meaning of the Second Amendment is nearly impossible as a result.

Tushnet, Mark V. 2008. *Dissent: Great Opposing Opinions in Landmark Supreme Court Cases.* Boston: Beacon Press.

The distinguished Supreme Court scholar explains sixteen influential cases throughout the Court's history. He offers a sense of what could have developed if the dissents instead of the majority opinions had won the case.

Van Cleve, Nicole G. 2016. *Crook County: Racism and Injustice in America's Largest Criminal Court.* Stanford, CA: Stanford University Press.

This award-winning book provides an intense look at the Chicago-Cook County criminal courthouse. The author takes readers inside the halls of justice, drawing on more than 1,000 hours of observing the court. She provides an intimate look at the types of everyday racial abuses that fester within the court. She documents how courtroom professionals classify and deliberate on the fates of mostly black and Latino defendants while racial abuse and due process violations are encouraged and justified.

Vile, John R. 2014. *Essential Supreme Court Decisions: Summaries of Leading Cases in U.S. Constitutional Law*, 16th ed. Lanham, MD: Rowman and Littlefield.

John Vile's book has become a standard resource for examining the most important Supreme Court cases in U.S. constitutional law. His book includes every facet of constitutional law, including powers and privileges of the three branches of the national government, federalism, war powers, and extensive briefs on civil rights and civil liberties. This new edition is revised and updated, and it covers cases organized by years, by Supreme Court Chief Justices who presided over the cases, and by type of cases.

Vile, John R. 2015. *Encyclopedia of Constitutional Amendments, Proposed Amendments, and Amending Issues, 1789– 2015.* 4th ed. 2 vols. Santa Barbara, CA: ABC-CLIO.

In this fourth and updated edition, Vile presents a comprehensive review of constitutional amendments and proposed amendments. It discusses the critical issues they deal with from 1789 to the present. He covers each of the twenty-seven amendments, as well as essays on proposed ones, and outlines proposals for more radical changes to the U.S. Constitution.

Wainwright, Susan, ed. 2019. *In Defense of Justice: The Greatest Dissents of Ruth Bader Ginsburg.* Fairhope, AL: Mockingbird Press.

Wainwright's book features a collection of Justice Ginsburg's most notable and fiery dissents. Each dissent presented is prefaced with an explanation of the case to aid the lay reader in approaching and understanding the legal prose. The book highlights Justice Ginsburg at the zenith of her passion to persuade future generations of the rightness of her positions on each of these cases.

Washington, Linn. 1994. *Black Judges on Justice: Perspectives from the Bench*. New York: New Press.

Washington's book is the first to present the views of leading African American judges on the way the judicial system works. It presents firsthand testimony of the judges to provide a penetrating analysis of the role of the jurist. It shows the daily malfunctioning of the courts and assesses the future of the judicial system itself.

Wheeler, Russell R., and Cynthia Harrison. 2006. *Creating the Federal Judicial System*, 3rd ed. Washington, DC: Federal Judicial Center.

Wheeler and Harrison explain the Judiciary Act of 1789, the evolution of the federal judicial system during the 1800s, and the three-tiered system that characterizes the federal court structure today. The book includes a series of highly useful maps showing the growth and evolution of the U.S. district and circuits from 1789 until the present.

Zotti, Priscilla H. M. 2005. *Injustice for All: Mapp vs. Ohio and the Fourth Amendment*. New York: Peter Lang.

Using original documents and extensive interviews, this book details the historical, legal, and political significance of *Mapp v. Ohio* (1961), the most famous and impactful Fourth Amendment case on search and seizure jurisprudence.

Leading Scholarly Journals

American Journal of Legal History was established in 1957 and is a peer-reviewed and peer-edited legal periodical published quarterly. Since 2016, it has been published by Oxford University Press. It publishes scholarly articles on all aspects and periods of legal history in both print and online format. Each issue regularly features book reviews. Since its relaunch in 2016, it has published contributions of a comparative, international, or transnational nature. The journal is edited by Professors Al Brophy (University of North Carolina School of Law, Chapel Hill) and Stefan Vogenauer (Max Plank Institute for European Legal History, Frankfurt).

American Journal of Political Science was established in 1956. It is published for the Midwest Political Science Association by Wiley. It is a quarterly, peer-reviewed journal publishing original articles advancing knowledge and understanding of citizenship, governance, and politics in all areas of political science, including, of course, judicial politics. It is ranked fourth among 180 political science–related journals by the American Political Science Association (APSA).

Boston College Law Review has been published since 1959. The highly regarded law journal is issued eight times per year. Publishing original articles on legal issues of national interest, it is the flagship scholarly publication of the Boston College Law School.

Columbia Law Review has been published since 1901 and is a leading publication of legal scholarship. It is published in eight issues a year and since 2008 has featured an online supplement, *Columbia Law Review Online*. The journal is edited and published by Columbia University Law School.

Cornell Law Review has been published since 1915 and contains original scholarship in all fields of law. It is a quarterly, peer-reviewed journal that is student run and edited. It publishes seven issues annually, with articles, essays, book reviews, and student notes, and is available in print and online versions.

Emory International Law Review is a leading journal of international legal scholarship known for its excellence in scholarship, legal research, analysis, and professionalism. It publishes articles on a vast array of topics from human rights to international intellectual property issues. It is published quarterly.

Emory Law Journal was founded in 1952 as the *Journal of Public Law*. It has been publishing academic, professional, and student-authored legal scholarship on the full range of legal subjects since 1978. It publishes six issues annually.

Fordham Urban Law Journal is a specialty law journal addressing policy issues affecting urban areas. It is the Fordham Law School's second-oldest publication and has been published since 1973 (and on a quarterly basis since 1980). In some years it features special thematic issues on various aspects of urban law.

Georgetown Journal of Legal Ethics was founded in 1987 and is published quarterly. It publishes interdisciplinary scholarship related to the future of the legal profession, issuing cutting-edge articles on ethical issues from diverse practical areas.

Georgetown Law Review is headquartered at Georgetown University Law School in Washington, D.C. It has published more than 500 issues since its inception in 1912 on the full spectrum of legal issues and cases. It employs one hundred law students and publishes its *Annual Review of Criminal Procedure.*

Harvard Law Review publishes eight regular annual issues of various legal articles by professors, judges, practitioners, and law students, and leading case summaries. It is run by an independent student group at Harvard Law School. It also publishes an *Online Harvard Law Review Forum*. One of the nation's oldest and most prestigious law reviews, it has been published since 1887. Alumni include President Barack Obama, seven Supreme Court justices, and a host of federal court judges, members of Congress, and other high-level federal government officials.

Hastings Law Journal has been published since 1949. It is the flagship law review of the University of California-Hastings. It is published six times per year. Its scholarly articles span a wide variety of legal issues and are written by experts in the legal community. It also publishes an occasional law symposium issue. It is run by ninety student members and reaches a large domestic and international audience.

Journal of Law and Courts is a publication of the University of Chicago Press and is published in association with the Law and Courts section of the American Political Science Association. Published biannually since 2013, it is an interdisciplinary journal aimed at the law and courts intellectual community.

Michigan Law Review publishes eight issues annually, seven of which are comprised of articles by legal scholars and practitioners, and notes by law students. One issue is devoted to book reviews. The review publishes important judicial decisions and legislative developments. It has been published by the University of Michigan Law School since 1902.

National Law Journal is a monthly U.S. periodical that has been published since 1978 by the American Lawyer Media. It reports on legal information of national importance to attorneys, including federal circuit courts, decisions, legislative issues, and legal news for business and private clients. Once every few years it publishes its list of the one hundred most influential lawyers.

Northwestern University Law Review was founded in 1906 as the *Illinois Law Review*. It is published quarterly in print and online and features articles on general legal scholarship. It is student operated with articles written by professors, judges, legal practitioners, as well as student pieces. It also hosts special symposium issues annually.

Notre Dame Law Review was founded in 1925, although it was known as the *Notre Dame Lawyer* until 1982. It is student edited and fosters scholarly discourse within the legal community mindful of its Catholic tradition. It is published quarterly, and annually has a symposium issue on federal courts, practice, and procedure as a forum exploring civil practice and procedures in the federal courts.

Review of Politics publishes articles primarily on political theory, interpretive studies of law, historical analysis on all aspects of politics: institutions, techniques, literary reflections on politics, and constitutional theory and analysis. It has been published quarterly since 1939 and is published by Cambridge University Press for the University of Notre Dame.

Stanford University Law Review is published both in print (since 1948) and online (since 2011). It fosters intellectual discourse among student members and contributes to legal scholarship by addressing important legal and social issues. It is published in six issues per year and features articles contributed by *Law Review* members as well as other Stanford Law School students, professors, judges, and practicing attorneys.

Supreme Court Review has been published by the University of Chicago Law School since it first appeared in 1910. It provides a sustained and authoritative survey of the Court's most significant decisions. It provides an in-depth critique of the Supreme Court and its work and on the ongoing reforms and interpretations of American law. It is written by and for legal academics, judges, political scientists, journalists, and sociologists. It is published annually in the spring.

University of California Law Review is the preeminent legal publication of the University of California, Berkeley School of Law. It was founded in 1912. It is published six times annually, covering a wide variety of topics of legal scholarship. It is edited and published entirely by students at Berkeley Law. It publishes research by the Berkeley Law faculty, centers, students, judges, and legal practitioners.

University of Chicago Law Review was founded in 1933. The quarterly journal is edited by the Law School's students and is one of the country's most prestigious and often-cited law reviews. Its authors include a host of Supreme Court justices, federal court judges, state supreme court judges, and preeminent legal scholars.

University of Minnesota Law Review has been published since 1917. It is solely student edited, publishes quarterly, and covers the entire range of legal issues. It also publishes an annual symposium issue.

University of Pennsylvania Journal of Constitutional Law provides a forum for the interdisciplinary study and analysis of constitutional law. It cultivates legal scholarship, promotes critical perspectives, and reinvents the traditional study of constitutional law. It has twenty student editors. It has been published quarterly since 1998.

University of Pennsylvania Law Review is a prestigious law review focusing on a wide range of legal issues. It was founded in 1852 and published its 165th volume in seven issues in the 2016–2017 academic year. It serves the legal profession, the bench, the bar, and the legal academy by providing a forum for publication of legal research. From about 2,000 submissions, it selects twelve articles in each volume.

University of Virginia Law Review has been one of the most prestigious publications in the legal profession since its founding in 1913. Published eight times annually, it covers law-related issues by and for judges, practitioners, teachers, legislators, students, and others interested in the law.

Yale Law and Policy Review has been published bi-annually since 1982. It features legal scholarship and policy proposals by lawmakers, judges, practitioners, academics, and students. It has an online companion called *Inter-Alia.*

Yale Law Journal has been published since 1891. It has been at the forefront of legal scholarship and shapes discussion of the most important and relevant legal issues through rigorous scholarship. It is published eight times per year, and its online companion has been published since 2005. It is one of the most widely cited law reviews in the nation.

Nonprint Sources

Websites

American Bar Association: www.americanbar.org
American Civil Liberties Union: www.aclu.org
American Constitution Society: www.acslaw.org
American Immigration Lawyers Association: www.aila.org
American Progress: www.americanprogress.org
Ballotpedia: www.ballotpedia.org
Brennan Center for Justice: www.brennancenter.org
Bureau of Justice Statistics: www.bjs.gov
Criminal Find Law: www.findlaw.com/criminal.html
Department of Justice: www.justice.gov
Economic Policy Institute: www.epi.org
Federal Judicial Center: www.fjc.gov
Federalist Society: www.fedsoc.org
The Gavel Gap: https://www.acslaw.org/analysis/reports/gavel-gap
Heritage Foundation: www.heritage.org
Justia: www.justia.com; supreme.justia.com
Lawjrank: law.jrank.org/
NAACP Legal Defense and Education Fund: www.naacpldf.org
National Association of Women Judges: www.nawj.org
National Center for State Courts: www.ncsc.org
National Constitution Center: constitutioncenter.org
National Institute of Justice: www.nij.ojp.gov

NOW Legal Defense and Education Fund: https://engage
.naacpldf.org/about-us.
Oyez.org: www.oyez.org
Pew Research Center: www.pewresearch.org
Politico: www.politico.com
Sentencing Project: www.sentencingproject.org
U.S. Courts: www.uscourts.gov
U.S. Supreme Court: www.supremecourt.gov

Films

Reversing Roe.
2018. This documentary film analyzes abortion laws in the
United States and the effects of *Roe v. Wade* (1973). Released on
Netflix, it presents interviews with several politicians, experts,
and activists involved in the abortion politics in the United
States. The film provides a clear and accessible overview of
some fifty years of social and legal history on this controversial
issue. It was nominated for an Emmy for Outstanding Politics
and Government Documentary.

RGB.
2018. This documentary film depicts the unlikely transfor-
mation of Justice Ruth Bader Ginsburg into a cultural icon,
as well as her tremendous contributions to American law. It
shows her early legal battles as a lawyer to advance women's
rights and dramatically and effectively explores many facets of
her exceptional life, including her enduring impact as an associate justice on the Supreme court. The film was nominated for
a Best Documentary Feature Academy Award.

7 Chronology

1641 Massachusetts colony's charter provides for the right to trial by jury.

1765 English Parliament, at urging of King George III, restricts trial by jury among its provisions. Colonists pass the Resolution of the Stamp Act, October 19, that declares "trial by jury is an inherent right of every British subject."

1776 Declaration of Independence written and signed on July 4. Lists grievances that include denial of trial by jury as one of the reasons colonies revolted from English rule.

1777 Articles of Confederation adopted.

1781 Articles of Confederation ratified. It establishes a government with a weak central government.

1783 Treaty of Paris signed, peace with England confirmed, sets the stage for the new constitutional convention.

1787 Second Constitutional Convention is held to revise the Articles of Confederation. It results in proposal of a new Constitution. Northwest Ordinance Act establishes territories and territorial courts.

1789 The Constitution is ratified, establishing a new federal government in the United States. Congress enacts the Judiciary Act of 1789 creating U.S. Supreme Court and federal "circuits." U.S. Department of Justice established as cabinet department.

The Colorado Supreme Courtroom located in the Ralph L. Carr Colorado Judicial Center in Denver, Colorado. Every state in the Union has its own supreme court or highest court of final appeal. (Glenn Nagel/Dreamstime.com)

1791 The Bill of Rights—comprised of the first ten amendments—is ratified. They establish many rights regarding judiciary, especially Fourth, Sixth, Seventh Amendments.

1796 Justice Samuel Chase appointed to Supreme Court.

1801 Judiciary Act of 1801, aka the Midnight Judges Act, is passed. John Marshall named chief justice of the Supreme Court.

1802 Judiciary Act of 1802 passed, setting a new number of Supreme Court justices.

1803 Louisiana Purchase adds territory and new territorial courts established. *Marbury v. Madison* decision handed down, establishing judicial review power. Justice Samuel Chase tried and acquitted in U.S. Senate in first impeachment trial of a Supreme Court Justice.

1807 Judiciary Act of 1807 passed.

1812 United States goes to war with England, a conflict often called "Madison's war" at the time.

1816 U.S. Senate establishes the Senate Judiciary Committee as standing committee.

1820 Missouri Compromise enacted to maintain balance between slave and free states.

1836 Roger Taney named chief justice of U.S. Supreme Court.

1837 Judiciary Act of 1837 passed.

1848 Treaty of Guadalupe Hidalgo signed, adding extensive territory to United States. Territorial courts established in new territories.

1849 The Know Nothing Party is founded. Supreme Court issues *Luther v. Borden* decision.

1850 The Compromise of 1850 regarding entry of slave states and free states passed.

1854 Republican Party established with an antislavery platform and a reform agenda regarding federal courts.

1855 U.S. Court of Federal Claims established.

1857 Supreme Court hands down *Dred Scott* decision, which states that "slaves" are property and must be returned to owners even if they are living in free states. The ruling heightens tensions that ultimately lead to outbreak of civil war.

1858 Union troops occupy Utah until 1862 to control Mormons there. Territorial courts established to do so.

1860 President Lincoln elected and Southern states secede from United States; Civil War begins.

1861 Lincoln suspends writ of habeas corpus.

1862 Homestead Act passed. Transcontinental Railroad construction begins. Morrill Anti-Bigamy Act signed.

1863 President Lincoln issues Emancipation Proclamation order freeing slaves in ten Confederate States. Congress enacts the Judiciary Act of 1863. The state of West Virginia, splitting off from Virginia, enters union as free state.

1864 Lincoln is reelected.

1865 Civil War ends with a Union victory. The postwar Reconstruction Era (1865–1877) begins. President Lincoln assassinated on April 15. Thirteenth Amendment ratified on December 6.

1866 Civil Rights Act enacted on April 6. Judiciary Act of 1866 passed.

1867 Congress enacts the Judiciary Act of 1867.

1868 Fourteenth Amendment is ratified.

1869 National Women's Suffrage Association is founded.

1870 Fifteenth Amendment is ratified.

1872 Jehovah's Witnesses begins. They soon challenge many laws in federal courts.

1873 Slaughter House cases are ruled on by the Supreme Court.

1875 Civil Rights Act of March 3, 1875, enacted—aka "the Enforcement Act."

1878   American Bar Association founded.

1879   *Reynolds v. United States* upholds polygamy laws against Mormons.

1889   The states of North and South Dakota and Washington all join the union, each with its own state constitution and its established state court systems.

1890   *Davis v. Beason* ruling again upholds bigamy laws against the Mormons. The states of Idaho and Wyoming enter the union with their constitutions and state court systems.

1891   U.S. Court of Private Land Claims established. Congress passes the Judiciary Act of 1891, aka the Evarts Act. Evarts elected to U.S. Senate from New York.

1893   U.S. Court of Appeals for District of Columbia established.

1896   *Plessy v. Ferguson* decision establishes "separate-but-equal" doctrine, legally justifying segregation, and spurring use of Jim Crow laws throughout the South. The state of Utah enters union with its constitution and its state courts.

1898   Spanish-American War. United States acquires new territory, new citizens. New territorial courts established.

1905   *Lochner v. New York* rules New York's labor law violates Fourteenth Amendment. *Rooney v. North Dakota* rules private execution does not violate ex-post-facto clause regarding capital punishment. *Beavers v. Haubert* decision regarding Sixth Amendment rights to fair trial handed down.

1906   U.S. Court for China established, runs until 1943.

1907   The state of Oklahoma enters union with its state constitution and state court system.

1909   National Association for the Advancement of Colored People is founded. NAACP begins their campaign of attempting to overturn discriminatory state laws via use of federal courts and gradual incorporation of several bill or rights amendments being applied to states via due process clause of

Fourteenth Amendment. The U.S. Court of Customs Appeals is established. William Howard Taft elect POTUS.

1910   U.S. Commerce Court established.

1912   The states of Arizona and New Mexico each enter the union with their respective state constitutions and state court systems.

1913   American Judicature Society founded.

1916   International Trade Commission established as a quasi-judicial agency.

1917   The Espionage Act is passed. The United States enters World War I.

1918   The Sedition Act is passed.

1919   Attorney General Palmer uses "Red Scare" raids to round up radical Socialists and Communists. *Schenck v. United States* upholds convictions of Socialists.

1920   The Nineteenth Amendment is ratified. The American Civil Liberties Union is founded. The League of Women Voters is founded.

1921   Former president William Howard Taft named as chief justice of Supreme Court, serving until his death in 1930.

1922   *Leser v. Garnett* upholds the constitutionality of Nineteenth Amendment. The Cable Act of September 22 passed granting citizenship to women when their husband is naturalized, but also stripping citizenship from women who marry foreigner who cannot become a citizen.

1923   Court holds in *United States v. Bhagat Singh Thind* that citizenship being open only to "free white person" means individual who looks white; East Indians are therefore not white and cannot naturalize.

1924   U.S. Tax Court created. And in recognition of their service in W.W. I, Congress enacts Act of June 4, "Citizenship for Non-citizen Indians." Citizenship allows them judicial rights previously denied to them.

1925 *Gitlow v. New York* sets "clear and present danger" test. Judiciary Act of 1925, aka the certiorari act, is passed.

1928 *Olmstead v. United States* finds wiretaps constitutional.

1929 Japanese American Citizens League is founded. League of United Latin American Citizens is founded. *United States v. Schwimmer* decides that a woman who refuses to swear oath because of pacifism can be denied citizenship. The Circuit Court of Appeals for the Tenth Circuit established. The stock market crash leads to the Great Depression (1930–1941) and FDR's New Deal's emphasis on economic rights.

1930 Charles Evans Hughes named chief justice of the Supreme Court.

1931 Act of March 3 restores citizenship of women lost when married to a foreign man or for residence abroad as per the Cable Act of 1922.

1935 Act of June 24 allows for naturalization of aliens who were veterans of World War I, explicitly giving citizenship to Asian veterans.

1936 Repatriation of Native-born women who lost citizenship by marriage.

1937 FDR proposes his "court-packing" plan to expand number of justices on Supreme Court to fifteen as means to get around Supreme Court's overturning a number of New Deal programs.

1938 Olin Foundation established.

1939 World War II breaks out in Europe. Congress passes the Administrative Office Act of November 6, which established executive agency to oversee many administrative functions regarding federal courts. William O. Douglas appointed to Supreme Court as associate justice.

1940 *Chambers v. Florida* holds compelled confessions are inadmissible.

1941 Pearl Harbor attacked; U.S. enters World War II.

1942 Japanese Americans relocated and internship camps opened, by Executive Order 9066, and Act of March 21, 1942. 120,000 incarcerated.

1943 *Hirabayashi v. United States* upholds constitutionality of relocation order by virtue of "military necessity." Chinese Exclusion Act repealed, and China is given quota. Chinese immigrants are able to naturalize.

1944 *Korematsu v. United States* ruled excluded zones order is constitutional. *Ex parte Mitsuye Endo* rules Endo and others cannot be detained in internment camps.

1946 American Association for Justice founded.

1947 Community Service Organization is founded. *Francis v. Resweber* rules execution after a failed attempt is not cruel and unusual punishment.

1948 Creation and Composition of Courts Act passed.

1949 *Brinegar v. United States* sets reasonableness test regarding probable cause. American Heritage Society founded.

1951 Court of Appeals for Armed Services established.

1953 *Burns v. Wilson* allows military courts to question suspects without informing them of their rights. Earl Warren appointed chief justice of Supreme Court.

1954 *Brown v. Board of Education* overturns *Plessy*; rules segregation of public school is unconstitutional, and "desegregation" movement begins.

1955 *United States v. Provoo* rules on fair trial clause. U.S. Court for Berlin established, runs until 1990.

1957 Montgomery, Alabama, bus boycott starts, and Montgomery Improvement Association begins. Southern Christian Leadership Council is founded by MLK. President Eisenhower sends troops to protect Little Rock, Arkansas high school desegregation students. Eisenhower signs the Civil Rights Act of August 9, aka the Eisenhower Civil Rights Act. *United States v. Pollard* rules on fair trial clause of Sixth Amendment.

1959   Congress establishes the Postal Service Board of Contract Appeals as special subject matter jurisdiction court. The states of Alaska and Hawaii are the last states to enter the union, each with its state constitution and state court system established.

1961   Vera Institute for Justice founded.

1962   Ted Kennedy elected to U.S. Senate from Massachusetts. Serves as chair of the Senate Judiciary Committee 1979–1981.

1963   The Judges of Circuit Court Act passed. The Supreme Court decides *Gideon v. Wainwright* on need to provide counsel to indigent person. On November 22, President John F. Kennedy is assassinated.

1965   Civil Rights Act of August 6 enacted; Voting Rights Act. *Griswold v. Connecticut* holds Connecticut's "Comstock" law is unconstitutional.

1966   The Black Panther Party is founded. *Miranda v. Arizona* decision sets test of "Miranda warnings" for police on arrest of suspect being read his rights. The Crusade for Justice starts in Colorado. *United States v. Ewell* decided regarding fair trial rules.

1967   *Afroyim v. Rusk* rules that a citizen may have dual citizenship with USA and Israel. *Klopfer v. North Carolina* rules on fair trial constraints of Sixth Amendment. *Loving v. Virginia* holds Virginia's interracial marriage ban is unconstitutional; it sets precedent for same-sex marriage. Congress establishes the Federal Judicial Center. Thurgood Marshall appointed associate justice of Supreme Court—the first Black so to serve.

1968   The Omnibus Crime Control and Safe Streets Act is passed. It established the Law Enforcement Assistance Administration that begins trend to "militarize" local police departments. On April 4, Martin Luther King, Jr. is assassinated. On June 5, former attorney general, then senator, and then presidential candidate Robert F. Kennedy is assassinated.

1969   *Smith v. Hooey* issues rules of fair trial constraints of Sixth Amendment.

1970   Twenty-Sixth Amendment is ratified, granting suffrage to eighteen-year-olds. Supreme Court rules in *Baldwin v. New York* that a trial by jury is required in any case where imprisonment exceeds six months' time.

1971   *United States v. Marion* regarding Sixth Amendment's requirements for a fair trial decided. The National Women's Political Caucus is established. The Southern Poverty Law Center is established.

1972   *Barker v. Wingo* decision on Sixth Amendment fair trial clause.

1973   Court decides *Roe v. Wade,* ruling right to privacy means abortion is legal. *Braden v. 30th Circuit* and *Strunk v. United States* decisions rendered regarding condition for fair trial rights of Sixth Amendment. Heritage Foundation begins. President Lyndon B. Johnson dies.

1974   The Asian American Legal Defense and Education Fund is established. Chief Justice Earl Warren dies. Law and Economic Center is founded.

1976   *Woodson v. North Carolina* rules state laws providing for mandatory death penalty are unconstitutional.

1977   *United States v. Lovasco* decided regarding Sixth Amendment's fair trial clause.

1978   *Zurcher v. Stanford Daily* decided. *Mincey v. Arizona* decided. The Human Rights Watch is founded. *Regents of University of California v. Bakke* holds fixed racial quotas unconstitutional but affirmative action plans are constitutional if one of several factors. Civil Service Reform Act passed. Congress establishes the U.S. Foreign Intelligence Court of Review. Congress establishes the Bankruptcy Appellate Court.

1979   Congress establishes the U.S. Merit System court; Bureau of Justice Statistics established; Alliance for Justice founded.

1980   Congress created the court of international trade as special subject matter jurisdiction federal court; and passes the Customs Courts Act of 1980. Ronald Reagan elected POTUS and begins the "conservative revolution" that gradually reshapes the federal judiciary through appointment of conservative ideological judges to all levels of the federal bench.

1981   U.S. Circuit Court of Appeals for the Eleventh Circuit established. Justice Sandra Day O'Connor appointed as associate justice, first woman to serve on Court.

1982   Federalist Society established. Congress creates the U.S. Court of Appeals for the Thirteenth Circuit, and the Canal District Court. Center for the Study of Law and Religion founded at Emory University.

1983   U.S. Supreme Court hands down decision in *INS v. Chadha* that rules the legislative veto is unconstitutional, impacting congressional oversight powers. Economic Policy Institute established.

1984   Supreme Court rules on series of cases on states search and seizure: *Oliver v. United States, Florida v. Meyers, Walter v. Georgia, Hudson v. Palmer, United States v. Leon, Massachusetts v. Sheppard;* and in *Spaziano v. Florida* regarding judge v. jury deciding on aggravating factors in death penalty case.

1986   *United States v. Loud Hawk* decided on Sixth Amendment fair trial clause. *Bowers v. Hardwick* rules on right of privacy to engage in homosexual activity. *California v. Greenwood* holds warrantless search of garbage is constitutional. William Rehnquist appointed chief justice. Antonin Scalia appointed as associate justice, soon leads Supreme Court's conservatives and advocates the "originalist" doctrine or approach to conservative activism on Court.

1987   *Sumner v. Shuman* holds death penalty cannot be mandatory even if prisoner already serving life sentence without parole.

1988 Court of appeals for veterans claims is established as special subject-matter jurisdiction federal appellate court; Center for Individual Rights is founded.

1989 Trademark trial and appeals court established; Cato Institute Center for Constitutional Studies founded.

1990 *Illinois v. Rodriguez* upholds warrantless search with third-party consent is constitutional. In *Walton v. Arizona,* Court rules a judge's finding of aggravating factors in death penalty is constitutional. It is overruled in 2002 by *Ring v. Arizona.* Pew Research Center established.

1991 *Gilmer v. Interstate/Johnson Lane* decision upholds the mandatory arbitration agreements. Supreme Court rules that the U.S. Tax Court is constitutional in *Freytag v. Commissioner of the IRS.* Institute for Justice founded.

1992 Legal Information Institute founded.

1993 Justice Thurgood Marshall dies. Ruth Bader Ginsburg appointed associate justice to the U.S. Supreme Court.

1994 Violent Crime Control and Law Enforcement Act is passed.

1995 *Harris v. Alabama* upholds law allowing judge to impose death penalty, making jury recommendation nonbinding even if it calls for life imprisonment.

1996 Office of Dispute Resolution for Acquisition is established by Congress.

1998 Center for Justice and Democracy is founded.

2000 *Apprendi v. New Jersey* rules that a jury trial is required to extend sentencing in criminal cases beyond the statutory limits. Supreme Court clarifies who may decide on extenuating circumstances in sentencing decision after conviction.

2001 The American Constitution Society is founded.

2002 *Florida v. J.S.* upholds use of stop and frisk based on anonymous tip. *United States v. Drayton* rules on consent and search on public bus. *Atkins v. Virginia* holds the execution of a mentally retarded offender is unconstitutional.

2003   *Sell v. United States* rules on Sixth Amendment fair trial factors. *Lawrence v. Texas* holds law banning homosexual activity between consenting adults in private is unconstitutional. Center for American Progress is founded. Constitution Center is founded.

2004   In *Blakely v. Washington*, the Supreme Court invalidates sentencing enhancement by judge alone. In *Rasul v. Bush,* the Court decides that foreign nationals detained at Guantanamo Bay could petition federal courts for writ of habeas corpus review. In *Hamdi v. Rumsfeld,* the Court holds U.S. citizens charged as enemy combatants have the right to due process to challenge their enemy combatant status.

2005   *Roper v. Simmons* holds death penalty for offender under eighteen at time of crime is unconstitutional. *Kelo v. City of New London* rules "taking clause" of Fifth Amendment on eminent domain seizure is legal even for private owner to another private owner. Congress enacts the Protection of Lawful Commerce-in-Arms Act. Chief Justice William Rehnquist dies. John Roberts appointed chief justice.

2008   *District of Columbia v. Heller* rules the D.C. handgun ban unconstitutional. *Kennedy v. Louisiana* rules death penalty unconstitutional for child rape with nonhomicidal crimes against the person.

2009   *Vermont v. Brillon* case decided on Sixth Amendment fair trial clause. On August 22, Senator Edward "Ted" Kennedy, leading icon on the Senate Judiciary Committee, dies. Barack Obama inaugurated POTUS.

2010   Court of Military Commission Review is established. In *Ontario v. Quon,* Court rules on right to privacy and electronic communication within a government workplace. Court rules on cases on Sixth Amendment right to fair trial in *Berghuis v. Smith* and *Thaler v. Haynes.* Court hands down ruling on the *Citizens United* case.

2011   *Bond v. United States* holds that individuals have standing to raise Tenth Amendment challenges to federal laws. In

AT&T Mobility LLC v. Concepcion et al., the Court upholds the mandatory arbitration clause in product/service contracts.

2012   In *United States v. Jones,* Court holds that the use of a GPS tracking device is a "search," and warrant is required. *Smith v. Cain* Sixth Amendment rule on fair trial clause.

2013   In *Maryland v. King,* Court holds that use of cheek swab is comparable to fingerprinting and is reasonable search under the Fourth Amendment. In *American Express Company v. Italian Colors Restaurant,* Court upholds mandatory arbitration for services.

2014   The National Center for Civil and Human Rights established.

2015   Senator Chuck Grassley, R-Iowa, becomes chair of the U.S. Senate Judiciary Committee and begins unprecedented series of judicial appointments of conservative justices.

2016   In *Hurst v. Florida,* Court holds law giving judge authority to decide facts relating to sentencing violates Sixth Amendment requiring jury to determine aggravating factors in death penalty case. Pew Research Center issues its report on minority judges on the bench. Donald Trump elected POTUS, soon launches appointment of hundreds of conservative judges to federal courts from list by Federalist Society and Heritage Foundation influence.

2018   *Carpenter v. United States* rules that cell-site location information requires a warrant be issued on probable cause to comply with privacy of historical cellphone location records.

2020   In *Ramos v. Louisiana* Court holds that for felony conviction, the jury's verdict must be unanimous.

Glossary

Administrative law   The body of law that pertains to the rules and regulations of the agencies of government, and to their promulgation and enforcement.

Amicus curiae   A Latin phrase meaning "friend of the court"; it refers to a person who is not a party to a case but who has an interest in the case and who provides expertise or advice to the court, typically in the form of a written brief, at the discretion of the court.

Appellant/Appellee   Terms that refer to parties to an appeals case. The appellant is the party who applies to a higher court for review challenging the decision of a lower court. The appellee is the party who responds to that appeal.

Arbitration   A clause inserted into a contract or agreement that requires the parties to resolve their disputes through an arbitration process. It binds the parties to a type of problem resolution outside the courts. The disputing parties agree that one or several individuals (arbiters) can make a binding decision about the dispute after receiving evidence and hearing arguments.

Bailiff   A court law enforcement officer (typically a sheriff's deputy) who maintains order in a courtroom at the direction of the judge; protects witnesses and jury members, lawyers and others present in the courtroom; and handles various errands, such as calling witnesses into the courtroom and serving summons.

Bench trial   A trial tried before a judge rather than a trial by a jury.

Certiorari   A legal order by which a higher court calls for the records of a lower court's decision for purposes of review.

Civil law   The system of law deriving from Roman law pertaining to private relationships between persons or parties who are members of a society. It is in contrast with criminal, military, or religious affairs. Violations of civil law are typically penalized with a fine.

Common law   The part of English law that is derived from custom and judicial precedents (referred to as "judge-made law") rather than from statutes. It is usually contrasted with statutory law.

Common pleas (or common bench)   Trial courts within the state court system deriving from the English legal system that cover legal cases that did not concern the king. In a state system, they are courts of general jurisdiction, for example, general, domestic relations, juvenile, and probate divisions.

Criminal law   That system of law concerning the punishment of persons who commit crime, and typically involving detention or imprisonment of those found guilty. Criminal law may be applied to both misdemeanor (minor) and felony (major) offenses.

De facto   Practices in fact or in effect (e.g., by social custom), whether right or not, that are not officially recognized by laws, statutes, ordinances, and so on. They are contrasted with de jure.

Defendant   A person, company, institution, or organization accused of a crime or legal violation in a court of law.

De jure   According to rightful entitlement or claim, by right, governed by a law, ordinance, or statute. It is contrasted with de facto.

Detainee   A person held in custody, especially for political reasons.

Dicta   The plural form of dictum and refers to a statement or ruling that is from an official source, such as a judge or court, that expresses a principle.

Doctrine of incorporation   A judicial, constitutional doctrine through which the Bill of Rights amendments are made applicable to the states through the due process clause of the Fourteenth Amendment.

Double jeopardy   The prosecution of a person twice for the same offense. It is a procedural defense that prevents an accused person from being tried on the same charges after a valid acquittal or conviction in the same jurisdiction.

Due process of law   A clause of the Fourteenth Amendment that specifies the judicial principle of fair treatment through the normal procedures of the judicial system—especially protecting a citizen's entitlements.

Equal protection of the law   Another phrase from the Fourteenth Amendment requiring states to guarantee the same rights, privileges, and protections to all citizens. It reinforces the principle of due process of law and prevents states from arbitrary discrimination against anyone.

Exculpatory material   Evidence in a criminal trial that exonerates or tends to exonerate the defendant of charges of which he or she is accused. It is the legal opposite of inculpatory evidence, which proves or supports guilt. In a criminal trial, the prosecution is obliged to present any exculpatory evidence it uncovers in its investigation of a crime.

Exempt   To be free from the obligation or liability imposed by others; for example, the payment of a tax or the obligation to perform certain duties imposed by a law.

Ex-parte   A Latin term that means a legal proceeding done with respect to or in the interest of one party or of an outside party. It is decided by a judge without all the parties to a dispute being present. It is not uncommon in cases involving national security issues.

Gubernatorial   An adjective pertaining to the office of the governor of a state.

Inalienable rights   Those rights that cannot be bought, sold, or transferred from one individual to another. For example, the Constitution guarantees the rights to life and liberty as inalienable, meaning that the government cannot take them away.

Injunction   A judicial order that restrains a person from beginning or continuing an action that 1) threatens or invades the legal rights of another, 2) may inflict irreparable harm, or 3) compels someone to carry out a certain action; for example, to make restitution to an injured party.

Judicial review   A procedure by which a court may review an administrative action by a public body; for example, the U.S. Supreme Court has the power to review the constitutionality of a legislative act by the U.S. Congress or a state legislature; and a state Supreme Court may review the state constitutionality of a state law or local government ordinance.

Jurisprudence   The theory or philosophy of law. Jurisprudence seeks to reveal the historical, moral, and cultural basis of a particular legal concept or principle.

Landmark decision   A decision that is notable and often cited because it significantly changes, consolidates, updates, or summarizes the law on a particular important topic and serves to guide future legal decisions or cases.

Litigation   The process of taking legal action.

Missouri Plan   The name for an assisted appointment plan for selecting judges, first developed in Missouri and now used in some version by thirty states. It has a nonpartisan judicial nominating committee that nominates potential judges, typically sending at least three names to the governor. The governor appoints the judge, who then must face (usually after one or two years) a retention election in which voters opt to retain the judge or not. In rare instances, voters opt not to retain the judge, and that judge is removed from the bench and the process begins anew to select another judge.

Nolle prosequi   A Latin legal term meaning "to be unwilling to pursue," and is a formal notice of abandonment by a plaintiff or a prosecutor of all or part of a lawsuit or other legal action.

Officer of the court   Any person who has an obligation to promote justice and uphold the law. These include judges, clerks, court personnel (such as bailiffs and court reporters), police officers, and attorneys.

Per curiam   A decision made by a judge or a court that is in unanimous agreement; such decisions are usually issued by an appellate court or a panel of judges in which the decision held is made by the court acting collectively.

Plaintiff   A person who brings a suit or case against another in a court of law.

Precedent   The doctrine and norm that when issuing decisions, all courts following binding precedent—meaning their decisions must follow any rulings made by courts above them. When different circuit courts reach contradictory results on the same issue, the Supreme Court usually grants certiorari on the issue, so that its decision establishes the law throughout the nation.

Pretextual   Constituting a pretext; that is, a dubious or spurious use of a half-truth or misleading fabrication to conceal the true purpose or rationale behind actions or words. It also refers to using minor charges to take the targets of a high-priority investigation into custody.

Prima facie   A Latin expression meaning on its first encounter or at first sight; it means that a first impression is accepted as correct until proven otherwise.

Prior restraint   The judicial suppression of material that would otherwise be published or broadcast on the grounds that it is libelous or harmful. In U.S. law, the government is severely limited in its ability to do this.

Racial profiling   Also sometimes called ethnic profiling, it is the act of suspecting or targeting a person for investigation solely on assumed characteristics or behavior of a racial or ethnic group rather than the behavior of the individual. It has also been used by police (and others) based on an individual's looks, name, religion, or national origin.

Remand   A committal into custody; that is, to place a defendant on bail or in custody, especially when a trial is adjourned.

Sheriff   An elected officer, usually at the county level, who is responsible for keeping the peace. A sheriff's deputy is often used as an officer of a court.

Stare decisis   The legal principle of determining points in litigation according to precedent; that is, a rule established in a previous case is binding or persuasive for a court when deciding subsequent cases with similar issues or facts even when they are not required to do so.

Statutory interpretation   The process by which courts interpret and apply legislation, often necessary when a case involves a statute, especially when the words of a statute have a plain or straightforward meaning.

Tort   In common law jurisdiction, a wrongful act or an infringement of a right that causes the claimant to suffer law or harm, leading to a civil legal liability. There are three categories of torts: negligent, intentional, and strict liability torts.

Venire   An entire panel of persons from which a jury is drawn to hear a court case.

Voir dire   A Latin phrase meaning to speak the truth. It refers to the process of questioning potential jurors as to their ability to be open-minded and fair and involves questioning by lawyers for both sides of a dispute and by the presiding judge in a case.

Writ   A formal, written command in the name of a court or other legal authority to act, or to abstain from acting, in some way.

Writ of certiorari   A court process in which a higher court seeks judicial review of a legal decision made by a lower court or government agency.

Writ of habeas corpus   A Latin phrase that means "to produce the body"; in legal parlance it is a court order demanding that a public official (usually a warden) deliver a prisoner to the court and to show a valid reason for the person's detention. It is a legal principle that has deep roots in English common law.

Writ of mandamus   An order from a court to a subordinate government official that orders the government official to properly fulfill their official duties or to correct an abuse of its discretion. It orders a subordinate court, corporation, or public authority to execute a specific act or duty for which they are legally responsible.

Index

Note: Page numbers followed by *f* indicate a figure; numbers followed by *t* refer to a table.

About the Author

Michael C. LeMay is professor emeritus of political science at California State University-San Bernardino (CSUSB), California. He also served as assistant dean and was director of an interdisciplinary master's degree program in national security studies. His published work includes immigration policy titles such as Praeger's *Doctors at the Borders: Immigration and the Rise of Public Health* (2015), *From Open Door to Dutch Door: An Analysis of U.S. Immigration Policy Since 1820* (1987), *Guarding the Gates: Immigration and National Security* (2006), and *Anatomy of a Public Policy: The Reform of Contemporary American Immigration Law* (1994); Greenwood's *U.S. Immigration and Naturalization Laws and Issues: A Documentary History*, with Elliott Barkan (1999); ABC-CLIO's *U.S. Immigration: A Reference Handbook* (2003), *Illegal Immigration: A Reference Handbook* (2015), and *Global Pandemic Threats: A Reference Handbook* (2016). He is a contributing author and editor of the three-volume *Transforming America: Perspectives on U.S. Immigration* (2012). LeMay received his doctorate from the University of Minnesota and his bachelor's and master's degrees from the University of Wisconsin.